WORLD MIGRATION REPORT

2015

Migrants and Cities:
New Partnerships
to Manage Mobility

International Organization for Migration (IOM)

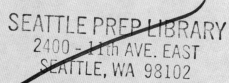

Contents

WORLD MIGRATION
REPORT 2015
Migrants and Cities:
New Partnerships
to Manage Mobility

iii

Editorial team

WORLD MIGRATION
REPORT 2015
Migrants and Cities:
New Partnerships
to Manage Mobility

VII

Editor-in-Chief
June J.H. Lee

Managing Editors
Jill Helke and Frank Laczko

Associate Editor
Asmita Naik

Copy Editor
Antoinette Wills

Writing Team
June J.H. Lee (Chapters 1–2 and 4–6)
Lorenzo Guadagno (Chapter 3)
Ann-Christin Wagner, Sansae Cho, and Yuka Takehana (Research assistance)

World Migration Report Advisory Committee
Gervais Appave (Chair), Mohammed Abdiker, Leonard Doyle, Carmela Godeau,
Bernd Hemingway, Davide Mosca, Akio Nakayama, Robert Paiva, Marcelo Pisani,
Bruce Reed, Pindie Stephen and Theodora Suter

Editorial Assistance
Paula Benea, Olivier Ferrari, Salvador Gutierrez, Barbara Rijks, Azzouz Samri and
Ezequiel Texido

Publication
Valerie Hagger

Layout
Carmelo Torres

Translators
Carmen Andreu, Fabienne Witt and the TRS team

Executive Assistance
Frances Solinap, Antoinette Wills, Ann-Christin Wagner, Sansae Cho
and Daniel Szabo

Cartography
Daniel Szabo

Acknowledgements

The Editorial Team wishes to thank all contributing authors, including mayors, local officials and city and migration practitioners. The Editorial Team is especially grateful to Mr William Lacy Swing, IOM Director General, for his vision and encouragement to produce this publication.

Special thanks go to all field offices for their tremendous effort in gathering the Migrants' Voices and relevant data, and to colleagues in IOM Headquarters for their assistance in data collection and analysis.

The Editorial Team is grateful also to Melissa Siegel (Maastricht University), Cecilia Tacoli and David Satterthwaite (both at the International Institute for Environment and Development) for their presentations in the framework of the WMR Inter-agency Seminar Series.

The Editorial Team is especially grateful to the Governments of Australia and the Netherlands for their generous financial support towards the development and publication of the *World Migration Report 2015*.

The Editorial Team would like to pay special tribute to Professor Graeme Hugo, Director of the Australian Population and Migration Research Centre at the University of Adelaide, who passed away on 20 January 2015, after finalizing his background paper for this report.

WMR 2015 seminars, background papers and text box contributors

SEMINARS

Migrant and Refugee Integration in Global Cities: The Role of Cities and Businesses.
Melissa Siegel, Head Migration Studies, Training and Research Projects,
Maastricht Graduate School of Governance| UNU-MERIT,
2 May 2014, Geneva, Switzerland.

Migration to Cities and New Vulnerabilities.
Cecilia Tacoli, Principal Researcher, Head of the Human Settlements Group,
International Institute for Environment and Development,
30 October 2014, Geneva, Switzerland.

Urbanization, Urban Poverty, and Rural-Urban Migration.
David Satterthwaite, Senior Fellow,
International Institute for Environment and Development,
30 October 2014, Geneva, Switzerland.

BACKGROUND PAPERS

Urban Migration Trends, Challenges and Opportunities,
by Ayşe Çağlar

Migration, Health and Urbanization: Interrelated Challenges,
by Caroline Schultz

Urbanization, Rural-urban Migration and Urban Poverty,
by Cecilia Tacoli, Gordon McGranahan and David Satterthwaite

Urban Migration Trends, Challenges, Responses and Policy in the Asia-Pacific,
by Graeme Hugo

Linkages between Urbanization, Rural–Urban Migration and Poverty Outcomes
in Africa,
by Mariama Awumbila

Cities Welcoming Immigrants: Local Strategies to Attract and Retain Immigrants in
U.S. Metropolitan Areas,
by Marie Price

Immigrant Entrepreneurship in Cities,
by Katrin Marchand and Melissa Siegel

Migrants and Cities in New Partnerships in sub-Saharan Africa,
by John Oucho

Urban Migration Trends, Challenges and Opportunities in India,
by Ram B. Bhagat

In situ Urbanization in China: Processes, Contributing Factors and Policy Implications,
by Yu Zhu

Migration and Urbanization Paths: Emerging Challenges of Reshaping the Human Geography of Latin America,
by Fernando Murillo

Urban Migration Trends in the MENA Region and the Challenge of Conflict-Induced Displacement,
by Mona Serageldin, François Vigier and Maren Larsen

TEXT BOX CONTRIBUTORS

Amina Benkais-Benbrahim,
Déléguée à l'intégration et Cheffe at Bureau cantonal pour l'intégration des étrangers et la prévention du racisme, Vaud, Switzerland

Arun Peter Lobo,
Deputy Director of the Population Division, Department of City Planning, New York City, United States of America

Atilla Toros,
Director General of the General Directorate of Migration Management, Ministry of the Interior, Turkey

Carlos Mora Álvarez,
Executive President of the State Council for the Attention of Migrants, Mexico

Cécile Riallant,
Programme Manager, Programme Management Unit, Joint Migration and Development Initiative, Brussels, Belgium

Fatma Şahin,
Mayor of Gaziantep Metropolitan Municipality, Turkey

Fritz Kuhn,
Mayor of Stuttgart, Germany

Michael Collyer,
Reader in Geography at the University of Sussex, Brighton, United Kingdom

Nava Hinrichs,
Managing Director at The Hague Process on Refugees and Migration, The Hague, the Netherlands

Pauline Texier,
Senior Lecturer at the Jean Moulin University Lyon III, Lyon, France and researcher at the UMR Laboratoire Environnement, Ville, Société

Wilfredo B. Prilles, Jr.,
Coordinator at the City Planning and Development Office, Naga City, the Philippines

Yasuyuki Kitawaki,
Mayor of Hamamatsu City (1999–2007), Japan

Text boxes, migrant voices, figures, tables and maps

TEXT BOXES

MIGRANT VOICES

FIGURES

WORLD MIGRATION
REPORT 2015
Migrants and Cities:
New Partnerships
to Manage Mobility

xvii

TABLES

MAPS

Acronyms

ACS	American Community Service
ADB	Asian Development Bank
AIDS	Acquired immune deficiency syndrome
APEC	Asia Pacific Economic Community
AS/COA	American Society/Council of the Americas
ASEAN	Association of South East Asian Nations
CIRD	China Institute for Reform and Development
CoE	Council of Europe
DREAM	Development, Relief and Education for Alien Minors
ECDC	European Centre for Disease Prevention and Control
EMHRN	Euro-Mediterranean Human Rights Network
EPF	Economic Policy Forum
EU	European Union
Eurostat	Statistical Office of the European Communities
GDP	Gross Domestic Product
GEM	Global Entrepreneurship Monitor
GIVE	Grassroots Integration through Volunteering Experiences
Habitat III	United Nations Conference on Housing and Sustainable Urban Development, Quito, Ecuador, 17-20 October 2016
HIV	Human immunodeficiency virus infection

WORLD MIGRATION
REPORT 2015
Migrants and Cities:
New Partnerships
to Manage Mobility

XIX

HLD	UN High-level Dialogue on International Migration and Development
IDP	Internally displaced person
IFRC	International Federation of Red Cross and Red Crescent Societies
IIED	International Institute for Environment and Development
ILO	International Labour Organization
IMAGE	Internal Migration Around the GlobE
IOM	International Organization for Migration
JMDI	Joint Migration and Development Initiative
LEP	Limited English proficiency
MMM	Malteser Migranten Medizin (Maltese Migrant Medicine)
NCD	Non-communicable disease
NGO	Non-governmental Organization
OECD	Organisation for Economic Co-operation and Development
OFW	Overseas Filipino Workers
PIC	Programme d'intégration cantonale (Cantonal Integration Programme)
Rio+20	United Nations Conference on Sustainable Development, Rio de Janeiro, Brazil, 20-22 June 2012
SAR	Special Administrative Region (*applicable to Hong Kong*)
TB	Tuberculosis
TECHO	Un Techo para mi País (A Roof for my Country)
THP	The Hague Process on Refugees and Migration
TVE	Township-village enterprise
UCLG	United Cities and Local Governments
UN	United Nations
UN DESA	United Nations Department of Economic and Social Affairs
UNDP	United Nations Development Programme
UNESCO	United Nations Educational, Scientific and Cultural Organization
UN-HABITAT	United Nations Human Settlements Programme
UNHCR	Office of the United Nations High Commissioner for Refugees
UNICEF	United Nations Children's Fund
WHA	World Health Assembly
WHO	World Health Organization
WMR	World Migration Report

Foreword

The *World Migration Report 2015: Migrants and Cities, New Partnerships to Manage Mobility* –the eighth report in IOM's World Migration Report (WMR) series– focuses on migrants and how migration is shaping cities and the situation of migrants in cities.

While much of the current international discussion about migration trends and migration policy tends to focus on the national level, this report takes migration enquiries to the city level and aims to raise understanding of the local socioeconomic dynamics of migration and the close connection between migration and urban development.

The main chapters of the *World Migration Report 2015* investigate both the challenges and opportunities arising from increasing migration to diverse urban settings. They present findings on the potential benefits of all forms of migration and mobility for city growth and development. The report showcases innovative ways in which migration and urbanization policies can be better designed for the benefit of migrants and cities.

The report particularly focuses on migrants' situations in the cities of the Global South, broadening the current focus on the cities of the Global North. It highlights how cities and migrants can work together in order to reduce the risks of migration to cities and take advantage of growing urban diversity in such areas as community resilience building and local economic, social and cultural development through migrants' connections between origin and host communities.

The report concludes with a set of recommendations for future city initiatives to include migrants as partners and migrants' issues in the discussion on urbanization and the post-2015 global development framework.

The *World Migration Report 2015* benefited, as previous editions, from the expertise and experience of IOM colleagues and external scholars. We are particularly grateful for the contribution of mayors and city government authorities to the report in sharing their perspective, experience and expertise. We also wish to thank the Governments of Australia and the Netherlands for their generous financial support.

We hope that this report will contribute to the policymaking for sustainable urban development and the ongoing discussion on the post-2015 global development agenda.

William Lacy Swing
Director General

Overview

OVERVIEW

We live in a world which is becoming increasingly urban, where more and more people are moving to cities. Over 54 per cent of people across the globe were living in urban areas in 2014 (UN DESA, 2014).[1] The current urban population of 3.9 billion is expected to grow in the next few decades to some 6.4 billion by 2050 (ibid.). It is estimated that three million people around the world are moving to cities every week (UN-Habitat, 2009). Migration is driving much of the increase in urbanization, making cities much more diverse places in which to live.

Nearly one in five of the world foreign-born population resides in established global gateway cities (Çağlar, 2014). In many of these cities such as Sydney, London and New York, migrants represent over a third of the population and, in some cities such as Brussels and Dubai, migrants account for more than half of the population. Other cities have seen a remarkable growth in migration in recent years. For example, the number of foreign residents in Seoul has doubled in the last ten years.[2] In Asia and Africa, rapidly growing small cities are expected to absorb almost all the future urban population growth of the world (UN DESA, 2014) and this mobility pattern to cities and urban areas is characterized by the temporality and circularity of the internal migration process (Hugo, 2014).

The fast rate of urbanization, and rising migration to cities, brings with it both risks and opportunities for the migrants, communities and governments concerned. The *World Migration Report 2015 – Migrants and Cities: New Partnerships to Manage Mobility* explores how migration and migrants are shaping cities, and how the life of migrants, in turn, is shaped by cities, their people, organizations and rules. This report examines the relationships between migrants and cities on such issues as employment, housing and health, and also considers how migrants help to build and revive cities with their resources and ideas, both in the origin and host countries. The report also identifies innovative examples of how some cities are seeking to manage the challenges of increased global mobility and social diversity with varying degrees of success. It will highlight new policy developments concerning urban partnerships among migrant groups, local governments, civil society and the private sector which are designed to meet the challenges posed by migration and cities.

Migration and how it is governed, should be an issue at the frontline of urban planning and sustainable development. However, migration is largely omitted from the global debate on urbanization. There is a glaring absence of the mention of migrants in international planning for a new global urban agenda, such as Habitat III.[3] Many city and local governments also still do not include migration or migrants in their urban development planning and implementation. Migrants are therefore still generally overlooked in global discourses on urbanization and cities.

---

1   The UN bases its reports on the definition of "urban" by the different national statistical offices as a spatial and demographic concept, which can vary from country to country.

2   Source: Seoul Metropolitan Government. Data taken from the database of Seoul Metropolitan Government, 2014: http://stat.seoul.go.kr/ (in Korean only).

3   The Third United Nations Conference on Housing and Sustainable Urban Development (Habitat III) will take place in 2016, as decided in General Assembly Resolution 66/ 207. For details, see: www.uclg.org/en/issues/habitat-iii.

The present report aims to address this challenge in three distinct ways:

- By documenting how migration is shaping cities and the situation of migrants in cities. Much of the current international discussion about migration trends and migration policy tends to focus on the national level. Taking the migration enquiry to the city level increases our understanding of the local political economies of migration, and the close connection between migration and urban development.

- By drawing attention to the livelihood of migrants in the cities of the Global South. The existing discussions on migrants and cities tend to focus primarily on the Global North and the integration of international migrants.

- By examining both internal and international migration. Cities across the development spectrum have growing mobile and diverse populations to manage. In the developed countries, one of the main sources of population diversity is international migration, while in the developing world it is most likely internal migration[4] and, to a lesser extent, growing international South–South migration.

The key features and messages of this report are presented as a contribution to address this lacuna in the ongoing global debate on urbanization and can be summarized under four key headings:

Migration is essentially an urban affair

We live in an era of unprecedented human mobility that has been markedly urban as migrants, both internal and international, move to cities and urban areas, bring diversity and connect communities within and across borders to create new linkages among localities. This calls for new approaches to urban governance and migration policies.

There are an estimated 232 million international migrants (UN DESA, 2013) and 740 million internal migrants (UNDP, 2009) in the world.

- About 50 per cent of international migrants reside in ten highly urbanized, high-income countries[5] such as Australia, Canada and the United States, several countries in Europe (France, Germany, Spain and the United Kingdom), the Russian Federation, Saudi Arabia and the United Arab Emirates (UN DESA, 2013). Migrants tend to concentrate in cities of these countries.

Almost all growth in the world's population over the next few decades of another 2.5 billion is expected to be in urban areas in low- and middle-income countries, particularly in Africa and Asia (UN DESA, 2014).

- Although Africa is not the world's fastest urbanizing region, its urban population has been growing at a historically unprecedented rate for decades. In 1960, Johannesburg was the only city in sub-Saharan Africa with a population of over a million; by 1970, there were four (Cape Town, Johannesburg, Kinshasa and Lagos) and, by 2010, there were 33 (UN-Habitat, 2013).

- Every day an estimated 120,000 people are migrating to cities in the Asia-Pacific region and, by 2050, the proportion of people living in urban areas

---

4   There is a serious lack of consistent, current and comparable data on foreign-born urban populations in most countries of the Global South.

5   http://data.worldbank.org/data-catalog/GNI-per-capita-Atlas-and-PPP-table

is likely to rise to 63 per cent. The Asia–Pacific region has added nearly 1 billion people to its urban population between 1990 and 2014, about half of whom in China alone (450 million). As part of a long-term trend, the urban population of the region has more than doubled between 1950 and 1975, and again between 1975 and 2000. It is anticipated to almost double once more between 2000 and 2025 (UN ESCAP, 2014).

Increased large scale migration to urban centres is inevitable due to the global realities of aging societies, slow and uneven economic growth among regions in a country and among nations, and environmental and climatic instability. For many cities, migration has become a more important determinant of population growth and age structures than fertility and mortality (Skeldon, 2013). Social networks are located in cities and newly arriving migrants can make use of these for survival and economic opportunities. It is in cities where migrant integration primarily takes place.

The geography of migration flows is changing in line with changes in the global economy. A much wider range of cities around the world have become destinations for migrants. For example, migrants are increasingly attracted to countries experiencing higher economic growth in East Asia, Brazil, southern Africa and western India. Cities everywhere are experiencing a constant ebb and flow of people between urban, regional, national and global communities. Thus cities face growing challenges of managing migration-induced diversity.

However, at the global level, migration policies and urbanization policies tend to be discussed in separate forums, which results in a lack of policy coherence. At the national level, with very few exceptions, there is a disjuncture between national and local policies. National governments may encourage migration to urban areas for economic development without sufficient coordination with local governments on the basic social service needs on the ground.

Cities, in the meantime, have taken their own initiatives to manage migration at the local level and directly interact with migrants, and even with their home communities through transnational partnership arrangements. For a small and growing number of cities, immigration policies and programmes are now integral to their urban development and management.

Migration to cities brings both challenges and opportunities

Almost all the growth in the world's population over the next few decades will take place in urban centres in low- and middle-income countries where poverty reduction is slow and large deficits in provision of basic services remain (UN DESA, 2012). Strong population growth in cities poses a great deal of pressure on infrastructure, the environment and the social fabric of the city. There is much concern about the pace of urbanization and the capacity of national and local governments among low-income nations to cope with its consequences. Policymakers in these countries tend to consider rural–urban migration as the main contributor to over-crowding, congestion, increasing exposure to environmental hazards and to shortfalls in basic infrastructure and services.

Over the last decades, particularly in the Global South, poorly managed urban migration has often resulted in the development of informal solutions to address gaps in the provision of basic needs and in the exclusion of migrants from access to formal land, housing and job markets as well as health and education services. UN-Habitat estimates that one out of every three people in cities in the developing world lives in slum areas accommodating migrants and other urban poor (UN-Habitat, 2007).

Migration policies of both origin and destination countries can affect cities in positive and negative ways. Restrictive, inadequate or unclear policies on labour mobility in Africa, Asia and Europe may give rise to irregular migratory flows and the growth of informal urban settlements. Strict border control policies can lead to urban "transit hubs" where migrants become stranded on their way to intended destinations.

Newcomers often have no choice except to settle in hazard-prone and poorly planned areas, where they have limited access to resources and opportunities that are essential for resilience. Furthermore, when disasters strike, they are among the worst affected.

Recent studies indicate that migrants are disproportionately represented among the urban poor in these informal settlements (Hoang, Truong and Dinh, 2013; Rigg, Nguyen and Luong, 2014). For example, in Accra, Ghana, 92 per cent of migrant households live in one slum, Old Fadama, without a ready supply of water or access to toilet facilities (Awumbila, 2014). In many cities in low- and middle-income countries, informal settlements commonly function as entry points for incoming migrants. Despite the hardships of living in such conditions, migrants are still able to find economic activity and opportunities to improve their current well-being and future prospects (Awumbila, Owusu and Teye, 2014) in these informal settlements or slums, such as Kibera in Nairobi, Kenya, or Old Fadama.

Moving to cities can greatly enhance people's well-being. It offers an escape from the impact of the hazards of a fragile rural livelihood, and an access to diverse employment opportunities and better health and education, all of which have the potential to reduce the poverty of the people moving as well as those who stay behind.

Urbanization clearly brings benefits, as it is hard to find sustained economic growth without urbanization. Cities can also turn urban diversity arising from migration into social and economic advantages. Migration can help increase productivity if it is strategically managed and linked to the formal economy. Fostering the inclusion of migrants into the labour market can have positive benefits both for the place of origin and of destination as links are maintained between the two.

Despite innovation in some cities, efforts for poverty reduction through the inclusion of migrants are not yet readily prioritized by city or municipal government authorities. Inclusive local plans, policies and measures, in particular at the city level, are critical in defining the well-being and resilience of migrants, while effective national and international instruments and institutions also need to be put in place.

A recent study found a strong correlation between effective provision of services and urban development in all of the major emerging economies (EPF and CIRD, 2013). In pursuing more inclusive urban governance, cities today link local urban social cohesion to economic growth and global competitiveness (Metropolis, 2011). The participation and inclusion of migrants in their host cities is an indispensable part of building stable, open and vibrant communities that assure the socioeconomic future of a country.

Migrants are resourceful partners in urban governance

Migrants make significant and essential contributions to the economic, social and cultural development of their host countries and of their communities back home. Yet oftentimes these contributions go unrecognized or, at best, are measured only in terms of the remittances they manage to send back home.

Migrants as builders of resilience: Migrants also play an important role in building the resilience of home and host communities through the exchange of resources and support. They and their networks can contribute to managing risk for the community at large. Migrants are often overrepresented in the healthy, productive age groups and provide diversified skills that can support disaster preparedness, response and recovery efforts, particularly in ageing societies.

Migrants as agents of local development: Migrants play a central role in forging the links between cities of origin and of destination and in mainstreaming migration into local development planning. City-to-city links are often created or maintained due to the presence of large migrant populations. Migrant and diaspora communities can play an important role in supporting local decentralized development partnerships between cities and in facilitating or undertaking some of the related activities such as the provision of expertise and information on the communities of origin.

Migrants as city-makers: Migrants can help strengthen the place of cities in the global economic and political hierarchy. They can do so by promoting historical, cultural, religious and socioeconomic assets of a city if opportunities exist to enable them to do so.

As reflected in the Declaration adopted at the UN High-level Dialogue (HLD) on International Migration and Development in New York in 2013, migrants need to be at the centre of national and global migration and development agendas. This has been a key message of international debates on migration since the UNDP *Human Development Report 2009* dedicated to human mobility and development. By examining how migration affects well-being, the WMR 2013 drew attention to the human development of migrants and its significance in policy debate.

Within the context of sustainable development, as identified at the Rio+20 conference in 2012[6] and other major summits including the 2013 UN HLD on International Migration and Development,[7] economic growth should be pursued equitably among all population groups. Sustained and inclusive economic growth is the goal most cities have striven to achieve with practical and innovative solutions. Furthermore, for an increasing number of cities, immigration policies and programmes are integral to their urban development planning and management. UNESCO and UN-HABITAT have undertaken joint research on the importance of migration for the growth of urban areas and how to enhance the inclusiveness of international migrants in cities (UNESCO and UN-Habitat, 2010 and 2012).

---

6   United Nations Conference on Sustainable Development, 2012: https://sustainabledevelopment.un.org/rio20

7   See: www.un.org/en/ga/68/meetings/migration/

Migrant-inclusive urban governance is needed

Urbanization is the dominant challenge of the twenty-first century. Most urban growth will come from both international and internal migration. Urban growth, however, can only be sustainable if cities invest in their communities, including migrants. Cities are well positioned to help manage human mobility. They have the authority to develop and implement policy frameworks for the inclusion of migrants. As service providers, they have direct access to migrants and can assess their needs.

Urban migration governance requires, however, a multi-stakeholder approach and governance structure so that diverse interests may be accommodated and cooperative action taken. It includes formal institutions as well as informal arrangements and the resources of residents including migrants. Partnerships with other cities and local governments, national government, civil society, migrant associations and the cities' own diasporas are necessary to reap the benefits of the human resources of each city. In particular, public–private partnerships involving businesses could foster the integration of migrants in the labour market and help prevent spatial segregation. These partnerships will make urban governance more flexible, cost-effective and increase both social cohesion and the economic competitiveness of cities.

Positive efforts are being made among city policymakers to promote social cohesion. There are good examples of institutional structures being formed with the commitment of federal and local-level authorities in a number of cities in Europe (such as Berlin, Athens, Bilbao and Dublin) and in Asia (Fuzhou in the Fujian Province of China, Singapore and a network of cities in Japan). Cities like Berlin, Dublin and Lille are also forging partnerships with migrant associations to promote citizenship and political participation among migrant groups. Another innovative approach to financing municipal inclusion policies is participatory budgeting. This is widely practiced by over 1,700 local governments in more than 40 countries, especially among low-income countries where municipal budgets remain low despite decentralization.

Platforms for exchange consultation and cooperation must be developed

As people increasingly live and work in more than one place, cities are challenged to manage their growing diversity and their strategic position within a country and the world at large. For example, openness to ethnic and cultural diversity has become an indicator of a city's ability to do business with the rest of the world along with such indicators of economic, investment and trade links to the global markets.[8] The capacity of a city to attract international populations and enable them to contribute to the future success of the city[9] is considered a key benchmark for a sustainable city of the future.

---

8   The "Global Cities Initiative" was launched by the Brookings Institution and JP Morgan Chase to strengthen the economic position, investment and trade links of US cities to the global network of metropolitan areas and which features immigration as one of its indicators of globality:
www.brookings.edu/about/projects/global-cities/about.
www.jpmorganchase.com/content/dam/jpmorganchase/en/legacy/corporate/Corporate-Responsibility/globalcities.htm

9   For more details: www.opencities.eu/web/index.php?why_openness_matters_en

Unfortunately, migration is still not taken into consideration in most urban development plans and policies, and vice versa; and there is a glaring absence of migrants in the major international planning for a new global urban agenda, such as Habitat III. This is in part a reflection of the chronic gaps and variances in definitions[10] as well as in data and empirical research on migration and urbanization. It may also be a consequence of the lack of coordination between central and local governments. The present report highlights the links between well-governed migration and well-managed development. This, in turn, shows that restrictive policies on migration and urbanization can be damaging for growth and development for both origin and destination cities and countries in a globalized context.

Relatively unencumbered by the lack of policy coherence at the global and national governance levels, cities are nevertheless taking their own initiative to create socially integrative communities and forge new intercity networks of good practice around migration and urban governance. They have been established in order to strengthen relations among local institutions and draw some collective good practices from their individual experiences, with the shared goal of sustainable urban development and governance. They include the Canada-based Maytree Foundation's Cities of Migration[11] and the OPENCities,[12] co-founded by the EU and the British Council.

In addition to these city networks (Eurocities, 2010 and 2014), various international organizations (Price and Chacko, 2012; UNESCO and UN-Habitat, 2010) and political think tanks (Kerr, McDaniel and Guinan, 2014; McHugh, 2014), as well as national and global forums for research and policy on migration and cities (Metropolis, 2011; Cities of Migration, 2012), have already published collections of good practices of inclusion policies, mostly from Europe and North America but also some from Latin America (Collett and Gidley, 2012).

Nevertheless, these efforts by cities and local authorities need to be complemented by action at the international level to ensure that migration is fully taken into account when setting goals for sustainable cities of the future in a post-2015 global urban development agenda.

It would be important to gather available information in a global database and promote more information-sharing and dialogue between cities and between multi-level government stakeholders and other partners. At the same time, an important question should be addressed – namely, can the good practices of more advanced countries be replicated in countries with limited resources which try to adjust to rapid urban transitions? Or, in other words, how far are best practices limited to certain national and regional contexts and to what extent could they be globally applicable?

In 2015, IOM will dedicate its high-level International Dialogue on Migration conference to migrants and cities. It aims to assemble the collective wisdom on migration, mobility and urban transition and, together with city leaders and other experts, to draw a clear policy path towards improved migration management at all governance levels, to benefit both migrants and cities.

---

10   See Chapter 1: 1.2. Definitions and Terminology.

11   See the Cities of Migration Conference in Berlin in June 2014 on "An Agenda for Shared Prosperity". For more details, see: http://2014conference.citiesofmigration.ca/

12   www.opencities.eu/web/index.php?home_en

A critical area for such a discussion is the improvement of data collection practices. Chapter 1 of this report highlights the paucity of city-level data. There is much work to be done to ensure that migrants are included in data sets covering urbanization and development. Having a clear understanding of where migrants reside and how they are organized is a critical first step in formulating an outreach strategy in order to foster their inclusion in the life of cities. Based on a good set of data on migrants, cities can then develop benchmarks for basic service provision as well as measure their levels of social and economic integration. This, in turn, could help formulate an effective policy from the numerous programmes and practices on the ground. As shown in Chapter 1, knowing the age structure of migrant communities helps a city to identify growing areas of financial and human resources needs.

REFERENCES

Awumbila, M.
2014   Linkages between Urbanization, Rural-Urban Migration and Poverty
            Outcomes in Africa. Background Paper for the *World Migration Report
            2015, Migrants and Cities: New Partnerships to Manage Mobility.*
            IOM, Geneva.

Awumbila, M., G. Owusu and J.K. Teye
2014   Can Rural-Urban Migration into Slums Reduce Poverty? Evidence from
            Ghana. Working Paper No 13. Migrating out of Poverty Consortium,
            University of Sussex, Brighton. Available from http://r4d.dfid.gov.uk/
            Output/196216/

Çağlar, A.
2014   Urban Migration Trends, Challenges and Opportunities, Background
            Paper for the *World Migration Report 2015:Migrants and Cities: New
            Partnerships to Manage Mobility*, International Organization for
            Migration (IOM), Geneva, Switzerland.

Cities of Migration
2012   *Practice to Policy: Lessons from Local Leadership on Immigrant
            Integration.* Maytree Foundation, Toronto. Available from http://
            citiesofmigration.ca/wp-content/uploads/2012/03/Practice-to-
            Policy.pdf

Collett, E. and B. Gidley
2012   *Attitudes to Migrants, Communication and Local Leadership
            (AMICALL), Final Transnational Report.* COMPAS, Oxford. Available
            from   www.compas.ox.ac.uk/fileadmin/files/Publications/Reports/
            Amicall_Report_ENG_v3_single_WEB_READY.pdf

Economic Policy Forum (EPF) and China Institute for Reform and Development
(CIRD)
2013   *Report 2013 Economic Policy Forum, Roundtable Meeting on
            "Urbanisation and Migration: Creating Equitable Access to Basic
            Services"*, 3 November 2013, Haikou, Hainan Province, People's
            Republic of China. Available from www.economic-policy-forum.org/
            wp-content/uploads/2014/02/Hainan_Documentation1.pdf

Eurocities
2010   *Cities Accommodating Diversity.* Findings and recommendations
            from the peer review project, 'Diversity and Equality in European
            Cities'. Eurocities, Brussels. Available from http://nws.eurocities.eu/
            MediaShell/media/DIVE_FinalPublication.pdf
2014   Integrating Cities Toolkits, Brussels. Available from www.
            integratingcities.eu/integrating-cities/resources/implementoring_
            toolkits

Hoang, X.T., T.A. Truong and T.T.P. Dinh
2013   Urban poverty in Vietnam – a view from complementary assessments.
            International Institute for Environment and Development (IIED)
            Working Paper, London. Available from http://pubs.iied.org/
            pdfs/10633IIED.pdf

Hugo, G.
2014   Urban Migration Trends, Challenges, Responses and Policy in the Asia-Pacific. Background Paper for the *World Migration Report 2015, Migrants and Cities: New Partnerships to Manage Mobility.* IOM, Geneva.

Kerr, J., P. McDaniel and M. Guinan
2014   *Reimagining the Midwest: Immigration Initiatives and the Capacity of Local Leadership.* The Chicago Council on Global Affairs and American Immigration Council. Available from www.immigrationpolicy.org/sites/default/files/docs/reimagining_the_midwest_report_2014.pdf

McHugh, M.
2014   *Immigrant Civic Integration and Service Access Initiatives: City-Sized Solutions for City-Sized Needs.* Migration Policy Institute, Washington D.C. Available from www.migrationpolicy.org/sites/default/files/publications/TCM_Cities_McHugh-FINAL.pdf

Metropolis
2011   *Integrated Urban Governance – The way forward, Commission 3, Manual.* Metropolis, Berlin. Available from www.stadtentwicklung.berlin.de/internationales_eu/staedte_regionen/download/projekte/metropolis/C3_Manual_barrier_free.pdf
Summary: http://old.metropolis.org/sites/default/files/publications/2011/summary_commissions_metropolis_2009-2011.pdf

Price, M. and E. Chacko
2012   *Migrants' Inclusion in Cities: Innovative Urban Policies and Practices.* Published in Spanish by the United Nations through UNESCO and UN-Habitat. Available from www.researchgate.net/publication/272023289_Migrants'_Inclusion_in_Cities_Innovative_Urban_Policies_and_Practices._Prepared_for_UN-Habitat_and_UNESCO_Marie_Price_and_Elizabeth_Chacko

Rigg, J., T.A. Nguyen and T.T.H. Luong
2014   The Texture of Livelihoods: Migration and Making a Living in Hanoi, *The Journal of Development Studies*, 50 (3):368–382. DOI: 10.1080/00220388.2013.858130.

Skeldon, R.
2013   Global Migration: Demographic Aspects and Its Relevance for Development. UN DESA Technical paper 2013/6. Available from www.un.org/esa/population/migration/documents/EGM.Skeldon_17.12.2013.pdf

United Nations Department of Economic and Social Affairs (UN DESA)
2012   *World Urbanization Prospects: 2011 Revision.* United Nations, New York. Available from www.un.org/en/development/desa/population/publications/pdf/urbanization/WUP2011_Report.pdf
2013   *International Migration 2013 Wallchart.* United Nations, New York. Available from www.un.org/en/development/desa/population/migration/publications/wallchart/docs/wallchart2013.pdf
2014   *World Urbanization Prospects, The 2014 Revision: Highlights.* United Nations, New York. Available from http://esa.un.org/unpd/wup/Highlights/WUP2014-Highlights.pdf

United Nations Development Programme (UNDP)

2009   *Human Development Report 2009 - Overcoming barriers: Human mobility and development*. United Nations, New York. Available from http://hdr.undp.org/en/content/human-development-report-2009

United Nations Economic and Social Commission for Asia and the Pacific (UN ESCAP)

2014   *Statistical Yearbook for Asia and the Pacific 2014*. United Nations. Available from www.unescap.org/sites/default/files/ESCAP-SYB2014_0.pdf

United Nations Educational, Scientific and Cultural Organization (UNESCO) and United Nations Human Settlements Programme (UN-Habitat)

2010   *How to Enhance Inclusiveness for International Migrants in our Cities: Various Stakeholders' Views*, UNESCO Mexico, 2010. [Accessed on 30 September 2014]. Available from http://unesdoc.unesco.org/images/0019/001905/190592m.pdf

2012   Migrants' Inclusion in Cities: Innovative Urban Policies and Practices. UN-Habitat.

United Nations Human Settlements Programme (UN-Habitat)

2007   *State of the World's Cities Report 2006/7 – Millennium Development Goals and Urban Stability*. UN-Habitat, page iv. Available from http://mirror.unhabitat.org/pmss/listItemDetails.aspx?publicationID=2101

2009   *State of the World's Cities Report 2008/9: Harmonious Cities*. UN-Habitat, Nairobi. Available from http://unhabitat.org/books/state-of-the-worlds-cities-20082009-harmonious-cities-2/

2013   *State of the World's Cities 2012/2013 - Prosperity of Cities*. Routledge, New York. Available from http://unhabitat.org/books/prosperity-of-cities-state-of-the-worlds-cities-20122013/

Acapulco	Kumashi
Accra	Lagos
Addis Ababa	Lansing
Agra	Laredo
Aisho	Lattakia
Aleppo	Lausanne
Allahabad	Leipzig
Amman	Lille
Amsterdam	Lisbon
Antwerp	London
Athens	Los Angeles
Atlanta	Los Cabos
Auckland	Lubumbashi
Austin	Ludhiana
Baltimore	Madrid
Bamako	Manila
Bangalore	Mardin
Bangkok	McAllen
Basel	Melbourne
Beijing	Mexico City
Berlin	Miami
Bilbao	Milan
Brisbane	Montreal
Brownsville	Moscow
Brunswick	Mumbai
Brussels	Naga City
Budapest	Nairobi
Buenos Aires	Nashville
Bujumbura	New Orleans
Calexico	New York
Cancun	Nogales
Canterbury	Nyon
Cape Town	Oakland
Casablanca	Ota
Charlotte	Paris
Chetumal	Philadelphia
Chicago	Phoenix
Chihuahua	Pittsburgh
Cirebon	Portland
Cleveland	Porto Alegre
Columbus	Puerto Vallarta
Copenhagen	Rabat
Dakar	Reggio Emilia
Dallas	Renens
Dara'a	Rio de Janeiro
Dayton	Rome
Delhi	Rotterdam
Detroit	San Diego
Dongguan	San Francisco
Dubai	San Jose
Dublin	Sao Paolo
El Paso	Seattle
Faridabad	Seoul
Fez	Shanghai
Fuqing	Shenzen
Fuzhou	Singapore
Gaziantep	St. Louis
Geneva	Stockholm
Glasgow	Stuttgart
Goma	Surat
Goslar	Sydney
Gottingen	Tallinn
Guangzhou	Tamaulipas
Guiguinto	Tangiers
Halifax	Tapachula
Hamamatsu City	Tenosique
Hanoi	The Hague
Harare	Tijuana
Ho Chi Minh City	Tokyo
Homs	Toronto
Hong Kong SAR	Toyota
Houston	Tripoli
Indianapolis	Tunis
Ipswich	Turin
Irbid	Vancouver
Istanbul	Venice
Izmir	Veracruz
Jakarta	Vevey
Johannesburg	Vienna
Kavarna	Warsaw
Kibera	Washington D.C.
Kinshasa	Wuppertal
Kobe	Yverdon-les-Bains
Kolkata	Zarqa
Kuala Lumpur	Zurich

Cities shaded are on the Global Map

Vancouver
Detroit Montreal
Chicago Toronto Halifax
New York City
San Francisco Dayton Washington, D.C.
Los Angeles Nashville
Phoenix Atlanta
Tijuana Austin
Houston Miami
Mexico City
Chetumal

Rotterdam Antwerp
Paris
Geneva
Dakar

Rio de Janeiro
São Paulo
Porto Alegre
Buenos Aires

Mega city (10 million or more)
Large city (5 to 10 million)
Medium-sized city (1 to 5 million)
Small city (up to 1 million)

Migrants and cities: At a glance

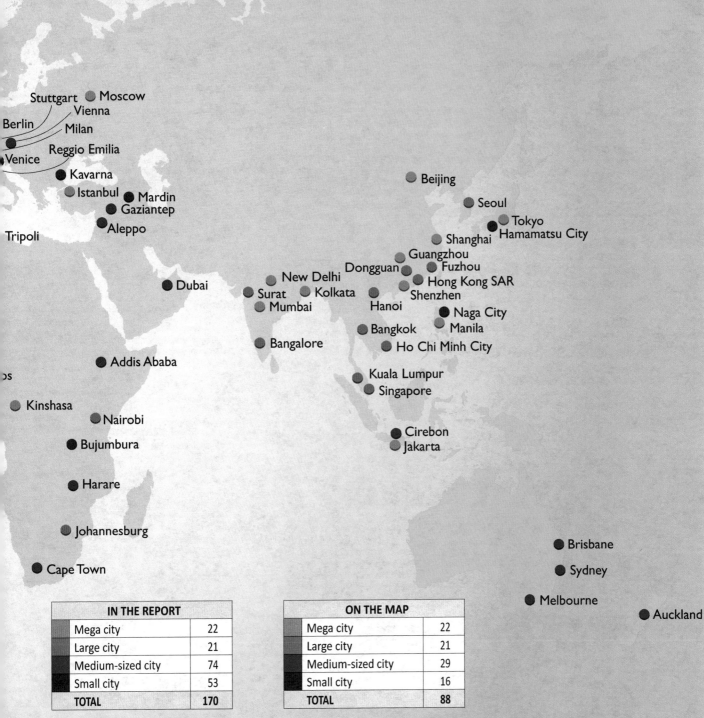

IN THE REPORT	
Mega city	22
Large city	21
Medium-sized city	74
Small city	53
TOTAL	**170**

ON THE MAP	
Mega city	22
Large city	21
Medium-sized city	29
Small city	16
TOTAL	**88**

Introduction

CHAPTER 1

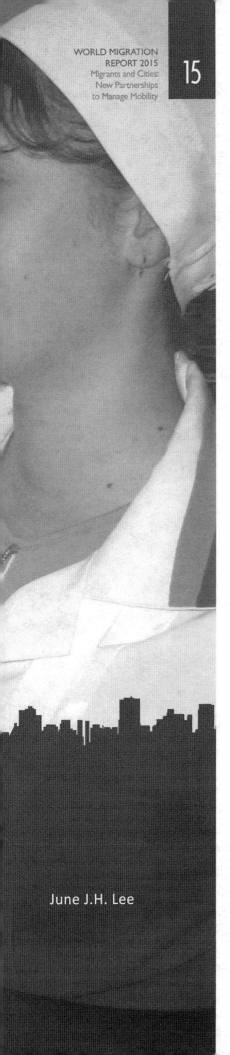

June J.H. Lee

HIGHLIGHTS

- Three million people around the world are moving to cities every week (UN-Habitat, 2009). The fast rate of urbanization brings with it both risks and opportunities for the migrants, communities and governments. The World Migration Report 2015 explores how migration and migrants are shaping cities, and how the life of migrants in turn is shaped by cities, their people, organizations and rules.

- It examines the relationships between migrants and cities on issues such as employment, housing and health, and also considers how migrants help to build and revive cities with their resources and ideas, both in the origin and host country. The Report also identifies innovative examples of how some cities are seeking to manage the challenges of increased global mobility and social diversity with varying degrees of success. It will highlight new policy developments concerning urban partnerships among migrant groups, local governments, civil society and the private sector which are designed to meet these challenges posed by migration and cities.

- Urbanization, defined as the increasing share of a population that is living in urban areas, can be attributed in general to natural population growth, net rural-to-urban migration, and also to the progressive extensions of urban boundaries and creation of new urban centres. Human mobility and migration clearly play an important part in the urbanization process as internal and international migrants gravitate to cities and urban areas. Yet there is no common method for analysing the interplay between migration and urbanization.

- Cities are generally conceived as settlements characterized by certain indicative features such as large populations, density, administrative functions and social diversity which make them distinct from non-city, suburban or rural areas. The traditional distinction between urban and rural areas in many developed countries has become blurred and the principal difference between urban and rural areas in terms of the circumstances of living, tends to be the degree of concentration of population. There is no internationally agreed definition of a "city" or any consensus on how to identify when a settlement is 'urban' or to determine its boundary.

- Overall patterns in migration and urbanization can be observed. There is however a lack of empirical data and the absence of systematically collected information of a comparative quality and content, especially in low income countries. This lack of data inhibits a deep understanding of migrants in urban environments. Cities, with their high concentration of migrants, often from different places of origin, offer a unique spatial domain for researching and understanding the dynamics of migration, urbanization and the intersection of national and local governance and policy.

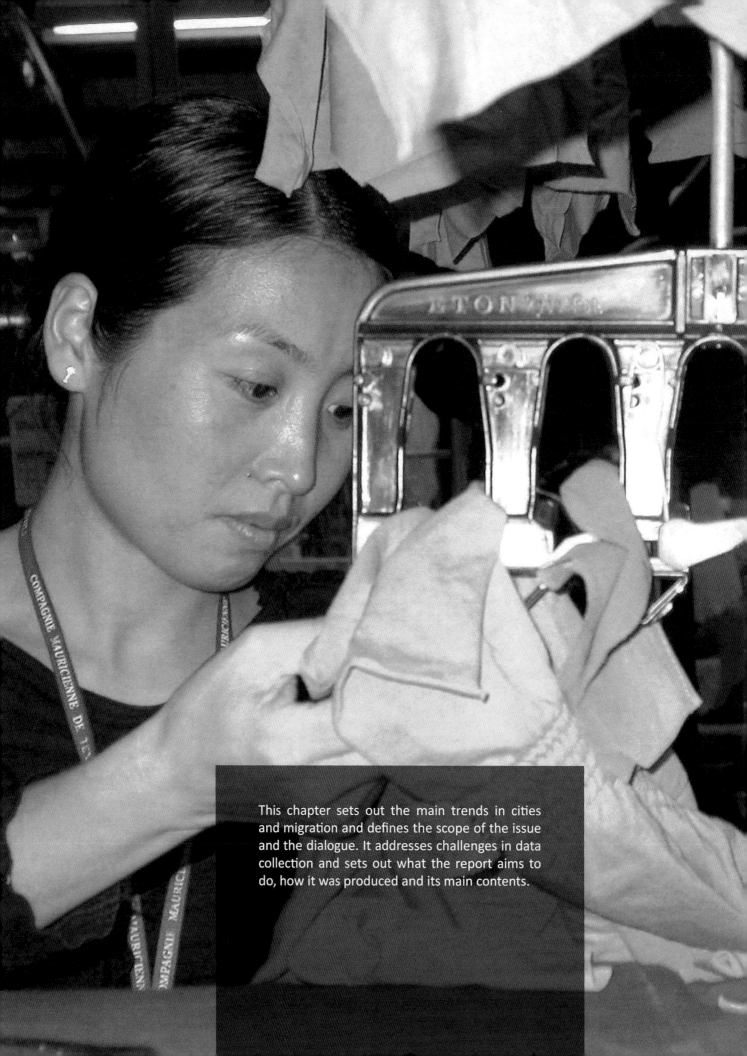

This chapter sets out the main trends in cities and migration and defines the scope of the issue and the dialogue. It addresses challenges in data collection and sets out what the report aims to do, how it was produced and its main contents.

MODERN DAY TRENDS

1.1 Statistics on migration and cities

We live in an era of unprecedented human mobility that has been markedly urban, as migrants, both internal and international, move to cities and urban areas, bring diversity and connect communities within and across borders to create new linkages among localities. This calls for new approaches to urban governance and migration policies.

There are an estimated 232 million international migrants (UN DESA, 2013) and 740 million internal migrants (UNDP, 2009) in the world.

- About 50 per cent of international migrants reside in ten highly urbanized, high-income countries[1] namely Australia, Canada and the United States, several countries in Europe (France, Germany, Spain and the United Kingdom), the Russian Federation, Saudi Arabia and the United Arab Emirates (UN DESA, 2013).

Almost all of the growth in the world's population over the next few decades, another 2.5 billion, is expected to be in urban areas in low- and middle-income countries, particularly in Africa and Asia (UN DESA, 2013).

- Although Africa is not the world's fastest urbanizing region, its urban population has been growing at a historically unprecedented rate for decades. In 1960, Johannesburg was the only city in sub-Saharan Africa with a population of over a million; by 1970, there were four (Cape Town, Johannesburg, Kinshasa and Lagos) and, by 2010, there were 33 (UN-Habitat, 2013).

- Every day an estimated 120,000 people migrate to cities in the Asia-Pacific region and, by 2050, the proportion of people living in urban areas is likely to rise to 63 per cent. The Asia-Pacific region has added nearly 1 billion people to its urban population between 1990 and 2014, about half of whom in China alone (450 million). The phenomenon is part of a long-term trend. The urban population of the region more than doubled between 1950 and 1975 and again between 1975 and 2000 and is projected to almost double once more between 2000 and 2025 (UNESCAP, 2014).

New partnerships for urban development

The *World Migration Report 2015* explores how migration and migrants are shaping cities, and how the life of migrants in turn is shaped by cities, their people, organizations and rules. A key message is that urban partnerships among migrant groups, local governments, civil society and the private sector are central to addressing the challenges and optimizing the opportunities presented by the growing trend of migration towards cities.

Sustained and inclusive economic growth is the goal most cities strive to achieve through practical and innovative solutions. Furthermore, for an increasing number of cities, immigration policies and programmes are integral to their urban development planning and management. UNESCO and UN-Habitat have undertaken joint research on the importance of migration for the growth of urban areas, and how to enhance inclusiveness of migrants in cities. Examples

---

1   See http://data.worldbank.org/data-catalog/GNI-per-capita-Atlas-and-PPP-table

are multiple of how migrants are helping to build cities, provide services and generally resuscitate the socioeconomic life of cities in decline, including some mid-size cities in the United States such as Dayton, Ohio, where Turkish migrants initiated cooperation with city authorities on a housing project. The authorities of such enterprising cities as Cleveland, Columbus, Detroit, Indianapolis, Lansing and Saint Louis have embarked on similar immigration-focused urban development experiments.

In recent years, there has been an increase in the number of networking initiatives among city authorities, urban practitioners, civil society leaders, business development communities and migrant/diaspora groups to discuss urban integration issues and foster participative economic growth. It is important to know to what extent these activities have been translated into effective urban policies to create "opportunity structures" for sustained and inclusive economic growth that empower both locals and newcomers.

For successful integration and community development, both cities of origin and destination are reaching out to each other. For example, Kavarna in Bulgaria concluded bilateral agreements with the four Polish cities where the majority of Roma from Kavarna were employed. These agreements give the Roma the right to work, register companies and facilitate tax collection. The Roma use their savings for improving their conditions of living, especially housing in Kavarna. In their destination cities, the Roma's economic success has changed the way they are perceived by the local population. Their new status as a prosperous group has improved inter-ethnic relations.

Urban governance in developing countries can be strengthened through city-to-city cooperation, particularly (but not only) with partner countries in the developed world. For example, the City of Rotterdam maintains strong partnerships with cities of the countries where most of Rotterdam's migrants come from, including Turkey, Morocco, Suriname, the Netherlands Antilles and Cabo Verde. In particular, Rotterdam also works on issues of water and climate change with their partner cities of Izmir, Istanbul and Casablanca. Similar initiatives have been developed over the past decade and are increasingly gaining popularity.

Global initiatives such as the Rockefeller Foundation's *Resilient Cities* programme and IBM's *Smarter Cities* programme view cities as drivers of sustainable national, regional and global economic growth to engage city governments, civil society and private sectors in partnerships on the ground and encourage cities to become smart to better respond to city and global challenges. The World Bank's *Project Greenback 2.0* identifies and works with "remittance champion cities" to improve transparency in the market for remittance services and to leverage the development effects of remittances.

However, many such public and private sector initiatives do not take full account of migrants as key players in city development, growth, resilience and sustainability. Migrants themselves can make significant and essential contributions to the economic, social and cultural development of their host countries and their communities back home. Yet oftentimes these contributions go unrecognized or at best are measured only in terms of the remittances they manage to send back home. As reflected in the Declaration adopted at the UN High-level Dialogue (HLD) on International Migration and Development in New York in 2013, migrants need to be at the centre of national and global migration and development agendas. This has been a core message of international debates on migration since the UNDP *Human Development Report 2009* on human mobility and development. By examining how migration affects well-being, WMR 2013 drew attention to migrants' human development and its significance in policy debate.

Migrants may be part of the challenge, especially during and after humanitarian crises, but they can also be part of the solution. As members of a global diaspora, migrants can act as bridge-builders, traders, business partners and humanitarian support between cities and countries. The economies of cities that have been built up by remittances of migrant workers are often more closely linked to the economies of the host country than the home country (Subohi, 2009; Klaufus, 2010). As cities plan for and manage the challenges of population growth (also from inflows) and increased sociocultural diversity, they need to include migrants in their planning and management for resilience.

1.2

DEFINITIONS AND TERMINOLOGY

Urbanization is defined mostly in demographic terms as the increasing share of a population that is living in urban areas. This increase can be attributed in general to three factors: natural population growth, net rural-to-urban migration, and the progressive extensions of urban boundaries and creation of new urban centres.

Very often, urbanization is primarily the result of migration. This is shown by the fact that fertility rates in urban areas tend to be lower than those of rural areas. This means that natural population growth of urban areas (the first factor mentioned above) is usually lower than that of rural areas. Furthermore, the extension of urban boundaries and creation of new urban centres (the third factor above) can also be often due to migration. Additionally, the term "urbanization" frequently refers to a broad rural-to-urban transition involving changes in population, land use, economic activity and culture. For example, on the periphery of urban centres, land becomes "urbanized" as it is developed for housing or manufacturing facilities and to where people move in order to live and work. However, these changes do not occur simultaneously, and the distinction between alterations in rural–urban economic activities and those involving cultural norms becomes less clear (McGranahan and Satterthwaite, 2014).

Urbanization and **urban population growth** are often conflated yet are still distinct concepts. Urban population growth is defined as the increase in the proportion of the urban population over time as part of the whole population. If the total population is not changing while the urban share is increasing, all urban population growth is the result of urbanization. Hence, in such simplified cases the rate of urbanization is equal to the rate of urban population growth. In most urbanizing countries in Asia and Africa, however, the situation is not so simple since the overall population is also growing. The fertility rates in these countries still remain higher than those of other regions where urbanization has slowed down and fertility rates are lower. Therefore, the contribution of migration to the urban population growth of Asian and African countries is relatively lower compared to natural population growth attributable to fertility rates. In Africa, migration only accounts for about one third of urban population growth whereas in Asia, the contribution of migration to urban population growth is higher than this due to a higher urbanization rate in Asia than in Africa (Tacoli, McGranahan and Satterthwaite, 2014).

Overall, about half of global urban population growth can be ascribed by experts to urbanization (that is, to net rural-to-urban migration) and the other half to natural population growth (McGranahan and Satterthwaite, 2014). Despite the fact that migration's contribution to urban population growth is moderate, there is much concern about the pace of urbanization and the capacity of national and local governments to cope with its consequences among low-income nations. Policymakers in these countries tend to consider rural–urban migration as the main contributor to over-crowding, congestion, increasing exposure to environmental hazards, and to shortfalls in basic infrastructure and services.

Cities are generally conceived as settlement types characterized by certain indicative features such as large populations, density, administrative functions, and social diversity which make them distinct from non-city, suburban or rural areas.   The traditional distinction between urban and rural areas in many developed countries has become blurred and the principal difference between urban and rural areas in terms of the circumstances of living tends to be the degree of concentration of population. The differences between urban and rural ways of life and standards of living tend to remain more significant in less developed countries. However, the rapid urbanization in the latter is increasingly linking the cities with their surrounding areas.   Key issues regarding definitions are as follows:

- No internationally agreed definition of a "city", nor any consensus on how to identify when a settlement is "urban" or to determine its boundary, as illustrated by the diversity of national urban definitions reported in the *World Urbanization Prospects, 2011 Revision* (UN DESA, 2012).

- Urban areas are defined differently in different countries. Some countries adopt a simple definition based on population size and density criteria, whereas other countries have multiple criteria including size, density and administrative level, and other indicators such as urban employment (for example non-agricultural workers), facilities (such as higher-level schools), and infrastructure (for instance street lighting). Not only are there diverse urban definitions, but countries change such definitions even from one census to the next.

- Most urban population thresholds fall between one and five thousand inhabitants. There are however, some extremes with Sweden defining 200 people as meeting the requirements of an "urban" population to Mali requiring 40,000 people to fulfil the same definition (McGranahan and Satterthwaite, 2014). This variation in the size definition can affect perceptions of regional over- or under-urbanization. For example, India, one of the top ten world economies, has one of the lowest urbanization rates at around 30 per cent. It is argued that it is undercounting urban population based on its restrictive urban definition.

- Using new monitoring technologies, attempts are being made to develop and apply more internationally comparable demographic definitions of urban and to move beyond simple rural–urban distinctions towards more complex settlement differentiation. The new methodology of the Organisation for Economic Co-operation and Development (OECD) for defining, monitoring and comparing "functional urban areas" (OECD, 2012) is one such example based on relative economic function rather than administrative boundaries. It uses population density to identify urban cores and travel-to-work flows to identify the hinterlands whose labour market is highly integrated with the cores. This may allow better understanding of the changes in settlement form and functioning in relation to changing social, economic and environmental complexity and especially in relation to other cities of different size and functions. However, the methodology is limited to the OECD countries and has not yet factored in migration or mobility.

The present report follows the general approach to cities of the United Nations taking into account national definitions and their size differentiation (UN DESA, 2014):

- **Megacities with more than 10 million inhabitants** are home to only about one in eight of the world's urban dwellers. Today the number of megacities has nearly tripled to 28 from a mere ten in 1990, with 453 million inhabitants, accounting for 12 per cent of the world's urban dwellers.

- **Large cities with 5 to 10 million inhabitants** account for a small, but growing proportion of the global urban population. In 2014, just over 300 million people lived in large cities, currently accounting for eight per cent of the urban population of the world.

- One in five urban dwellers worldwide lives in a **medium-sized city with 1 to 5 million inhabitants.** The global population living in medium-sized cities nearly doubled between 1990 and 2014, and is expected to increase by another 36 per cent between 2014 and 2030, growing from 827 million to 1.1 billion.

- The number of people living in cities of between 500,000 and 1 million inhabitants is expected to hold only around 10 per cent of the global urban population. In 2014, close to **one half of the world's urban population lives in settlements with fewer than 500,000 inhabitants.** While this proportion is projected to shrink over time, by 2030 these small cities and towns will still be home to around 45 per cent of urban dwellers.

Global urban population growth is propelled by the growth of cities of all sizes, as the UN DESA *World Urbanization Prospects, 2011 Revision* report mentioned above noted. Migration does contribute to urbanization, although the precise characteristics of migration flows remain inadequately studied. As such, cities of all sizes, municipalities, small towns, and even rural areas with their growing linkage to urban centres, are dealt with in the present report. As migrants, especially international migrants, tend to gravitate toward cities rather than small towns, medium-sized and large cities are discussed more often than other localities in this report. (See Global map: Migrants and cities: At a glance.)

1.3

RESEARCH GAPS ON NEW URBAN DESTINATIONS

Overall patterns in migration and urbanization can be observed. There is, however, a lack of empirical data and the absence of systematically collected data of a comparative quality and content, especially in low income countries. This lack of data inhibits a deep understanding of migrants in urban environments. Cities, with their high concentration of migrants, often from different places of origin, offer a unique spatial domain for researching and understanding the dynamics of migration, urbanization and the intersection of national and local governance and policy.

Frameworks for studying migration

As migration destinations change and diversify with people moving to different areas, especially to low- and middle-income countries, binary models which define migration as global South–North or developing–developed country movements do not aid the understanding of the heterogeneous nature of movements towards these new destinations. Currently there is no theoretical framework to help understand the complexities created by such rapidly shifting patterns of migration. A shift to cities as a unit of analysis may help reveal a more nuanced picture instead of using the "nation" as a marker given the significant differences that can exist between regions even within a country. Due to the lack of jurisdiction on immigration, cities can offer a natural spatial field for studying the dynamics and outcomes of migration on the ground. The new immigrant destinations, both in low- and high-income countries, present opportunities to re-examine key aspects of the migration process and outcomes in contexts which offer different reception conditions and local and institutional capacities. This shift will help shed light on migration as an actual social process – how migrants arrive, how they search for work and how they are accommodated – rather than aggregate demographic phenomena resulting from national policies. Importantly, research on migration at subnational level can highlight the critical role of local, regional and national governance, both of migrant selection and urban planning, in influencing migration outcomes. Human mobility transfers human capital. It also transfers knowledge and material capital. The changes in the nature of mobility have implications for uneven development among cities. Urban governance impinges on and mediates the key relationships between mobility and uneven regional development.

Data sources, limitations and good practices

Despite the fact that migration to cities is rapidly increasing, with more than half the world's population now residing in them and migrants playing a crucial role in the city-making and globalization processes, there is little data on these trends especially on foreign-born urban populations in the most low-income countries. The reasons for this are as follows:

- **Lack of census data.** The best data on migration in general, and on migration to cities in particular, often comes from censuses, but as many low-income countries do not have the resources to conduct censuses on a regular basis, information on migration is often out-of-date. In sub-Saharan Africa, for example, only 12 countries have conducted a census during the last ten years;[2]

---

2   See http://www.theguardian.com/global-development/poverty-matters/2014/jan/31/data-development-reliable-figures-numbers

- **Definitions of foreign-born in cities vary.** While in most cases, foreign-born refers to those born outside of the borders of the territorial residence, some countries like the Netherlands include second- and third-generation migrants in this category despite the fact that they are born in the country of settlement (Hagendoorn, Veenman and Vollebergh, eds., 2003). Some sources differentiate foreign-born in terms of their legal status, for instance, illegal, refugees, asylum-seekers (Çağlar, 2014);

- **Definitions of what constitutes "rural" and "urban" vary** between countries and can affect perceptions of over- or under-urbanization as noted above;

- **The quality and content of data varies** widely among countries thus limiting the ability to make comparisons across countries and cities.

Text box I

How the American Community Survey is used in New York, United States

Detailed information on New York City's population and housing attributes used to be obtained once a decade from the "long form" of the United States decennial census. The long form was eliminated after the 2000 census, and this information is now obtained annually from the American Community Survey (ACS). The ACS has a national sample of 3.54 million households and provides detailed social and economic information not only for the city, its boroughs, and community districts, but also for census tracts and block groups that comprise neighbourhoods.

The ACS is a rich source of information on New York's 3.1 million immigrants who account for 37 per cent of the city's 8.4 million residents. Latin Americans comprise nearly one-third of the city's immigrants, followed by immigrants from Asia (28%), the Caribbean (19%), Europe (16%), and Africa (4%). These immigrants play an important role in driving the demand for housing: close to one-half of all housing units occupied for the first time after 2000 had an immigrant householder. These facts are drawn from the New York City Department of City Planning's Population Division's 2013 report in the series, *The Newest New Yorkers*. The report uses ACS data, particularly the public use micro-data sample, which allows for an in-depth analysis of various immigrant groups. Information about age, sex, household type, education, labour force, occupation and income characteristics of immigrant groups provides perspective on where each immigrant group fits along the city's social, demographic, and economic spectrums. A major finding of the report was that the elderly population is now disproportionately comprised of immigrants. While immigrants primarily arrive in the young working ages, earlier cohorts have now aged and, for the first time, the city has an elderly population with a growing immigrant component with origins in Latin America, Asia, and the Caribbean. This context is extremely useful to those responsible for developing policies, planning programmes, or targeting services to the elderly.

Nearly one-half of New York City's foreign-born population has limited English proficiency (LEP) and this can be an impediment to interactions with government agencies. An executive order, signed by the mayor in 2008, requires every city agency that has direct interaction with New Yorkers to provide language assistance in the top six languages (other than English) spoken by New Yorkers: Spanish, Chinese, Russian, Korean, Italian and French Creole. These languages were identified, and are updated periodically, using the ACS. While this is a city-wide list, it is important to note that languages spoken differ dramatically across neighbourhoods. Whenever a service need arises at the neighbourhood level, languages appropriate to the neighbourhood are identified using the ACS. Public libraries often use this information to make decisions on which foreign language books need to be ordered and to determine the branches in which they need to be placed. ACS language data are also used in tandem with voter data to provide interpreter services for voters who are LEP, thus ensuring the city complies with voting rights statutes.

The ACS is a rich source of information for not only the city, but also for its 59 community districts, which are part of the city's government structure. Each district has a board, whose members are charged with identifying needs in their district and articulating local neighbourhood concerns. The division uses ACS "summary tables" to paint a comprehensive sociodemographic profile of each community district, as well as of the city overall. Data provided include information on educational attainment, poverty, the number and origins of immigrants, and languages spoken in each community district – and how this has changed over time. This information provides a vital framework for the deliberations of each community board. Compared with the information from the decennial census, the annual information from the ACS provides a timely snapshot of a constantly evolving city.

Contributed by Arun Peter Lobo, Deputy Director, Population Division, New York City Department of City Planning

The lack of credible data has been a major constraint which has hampered the formulation of proper policies in both sending and receiving countries. In destination countries, census data provide the basis for most of the available global databases on migration stocks, especially in terms of traditional migration routes. See, for example, the micro sample of the United States Census and the American Community Survey (text box 1). In countries of origin, surveys with special migration questions or modules generate relevant data about the impact of migration and remittances on poverty reduction, education and health in sending communities. There is, however, a particular dearth of reliable global data on internal migrants. Cross-national comparisons of internal migration are hindered by widespread variation in data collection practices (Esipova, Pugliese and Ray, 2013). The IMAGE project, which identifies forms of data on internal migration, found that 109 out of 193 UN Member States were collecting data from multiple sources, linking data from population registers and national surveys (Bell et al., 2014). Table 1 sets out the advantages and disadvantages of different data sources – censuses, surveys, population registers and other administrative sources – in terms of gathering information on migration flows.

Table 1 | **Comparison of data sources**

Data source	Advantages	Disadvantages
Censuses	• Universal coverage • High degree of standardization • Wide geographic coverage	• High cost and infrequently conducted • No disaggregated migration data • Only contain basic variables • Snapshot; not useful for examining trends • Do not capture irregular migrants • City-level data does not capture migrants in peri-urban areas • Possible underreporting of foreign-born population in some cities
Surveys (labour market or specialized and multitopic surveys)	• Most reliable data source in origin countries • Rich source of data • Useful identifying microeconomic linkages between migration and other aspects • Better capture undercounted migrants	• Small sample sizes • Do not capture migrants from smaller corridors • Absence of a proper sampling frame • High costs of tracking down migrants • Lack of statistical capacity in origin countries • Reliance on proxy respondents
Population registers	• Record both internal and international migration • Provide detailed up-to-date demographic and socioeconomic information	• High degree of heterogeneity across countries • Do not capture irregular migrants • Departures are underreported
Administrative data sources, (border statistics, residency permits, naturalization records, etc.)	• Disaggregated data available	• Residency permits only; possible undercount • Rarely made public by governments • Do not capture irregular migrants

Source: Based on C. Carletto, J. Larrison and Ç. Özden, (2014) Informing Migration Policies: A Data Primer. World Bank Policy Research, Working Paper 7082.

The way forward

Cities offer a natural space for studying the dynamics and outcomes of growing diverse migration and mobility patterns on the ground. Looking at migration from a city perspective shifts the focus from why people move to how they work, live and shape their local habitats. This type of enquiry is at a nascent stage and has major limitations due to the critical lack of available, accurate, comprehensive and comparable data (Winders, 2014). Such migration enquiries need to highlight multiple dimensions of urban diversity beyond the country of origin or ethnic group of migrants. Additional variables, such as migration status and concomitant entitlements/restrictions of rights, labour market experiences, gender and age profiles, patterns of spatial distribution, and mixed local area responses by service providers and residents, need to be considered. This will produce much richer analyses of the diverse migration and mobility patterns and help improve urban migration policymaking practices.

1.4
GUIDE TO THE REPORT

1.4.1. Contribution of the report

This report explores how migration and migrants are shaping cities, and how the life of migrants in turn is shaped by cities, their people, organizations and rules. It examines the relationships between migrants and cities on such issues as employment, housing and health, and also considers how migrants help to build and revive cities with their resources and ideas, both in the origin and host country. The report also identifies innovative examples of how some cities are seeking to manage the challenges of increased global mobility and social diversity with varying degrees of success. It will highlight new policy developments concerning urban partnerships among migrant groups, local governments, civil society and the private sector which are designed to meet these challenges posed by migration and cities. Migrants are still largely absent from global discourses on urbanization and cities are not a major part of global migration debates.

The present report aims to address these gaps in three distinct ways:

- By documenting how migration is shaping cities and the situation of migrants in cities. Much of the current international discussion about migration trends and migration policy tends to focus on the **national level**. Taking the migration enquiry to the city level has increased the understanding of the local political economies of migration, and the close connection between migration and urban development. It has shifted the focus from why people move to how they work, live and shape habitats that connect the world as their migration and mobility patterns diversify.

- By paying attention to the livelihood of migrants in the cities of the **Global South**. The existing discussions on migrants and cities are limited as they tend to focus primarily on the Global North and the integration of international migrants. This is due to the traditional focus on migration from low- and middle-income countries to more affluent ones. But this report takes a global perspective and particularly focuses on the situation of migrants in the cities of the Global South.

- By examining both **internal and international** migration. Cities across the development spectrum have growing mobile and diverse populations to manage. In the developed countries, one of the main sources of population diversity is international migration, while in the developing world, it is most likely internal migration[3] and to a lesser extent, growing international South–South migration.

While acknowledging the vast differences between international and internal migration scenarios, and between the ability of rich, emerging and poorer countries to deal with these, the present report highlights the growing evidence of potential benefits of all forms of migration and mobility for city growth and

---

3   There is a serious lack of consistent, current and comparable data on foreign born urban populations in most countries of the Global South.

development. It showcases innovative ways in which migration and urbanization policies can be better aligned for the benefit of migrants and cities.

This report's examination of migrants and cities is not exhaustive. It is indicative of the immense scope and complexity of the field. As such the report does not deliver easy policy lessons. It acknowledges that the policy challenges are complex – how to maximize the benefits of migration for city development whilst reducing the risks of migration for cities and migrants. The report highlights some innovative ways in which cities have addressed these challenges.

Proviso

There is a renewed enthusiasm and interest in focusing on cities and their diversity, especially defined by ethnic diversity. This often involves a consideration of rich cities in the Global North, urban elites and skilled migrants.

According to UN-Habitat, cities are economic engines which can steer the world towards prosperity, especially in developing regions (UN-Habitat, 2013; UN DESA, 2012). In North America migrants are seen as agents of city growth and competitiveness (AS/COA, 2014). Europe sees diversity, partly induced by international migration, as an asset for the development of a city and the Council of Europe strongly supports public discourse and urban institutions that take diversity positively into account.[4]

In this context, there are quite a few and a growing number of city networks that strengthen relations among local institutions and draw collective good practices from their individual experiences, with the shared goal of sustainable urban development and governance. They include the Canada-based Maytree Foundation's "Cities of Migration"[5] and the OPENCities, co-founded by the EU and the British Council.

In addition to these city networks (Eurocities, 2010, 2014), various international organizations (Price and Chako, 2013; UNESCO and UN-Habitat, 2010), political think tanks (Kerr, McDaniel and Guinan, 2014; McHugh, 2014) and national and global forums for research and policy on migration and cities (Metropolis, 2011; Cities of Migration, 2012) have already published compilations of good practices of inclusion policies, mostly from Europe and North America, and also some from Latin America. Some of these collections have a specific thematic focus, for example, the communication strategies of local authorities for the promotion of positive attitudes towards migrants (Collett and Gidley, 2012).

The present report aims to build on these important initiatives and to address the challenges faced by cities of the Global South, particularly in capitalizing on inward migration flows. Many important questions remain in this discussion about cities and migration, for instance:

- How can the good practices of developed countries be replicated in other countries with limited resources, including small island developing States that are adjusting to rapid urban transitions?

- How useful are the lessons of more advanced States in managing diversity?

- How are local and central governments and their numerous non-State partners able to achieve optimal practice-to-policy outcomes?

---

4   See the Council of Europe's website at: www.coe.int/t/dg4/cultureheritage/culture/cities/default_EN.asp? Intercultural cities: governance and policies for diverse communities.
5   See the Cities of Migration Conference in Berlin in June 2014 on "An Agenda for Shared Prosperity" : http://2014conference.citiesofmigration.ca/

1.4.2. Sources of information

There are two main factors which limit the discussion on migrants and cities. Firstly, basic subnational data on migration is seriously limited in terms of availability, accuracy, comprehensiveness and comparability. Secondly, research on migration at subnational level has focused predominantly on localities in North America. Most studies on new destinations in Europe and other regions are conducted on a national scale. Analyses of different scale levels pose a challenge for a comparative study (Winders, 2014). Much groundwork is therefore needed on a wide range of new destinations especially in the Global South for insightful comparison.

With these caveats, the present report intends to discuss some of the compelling empirical realities of a wide range of locations around the world as migrants move among a range of destinations, especially urban areas, and maintain social connections across them. Both international and internal migrants gravitate to and invest their resources in urban areas, where more and more of the global population is expected to reside (UN DESA, 2014).

The present report draws on a variety of primary and secondary sources of information to discuss new urban migration trends and mobility patterns and to explore their development implications and governance challenges.

- A literature review was conducted on a wide range of topics from urbanization, slum upgrading, migration and development, migrant inclusion policies and practices, diversity management, to urban governance and citizenship in order to identify the report's sub-themes and experts. The serious shortage in existing studies that examine migration dynamics at subnational level and migrant life and work in cities, especially in the cities of the Global South, was noted.

- Experts were identified to provide background papers reviewing urban migration trends in major regions and countries, their challenges and opportunities and urban migration policy and partnership examples. Specific topics such as migrant entrepreneurship, migrant health, and migrant-specific vulnerability and resilience in urban settings were included in the set of background papers, as there is particular dearth of research on these topics.

- In addition to the background papers, local authorities, including several mayors, contributed text boxes in order to share their experiences and perspectives on specific challenges posed by urban migration as well as innovative local solutions.

- IOM Regional Offices provided relevant background information as well as interview cases with urban migrants in order to add the critical migrant voices to the present report.

1.4.3. Report structure

- Chapter 2 examines the various urban settings which have experienced recent growth of either internal or international or even both types of migration flows. It highlights the diversifying migration flows and underlines some of the challenges both migrants and their new host communities and cities are facing.

- Chapter 3 looks at aspects of urban vulnerabilities in general – livelihood and mobility strategies, barriers to accessing resources and specific forms of vulnerabilities, as they affect the populations most at risk including migrant women. It highlights how mobile populations become more vulnerable to disasters by movement into cities, and how partnerships among migrants, non-governmental organizations and local governments can help build resilience to natural hazards.

- Chapter 4 explores how urbanization and new mobility patterns can contribute to urban poverty reduction, growth and development and enhance migrant well-being. Mobility is an essential part of livelihood strategies for families and communities. Migration helps to build bridges across urban–rural divides and foster closer links between the two. It also examines how cities can turn urban diversity into social and economic advantages, by facilitating migrant access to formal labour markets and encouraging migrant-led businesses.

  The chapter then turns to the emerging innovative partnerships around cities dealing with and potentially enhancing development impacts of migration and well-being among migrants. The central role of migrants is highlighted in forging the links between cities and communities of origin and destination and mainstreaming migration into local development planning.

- Chapter 5 studies some of the urban governance conditions for migrant inclusion and partnerships. How national and local government relations work and how the different governance entities share financial, budgetary and administrative authority and flexibility for migration governance to shape the opportunities structure that helps link migrant inclusion to economic growth and global competitiveness. Urban citizenship is a pragmatic policy tool to further enable migrants' inclusion and an important element of such opportunities structures. The chapter highlights migrants as city-makers in the context of local opportunity that articulates the urban and migration policies and the global dynamics.

- Chapter 6 brings together reflections and conclusions arising from the Report and proposes ideas and recommendations for the future.

A tale of many cities – Living and working in Ypejhú, Buenos Aires and Madrid

Mercedes was born in Ypejhú, Paraguay, in a large family with twelve brothers and sisters. Her father worked cultivating wheat and her brothers helped him from a very early age in order to support the family finances. When she was 18, Mercedes left home and went to live with her boyfriend, Pedro. Some years later, Maicol, her only son, was born but the couple decided to split up. Since she was unable to maintain her household, Mercedes decided to migrate to Argentina in the footsteps of her sisters and school friends. Her son stayed in Paraguay and Mercedes' mother took care of him as she was already caring for her other grandchildren.

Mercedes has been living in Buenos Aires for 15 years now, working as a cleaner, domestic help and babysitter. At the beginning, her housing and working conditions were difficult: "I was working informally, many hours a day, living in a rented room, sharing with other three Paraguayan women whom I didn't know, and I was missing my son a lot". When the economic situation became difficult in Argentina, Mercedes used all her savings to buy a ticket to Madrid, Spain, and moved there looking for new horizons: "It was 2001, my boss had suddenly fired me, and the owner of my rented room asked me for more money to stay. I didn't think twice: I took my savings, bought the ticket and left with the only suitcase I had."

In Madrid, Mercedes' first job involved cleaning in a bar and then cooking in a restaurant. However, her employer was not treating her well and she was missing her family and son: "When I was living in Buenos Aires, I always tried to escape to Paraguay to visit Maicol and spend time with my mum. I went by bus and it wasn't that expensive. While in Spain, it was impossible to travel home and I started to feel very lonely". That was when Mercedes decided to return to Argentina after two years in Madrid: "I came back to Buenos Aires and it was starting from zero again. But the country's situation was a bit better after recovering from the financial crisis".

Currently, Mercedes lives in an apartment that she rents in the district of San Fernando, Buenos Aires Province, where other Paraguayan migrants also live. Although it is small, she lives by herself and has running water, electricity and a toilet, something that she did not have in Ypejhú, where almost 45 per cent of the population does not have access to sanitation. "My apartment is small but nice. I have to travel two hours to get to my job, but I don't care. I have decorated the room and it is now cosy. I feel good to have a little place for when my son visits me". However, Mercedes admits that she feels unsafe and is afraid of walking alone at night.

Thinking about the future, Mercedes imagines herself with a foot in Buenos Aires and a foot in Asunción, where her son currently resides: "When I'm in Buenos Aires, I miss the Paraguayan rhythm, the calm, the tranquility and the warm temperatures all year round. But when I'm there, I miss the movement of the city, the bars, the streets, the buildings. I think that, as a popular song says, I'm not from here, not from there".

REFERENCES

Americas Society / Council of the Americas (AS/COA)
2014   *Immigrants & Competitive Cities,* Get the Facts Series. Available from www.as-coa.org/sites/default/files/ImmigrantsandCompetitive Cities.pdf

Bell M. et al.
2014   *Internal Migration Data around the World: Assessing Contemporary Practice.* Population Space Place, published online in Wiley Online Library (www.wileyonlinelibrary.com) DOI: 10.1002/psp.1848, Vol. 21 (1).

Çağlar, A.
2014   Urban Migration Trends, Challenges and Opportunities, Background Paper for the *World Migration Report 2015: Migrants and Cities: New Partnerships to Manage Mobility,* International Organization for Migration (IOM), Geneva, Switzerland.

Cities of Migration
2012   *Practice to Policy. Lessons from Local Leadership on Immigrant Integration.* Maytree Foundation, Toronto. Available from http://citiesofmigration.ca/wp-content/uploads/2012/03/Practice-to-Policy.pdf

Collett, E. and B. Gidley
2012   Attitudes to Migrants, Communication and Local Leadership (AMICALL). Final Transnational Report. COMPAS, Oxford. Available from www.compas.ox.ac.uk/fileadmin/files/Publications/Reports/Amicall_Report_ENG_v3_single_WEB_READY.pdf

Esipova N., A. Pugliese and J. Ray
2013   *The Demographics of Global Internal Migration,* Migration Policy Practice, IOM and EurAsylum, Stockport, UK, 3(2):3–5. Available from http://publications.iom.int/bookstore/free/MigrationPolicyPracticeJournal10_15May2013.pdf

Eurocities
2010   *Cities Accommodating Diversity.* Findings and Recommendations from the Peer Review Project 'Diversity and Equality in European Cities'. Eurocities, Brussels. Available from http://nws.eurocities.eu/MediaShell/media/DIVE_FinalPublication.pdf
2014   Integrating Cities Toolkit, Brussels. Available from www.integrating cities.eu/integrating-cities/resources/implementoring_toolkits

Hagendoorn L., J. Veenman and W. Vollebergh (eds.)
2003   *Integrating Immigrants in the Netherlands: Cultural Versus Socio-economic.* Ashgate, Aldershot. (Cited in A. Çağlar, *Urban Migration Trends, Challenges and Opportunities*, Background Paper for the World Migration Report 2015: Migrants and Cities: New Partnerships to Manage Mobility, IOM, 2015.)

Kerr, J., P. McDaniel and M. Guinan
2014   *Reimagining the Midwest: Immigration Initiatives and the Capacity of Local Leadership*. The Chicago Council on Global Affairs and American Immigration Council, Chicago. Available from www. immigrationpolicy.org/sites/default/files/docs/reimagining_the_ midwest_report_2014.pdf

Klaufus, C.
2010   *Watching the city grow: remittances and sprawl in intermediate Central American cities*, CEDLA (Centre for Latin American Research and Documentation). Available from http://eau.sagepub.com/ content/22/1/125.refs (Accessed 19 Jan 2014) Environment & Urbanization, Vol. 22, pp 125–137.

McGranahan, G. and D. Satterthwaite
2014   *Urbanisation concepts and trends*, International Institute for Environment and Development (IIED) Working Paper. Available from http://pubs.iied.org/pdfs/10709IIED.pdf

McHugh, M.
2014   *Immigrant Civic Integration and Service Access Initiatives: City-Sized Solutions for City-Sized Needs*. Migration Policy Institute, Washington D.C. Available from www.migrationpolicy.org/sites/default/files/ publications/TCM_Cities_McHugh-FINAL.pdf

Metropolis
2011   *Integrated Urban Governance, The way forward*, Commission 3 Manual. Metropolis World. Available from http://old.metropolis.org/ sites/default/files/initiatives/2932/documents/c3-metropolis-urban-governance-eng.pdf
             Summary: http://old.metropolis.org/sites/default/files/publications/ 2011/summary_commissions_metropolis_2009-2011.pdf

Organisation for Economic Co-operation and Development (OECD)
2012   *Redefining Urban Areas in OECD Countries, A New Way to Measure Metropolitan Areas*, pp 19–55. OECD, Paris. Available from www. oecd.org/gov/regional-policy/redefiningurbananewwaytomeas-uremetropolitanareas.htm

Price, M. and E. Chacko
2013   *Migrants' Inclusion in Cities: Innovative Urban Policies and Practices*. UNESCO and UN-Habitat. Available from www.researchgate.net/ publication/272023289_Migrants'_Inclusion_in_Cities_Innovative_ Urban_Policies_and_Practices._Prepared_for_UN-Habitat_and_ UNESCO_Marie_Price_and_Elizabeth_Chacko

Subohi, A.
2009   *Workers' Remittances Build a New City*, 23 February 2009. Available from www.dawn.com/news/446247/workersae-remittances-build-a-new-city-2

Tacoli, C., G. McGranahan and D. Satterthwaite
2014   Urbanization, Rural-urban Migration and Urban Poverty. Background Paper for the *World Migration Report 2015: Migrants and Cities: New Partnerships to Manage Mobility*, International Organization for Migration, Geneva.

United Nations Department of Economic and Social Affairs (UN DESA)

2012   *World Urbanization Prospects: 2011 Revision.* United Nations, New York. Available from www.un.org/en/development/desa/population/publications/pdf/urbanization/WUP2011_Report.pdf

2013   *International Migration 2013 Wallchart.* United Nations, New York. Available from www.un.org/en/development/desa/population/migration/publications/wallchart/docs/wallchart2013.pdf

2014   *World Urbanization Prospects, The 2014 Revision - Highlights.* United Nations, New York. Available from http://esa.un.org/unpd/wup/

United Nations Development Programme (UNDP)

2009   *Human Development Report 2009, Overcoming barriers: Human mobility and development.* United Nations, New York. Available from http://hdr.undp.org/en/content/human-development-report-2009

United Nations Economic and Social Commission for Asia and the Pacific (UNESCAP)

2014   *Statistical Yearbook for Asia and the Pacific 2014.* United Nations. Available from www.unescap.org/resources/statistical-yearbook-asia-and-pacific-2014

United Nations Educational, Scientific and Cultural Organization (UNESCO) and United Nations Human Settlements Programme (UN-Habitat)

2010   *How to enhance inclusiveness for international migrants in our cities: various stakeholders' views.* UNESCO, Paris. Available from. Available from http://unesdoc.unesco.org/images/0019/001905/190592m.pdf

United Nations Human Settlements Programme (UN-Habitat)

2009   *State of the World's Cities 2008/2009 – Harmonious Cities.* United Nations. Available from http://unhabitat.org/books/state-of-the-worlds-cities-20082009-harmonious-cities-2/

2013   *State of the World's Cities 2012/2013 – Prosperity of Cities.* Routledge, New York. Available from http://unhabitat.org/books/prosperity-of-cities-state-of-the-worlds-cities-20122013/

Winders, J.

2014   "New Immigrant Destinations in Global Context", *International Migration Review* 48(S1):149–179 (2014).

Migration and urban diversity

CHAPTER 2

June J.H. Lee

HIGHLIGHTS

• Urbanization and migration go hand in hand. Urbanization, which is the increasing proportion of a population living in urban as opposed to rural areas, usually involves some form of migration whether it be internal or international. The current high levels of urbanization around the world have not been achieved only by changes in natural population levels arising from variations in fertility and mortality rates. Rather the increase in migratory flows around the world – within and between countries, between rural and urban areas, between the Global North and South in all directions – is a key force behind modern day urban growth.

• These migratory movements are shaping a diverse form of urban settlement, ranging from the emergence of global cities like London, New York and Tokyo as powerhouses of the international economy to forgotten informal settlements like Kibera in Kenya where inhabitants struggle to meet the most basic of human needs. Other trends include movements to secondary towns, depopulated cities, peri-urban areas and transit cities.

• The common theme across all these diverse examples is that the vast majority of this urban growth is organic and unplanned. Cities around the world are struggling to manage this unexpected growth and put in place adequate services and infrastructure to meet the needs of fast-growing populations.

• The problem is sometimes compounded by a disjuncture between national and local policies. For instance, migration to urban areas may be promoted by central government as a way of strengthening national economies, but without ensuring coordination of local policies on health, education and social care to meet the needs on the ground. Aside from a few examples where city-level policymakers proactively incentivize migration to depopulated towns, local policymakers are usually at the receiving end of higher level policy decisions rather than the architects of migration and urbanization policies themselves.

• Even if this urban growth is organic and unplanned, the key question for policymakers is what lessons can be learned from around the world on managing migration and urban growth effectively in order to alleviate the severe difficulties being experienced on the ground in many cities.

• Increasing diversity within cities is another feature of modern day trends in migration and urban growth. The major cities of the industrialized world in particular have very diverse populations living side by side. In developing countries too, the ethnic and racial mix can be considerable as migrants are drawn from nearby countries and across the region. Managing diversity effectively poses a challenge for both local and national governments.

Bushalte
Busstop

B12

B14

This chapter examines the various urban settings which have experienced recent growth either due to internal, international or mixed migration flows. It highlights the diversifying migration flows and underlines some of the challenges both migrants and their new host communities and cities are facing.

2.1

INTRODUCTION

The geography of migration flows is changing as new destinations emerge globally. In addition to the traditional migrant corridors from the Global South to the advanced economies of North America and Europe (Münz, 2014), migrants are attracted to the fast-growing economies of new growth centres in East Asia, South Africa, Brazil and India. Map 1 highlights the traditional and new migrant destinations areas. Population movements among low- and middle-income countries, known as South–South migration, have gained importance with developing countries themselves becoming places of both immigration and emigration. China, for example, is a country which receives immigrants from Nigeria while, at the same time, being a country of emigrants to the Middle East. Internal migration is also on the rise in these countries and is leading to the fast expansion of cities (UN DESA, 2014). New migrant destinations are also emerging at subnational level as migrants move to smaller, second-tier metro areas (Walton-Roberts, 2011).

This mass migration, both between and within countries, is shaping the type of urbanization taking place, from the development of central inner city areas through to counter-urbanization measures which foster growth in outlying areas and suburbs. Urbanization can be planned or organic but the reality in today's world is that much urban growth is fast and chaotic and placing a strain on the existing infrastructure and resources. The following section describes the diversity of urban settings around the world, from global cities through to peri-urban development and shanty towns, and shows that local administrations are not always equipped with the policies, infrastructure or know-how to cope with unforeseen arrivals.

Map 1 **Global diversification of migration destinations**

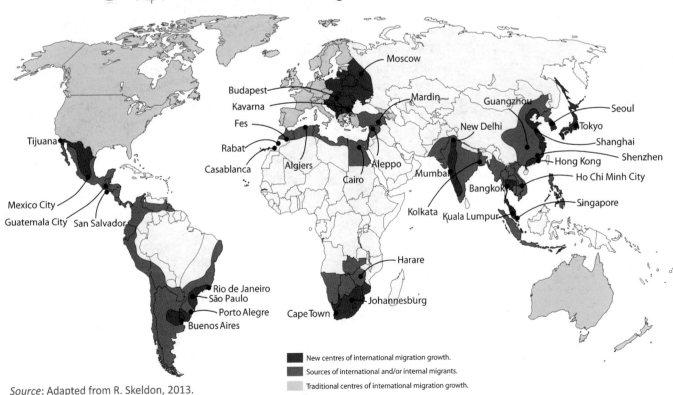

■ New centres of international migration growth.

■ Sources of international and/or internal migrants.

■ Traditional centres of international migration growth.

Source: Adapted from R. Skeldon, 2013.

2.2

DIVERSITY OF
URBAN SETTINGS

2.2.1. Global cities

Global cities like London, New York and Tokyo play a vital role in the international economic system. They are crucial also to the economies of the countries in which they are situated and form a central part of national economic strategy and planning. However, the cities themselves may be differentially equipped to deal with the often high concentrations of international migrants attracted to such places.

Global cities such as London, New York, Tokyo and Hong Kong Special Administrative Region (SAR) lie at the heart of the international economic system (Sassen, 1991). They are recognized as important nodes in the global economic system by virtue of their connections with international financial markets and multinational corporations. Cities are classified according to their degree of integration within the global economy. Rankings from 2014 show that the top 20 global cities in the world are fairly evenly split between Europe (London, Paris, Brussels, Madrid, Vienna, Moscow and Berlin), Asia-Pacific (Tokyo, Hong Kong SAR, Beijing, Singapore, Seoul, Sydney and Shanghai) and the Americas (New York, Los Angeles, Chicago, Washington D.C., Toronto and Buenos Aires).[1]

Global or "world" cities of this type are a major draw for migrants; some 19 per cent of the world's foreign-born population is estimated to live in them (Çağlar, 2014). Figure 1 shows the size of the foreign-born population in major world cities; some cities with highly mobile workforces have particularly high proportions of foreign-born populations, for instance, Dubai (83%) or Brussels (62%) which is the headquarters of the European Commission. The high number of migrants from many different countries adds to the global character of such cities in terms of cultural outlook and social norms, although these factors are not part of the consideration in the usual global city classification systems.

Where global cities exist, migrants tend to be particularly concentrated in them as compared to other parts of the country: for example, of Canada's 6.8 million foreign-born population (The Canadian Press, 2013), 46 per cent live in Toronto (Statistics Canada, 2011). Statistics from the United States show that, as at 2010, just over 40 per cent of the nation's foreign-born population was living in New York, Los Angeles, Miami, Chicago and San Francisco (Singer, 2013). Moreover, the foreign-born population may sometimes outstrip the native population in cities of this type: 28 per cent of Australia's 6.6 million people were born overseas (Australian Bureau of Statistics, 2015) and are mainly concentrated in Sydney (1.4 million) and Melbourne (1.2 million) (Australian Bureau of Statistics, 2014).

---

1   See www.atkearney.com/research-studies/global-cities-index#sthash.nebCorKC.dpuf

Figure 1   **Foreign-born population in major cities**

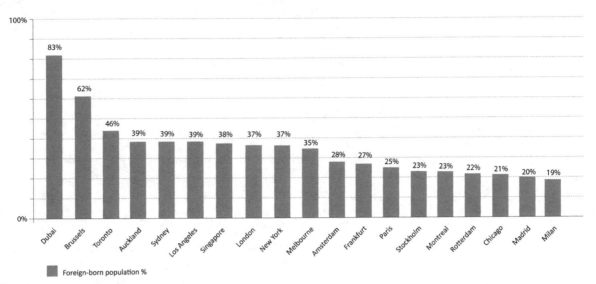

Source: Compiled by IOM from various sources – see list at the end of the References section.

The composition of these cities has changed over time. Data from the United States shows that its five largest "gateway" cities, New York, Los Angeles, Miami, Chicago and San Francisco, the main entry points for migrants from various countries of origin, have experienced more domestic migration out than in during 2000–2009 thus shifting the balance between foreign- and native-born populations in these places. In Europe, the increase of foreign-born populations is a relatively recent phenomenon as compared to the United States. In the United Kingdom, the foreign-born population doubled from 3.8 million to around 7.8 million between 1993 and 2013. Thirty eight per cent of the entire foreign-born population live in London, and whose number has increased from 1.6 million in 1995 to a current total of nearly 3 million (Rienzo and Vargas-Silva, 2014).

National policy in Europe, North America and Australia may see immigration to global cities, especially of highly skilled migrants, as part of a development strategy aimed at enhancing economic competitiveness. However, the cities themselves are differentially equipped to deal with the arrival of foreign-born populations. Among cities in the United States, New York, Chicago and San Francisco have been attractive destinations for over a century and have robust institutions in place to serve diverse migrant groups, including those who are undocumented (Price, 2014). There are strong partnerships between local authorities and non-governmental organizations (NGOs) as well as forums for learning and exchange between cities such as the Cities for Citizenship or the Partnership for a New American Economy which brings together mayors and corporate leaders. By comparison, Washington D.C. and Atlanta, which have experienced a rapid growth of immigrant population since 1980 yet lack explicit strategies to attract and settle new foreign-born arrivals, have seen a backlash, especially over the numbers of unauthorized immigrants, as a result of these sudden demographic changes (ibid.).

2.2.2. Secondary cities

Migrants are also moving to secondary smaller scale cities which may not be known outside the country or region. Such cities can be an attractive option for migrants; they can offer better value amenities which can offset the loss of cultural and social facilities afforded by larger conurbations. Secondary cities, however, may be ill-equipped to adjust to and optimize the opportunities presented by migrant arrivals.

The last two decades have seen growing numbers of migrants in the Global North moving to smaller, "second tier" metropolitan areas (Walton-Roberts, 2011). These secondary cities have between 500,000 to 3 million inhabitants and may not be known outside their national or regional context. This emerging trend can be seen across North America and Europe (Esipova, Pugliese and Ray, 2013):

- In the United States, the largest increase in internal migration in 2012–2013 was to secondary cities (US Census Bureau, 2013) while the three largest metropolitan cities experienced a net outflow of residents in the same period - New York (100,000 persons), Los Angeles and Chicago (both roughly 50,000 persons). There were net losses of American residents from the high-tech industrial conurbations of San Jose and San Diego as well as from cities like Detroit in the post-industrial Rust Belt region of America. Net gains, however, were registered among the low-cost Sun Belt cities of Phoenix, Dallas and Houston, and also in the leading knowledge-hubs such as Austin, Seattle, San Francisco and Washington D.C. (Florida, 2014). The United States 2000 Census recorded a substantial increase of international migrants in the secondary cities of Atlanta, Charlotte and Nashville (Price, 2014).

- In Canada, while Toronto, Montreal and Vancouver continue to receive the majority of international migrants, both recent and established migrants are shifting to suburban areas and smaller communities (Federation of Canadian Municipalities, 2009).

- In Europe, migrants are settling in small towns instead of gateway cities (Bayona and Gil-Alonso, 2011), for instance in the smaller municipalities of the Italian provinces of Lazio or Lombardy instead of the major hubs of Rome or Milan respectively (UNESCO SSIIM, n.d.).

Migrants may be drawn to smaller towns, suburban, exurban or rural locations because of, for instance, employment opportunities, affordable housing, personal safety, family links, schools, universities, public transport, medical facilities and clean air (The Demographia, 2015). These advantages may offset the loss of access to economic, political or cultural facilities, including established migrant networks, which can be found in primary gateway cities (Glick Schiller and Çağlar, 2011). However, these secondary cities are not always equipped with the policy frameworks, governance structures and administrative arrangements needed to maximize the capacity and resources that new migrants can bring.

2.2.3. Depopulated cities and rural areas

Depopulated urban areas which have suffered from unsustainable population loss, for instance due to industrial decline, may benefit from policies incentivizing migrants to come and settle in their areas in order to help revitalize local economies.

Depopulated or shrinking cities are those which have experienced notable population loss, often due to emigration. This depopulation can be a concern if labour shortages undermine the remaining economy even further or make it difficult to maintain the level of infrastructure that exists. This is a problem that has afflicted a number of mid-western (formerly gateway) cities in the United States such as Baltimore, Pittsburgh, Philadelphia, Cleveland and St. Louis. Detroit, once the fourth-largest city in the United States and manufacturing power house, lost one-quarter of its population between 2000 and 2010 along with its automobile industry base. Job and population losses reduced the city's finances and led to the underinvestment and decline in public services.

In some cases, international migrants have been encouraged to move to such areas to revive ailing economies and populations. Detroit and other Rust Belt cities in the United States have turned to immigration as one of the main strategies for spurring revitalization, stabilizing failing neighbourhoods and boosting economic development (Tobocman, 2014). Turkish immigrant families have been welcomed to Dayton, Ohio, to help revitalize the economy. In Germany, the mayor of Goslar, a small town with a population of approximately 50,000, offered to take refugees from the neighbouring cities of Göttingen and Brunswick in order to counter the decline in its own population and labour shortages which were undermining the town's economy based around a high-end spa. See text box 2 for a similar example from Spain.

Depopulation has also affected rural areas. In Europe, one of the emergent trends is the rapidly increasing migration to rural areas after the enlargement of the European Union in 2004. This immigration has taken place concurrently with outmigration from the same areas. The restructuring of local economies, the creation of new jobs characterized by low pay, insecure, uninsured, seasonal and mostly part-time work has led to the outflow of native populations and the arrival of migrants, mostly from the new European Union member states, willing to take on these jobs. Thus immigration flows to depopulated rural regions have contributed to the sustainability of public and private services in those areas, and mitigated the effects of the depopulation dynamics (Kasimis, 2010). Likewise in the United States, industrial bases, particularly for meat packing and construction, located in remote rural areas are a draw for international migrants, mainly from Mexico (Brown, 2012). In rural Arkansas, where year-round employment is available, Mexicans, who often maintain a back-and-forth binational lifestyle in other parts of the United States, are now settling down more or less permanently, especially as border security becomes tighter (Striffler, 2007). The international and internal migration flows back and forth to depopulated cities and rural areas in Europe and North America is reconfiguring the demographic composition of the population in those places. The position of migrants and the opportunity structures available to them in depopulated small towns and rural areas will inevitably be different from those provided by gateway cities.

Migration to the depopulated Aragon region, Spain[2]

Aragon, a depopulated region in the north-east of Spain, attracted foreign-born immigrants to fill labour shortages following a restructuring of the economy. It now has a high per capita income thanks to its emergent tourist trade. The foreign-born population constituted less than 1 per cent in 1999 and had reached up to 8 per cent by 2004 making up the majority of the new inhabitants. Although population growth still remained negative, the immigration of foreign-born to Aragon and their contribution to the restructured economy of the region has also attracted the internal migration of native Spaniards from cities near to Aragon. The immigration of foreign-born populations has clearly contributed to local development and further employment opportunities.

2.2.4. Peri-urbanization

The urbanization of former rural areas on the fringes of cities and towns (peri-urbanization) can result from the need for a mobile workforce to service growing export-led industries. Such rapid urban growth can place a major strain on infrastructure and services especially where local administrations are ill-equipped to cope with such change.

Peri-urbanization, that is urbanization of former rural areas on the fringe of cities and towns, can be observed in many parts of the world, for instance in Asian cities such as Shenzhen in China, Jakarta in Indonesia and Bangkok in Thailand. Migration is likely to play a larger role in the growth of these types of low-income (usually informal) settlements in peri-urban areas rather than in the growth of existing urban areas. Population growth in peri-urban areas is therefore due not only to the migration of people from rural localities towards urban centres but also to people who are already in such centres and seek to move away. Peri-urbanization thus reflects population movements both towards and out of cities (Tacoli, McGranahan and Satterthwaite, 2014).

Peri-urbanization is often driven by export-led economic development and the need for land to accommodate production activities and workforces. Such workforces may be comprised of mobile populations with dual residences in rural and in urban areas and whose rights of residence in cities and access to welfare may be in dispute and cause contention among locals. In China, peri-urbanization has been driven by policy as authorities have sought to redistribute growth by decentralizing services and production. However, this has brought with it, huge social and administrative challenges, especially in terms of financing as shown in text box 3 (Gross, Ye and Legates, 2014).

The challenges of peri-urban development can be seen in sub-Saharan Africa with the growth of large multi-ethnic, multicultural, multilingual and multi-

---

2   Taken from A. Çağlar, Urban Migration Trends, Challenges and Opportunities, 2014. Background Paper for the *World Migration Report 2015: Migrants and Cities: New Partnerships to Manage Mobility*, International Organization for Migration, Geneva.

faith settlements. In West African cities, the largely poor urban and peri-urban population is essentially excluded from socioeconomic development opportunities. The continued rapid growth of East African primary cities, such as Nairobi, has had repercussions which include acute housing shortages, traffic congestion, pollution and uncontrolled peri-urban sprawl (UN-Habitat, 2014). Many cities faced with this type of peri-urbanization find it difficult to meet the rapidly increasing demands on infrastructure and services caused by new arrivals due to the lack of resource allocation in city administrative budgets. Cirebon in Indonesia, for example, has 300,000 residents but an additional 400,000 people live on the outer edges of the city and face a real challenge in accessing services and infrastructure (Fahmi et al., 2014) in part due to absence of or conflicting formal political boundaries, city planning and policy procedures. Efforts by some countries to halt or redirect internal migration in order to prevent peri-urban development have had mixed results.

Text box 3

In situ urbanization in China

Urbanization in China over the last three decades has been unprecedented in scale: 260 million migrants have moved to cities from rural areas, driving much of the country's rapid economic growth. Between 2000 and 2010 alone, 117 million Chinese moved from rural to urban areas to seek better employment opportunities. Coastal regions, the engines of China's growth, accounted for more than half of migrant inflows. The largest and fastest-growing internal migrant populations are in the Beijing, Dongguan, Guangzhou and Shanghai metropolitan regions, with more than 52 million migrants in 2010, or 35 per cent of all migrants in China.

Since the late 1970s, China has embarked on small town development in rural areas in order to redistribute growth and mitigate the population exodus to large cities. The Government relaxed restrictions on small town development in rural areas as well as the *hukou* urban registration system and encouraged a shift from state-owned enterprises to township-village enterprises (TVEs). Numerous rural communities have rapidly been transformed into towns with urban communities and TVEs providing employment opportunities and increased welfare. Local governments were vested with the responsibilities to lead this long-term urbanization plan.

Chinese urbanization has been successful in avoiding large-scale urban poverty and unemployment, often associated with urbanization, yet complex challenges have arisen relating to property rights, central-local division of responsibilities and cost-sharing. Property ownership laws continue to remain unclear for many. Also many local governments lack the finances and capacities to deliver on the central government's commitment to give urban registration to one hundred million rural migrants by 2020 and address their social and labour rights (Zhu, 2014). Local governments reportedly receive half the country's fiscal revenue but are responsible for eighty per cent of national spending. As a result, many have incurred major debts in their expansion and have speculated with expropriated villagers' property to cover their costs (The Economist, 2014).

Currently, China's vast migrant population makes up almost one-third of the urban total of 730 million. These migrants, however, face difficulty in gaining official recognition as city-dwellers and are excluded from welfare benefits and access to public services. By 2030, China's cities will be home to close on 1 billion people or about 70 per cent of the population, compared with 54 per cent today. China's internal migrants are one of the key factors in the contest among towns and cities to grow and be economically competitive.

2.2.5. Informal settlements and slums

The proliferation of informal settlements suffering from overcrowding and a lack of basic amenities, such as water, sanitation and housing, has accounted for much of the physical growth of cities. The growth of slums is in part a marker of a lack of proactive city planning.

In many parts of the world, the proliferation of informal settlements has accounted for the physical growth of cities throughout most of the twentieth and the beginning of the twenty-first century. The expansion of urban settlements that lack access to water, adequate sanitation, durable housing and sufficient living space has contributed to the growth of slums (UN-Habitat, 2013a). It is now estimated that some 863 million people are living in slums, as compared to 650 million in 1990 and 760 million in 2000. In sub-Saharan Africa, 61.7 per cent of the urban population lives in slums (UN-Habitat, 2013b). Figure 2 shows the proportion of urban populations living in slums.

Figure 2 **Proportion of urban population living in slums per region**

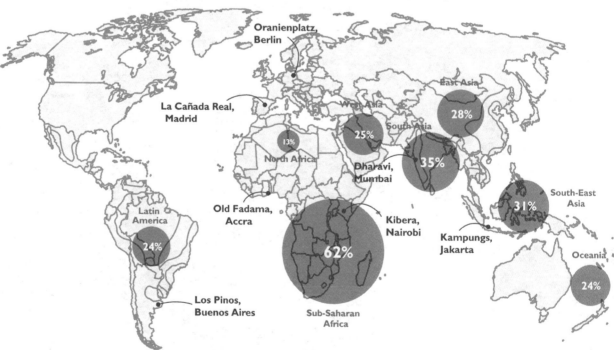

Source: IOM calculations based on UN-Habitat, 2013b.

Recent studies indicate that migrants are disproportionately represented among the urban poor in these informal settlements (Hoang, Truong and Dinh, 2013; Rigg, Nguyen and Luong, 2014). For example, in Accra, Ghana, 92 per cent of migrant households live in one slum, Old Fadama, without a ready supply of water – water has to be purchased daily or drawn from nearby wells – and 94 per cent of migrants in the same slum do not live in accommodation with toilet facilities (Awumbila, 2014). In many cities in low- and middle-income countries, informal settlements commonly function as entry points for incoming migrants. Despite the hardships of living in such conditions, migrants are able to find economic activity and opportunities to improve their current well-being and future prospects in these informal settlements or slums, such as Kibera in Nairobi, Kenya, or Old Fadama (Awumbila, Owusu and Teye, 2014).

Early migration models viewed the informal opportunities found in urban settlements as a temporary staging post for new migrants on their way to formal sector employment. However, it can typically take migrants generations to build assets and invest in education and skills, and the differences in the circumstances between recent and settled migrants can be striking. Older settlements are often home to the descendants of migrants whereas newer ones tend to be home to recent migrants (see text box 4 for an example from India).

Text box 4

Comparing "first" and "fourth" generation slums in Bangalore, India[3]

In India, low-income urban settlements are officially divided in two categories: "notified" or "recognized" slums and non-notified slums, effectively a residual category. However, this distinction does not reflect the vast differences between settlements. A recent study compares long-established notified slums and recent non-notified ones in Bangalore. In the notified slums, hardly anyone has arrived recently in the city: indeed, more than 70 per cent of residents have lived in Bangalore for four or more generations. This is reflected in the settlements' housing and infrastructure: permanent constructions prevail and electricity and drinking water connections are commonly available. Residents are better described as settled lower middle-class rather than poor, and most of them have house appliances and their own mobile phones. Education and home ownership are the main categories of expenditure.

The contrast with the "first generation" slum is striking. These are home to recent migrants from rural areas who retain strong links with their villages, with many families split between the two locations. Migration is primarily a response to the growing uncertainty of rural livelihoods, with droughts and erratic rainfall resulting in the accumulation of debts; these residents represent some of the poorest people in rural India. The typical shelter is a tent shared by tenants who pay rent in cash, with no written lease and the constant fear of eviction. About 40 per cent of residents have been in Bangalore from one to five years, and another 40 per cent between five and ten years. The vast majority belong to the lowest social strata – between 70 and 100 per cent, compared to 11.4 per cent of Bangalore's total urban population – and are mainly landless or own very small plots in their villages.

---

3   Taken from K. Anirudh, M. S. Sriram and P. Prakash, Slum types and adaptation strategies: Identifying policy-relevant differences in Bangalore. *Environment and Urbanization*, 26(2): 568–585, 2014. Cited in C. Tacoli, G. McGranahan, and D. Satterthwaite, Urbanization, rural-urban migration and urban poverty, 2014. Background Paper for the *World Migration Report 2015: Migrants and Cities: New Partnerships to Manage Mobility*, International Organization for Migration, Geneva.

Infrastructure in these settlements is non-existent: there is no electricity, water is purchased from vendors, and garbage removal and security services are unknown. Bus stops are more than three kilometres away as are health centres, and there is no evidence of any government, NGO or other outside support. The primary category of expenditure is the repayment of debts and support of relatives in home areas, leaving very little for education and housing – and consequently opportunities to access better employment. These kinds of settlements hardly serve as locations to build a better life for newly arrived migrants. Lacking identity papers in the city and not being registered as voters, they are unable to attract political patronage or official support. From being the poorest groups in rural areas, they have become the poorest in urban centres. At the same time, however, migration remains an important survival strategy even though it does not result in the accumulation of assets.

The rapid growth of informal settlements is not an inevitable part of rapid urbanization; many cities that have grown rapidly have a low proportion of their population in informal settlements and close to universal coverage for basic infrastructure and services (UCLG, 2013). The lack of proactive planning of low-cost settlements in order to accommodate rapid urban growth is the issue and this may stem from deliberate policy measures aimed at deterring migrants through the provision of low quality living conditions. Such policies can in turn fuel negative public opinion and xenophobia against migrants (Ostanel, 2011).

In many urban areas of Latin America, Asia and Africa, government restrictions on land has limited the supply of affordable housing which has contributed to the growth of informal settlements. Informal settlements, squatting and slums are in part a response to the lack of low-income public housing or subsidies (UN-Habitat, 2013c) and reflect weak urban planning and governance both at the local and national level (UN-Habitat, 2013a).

The situation can be improved by conferring secure land tenure through the regularization of land markets and the residential status of people. This can lead to improved livelihoods for the urban poor including migrants as well as local development. The relatively fewer slums in North Africa are largely attributed to better urban development strategies, including investment in infrastructure and the upgrading of urban settlements. Morocco's national urban improvement plan has sought to rehouse slum dwellers through the "Cities without Slums" programme (UN-Habitat, 2012). Likewise in China, at a time when the urban migrant population grew more than 80 per cent (2000–2010), the number of urban slum dwellers dropped, in part due to state controls on the building of shanty towns (The Economist, 2014).

Cities in West and Central Africa are now reportedly integrating customary land transactions into formal land markets but poor immigrants are unlikely to benefit from this. Comparative studies of the regularization of informal settlements in Latin America have found that, rather than applying one single approach, urban planners should present alternative options for secure land tenure for slum dwellers, such as communal land tenure as an option for the lowest income group (Murillo, 2014). There is a dearth of data on migrants and slums, including on their role in transforming slums into mainstream communities (ibid.).

2.2.6. Transit cities

Transit cities were traditionally staging posts for migrants wishing to seek access to the industrialized economies of the Global North. As border controls have become more restrictive, border towns in places like Mexico or Morocco are becoming long-stay destinations in themselves for migrants unable to reach the United States and Europe respectively.

Strict border control policies can give rise to involuntary urban "transit hubs", where temporary populations are stranded in towns on their way to their intended destinations (Marconi, 2008). In Africa and Asia, some cities also serve as staging posts for internal migrants to become international ones (Hugo, 2014; Bakewell and Jónsson, 2011). In West Africa, former destination countries like Côte d'Ivoire and Nigeria have become transit countries while people accumulate sufficient resources to move further afield (UN-Habitat, 2010).

These transit hubs can become places of long-term stay if options for moving on are closed down. For example, as European border security has tightened and employment opportunities dwindled after the European financial crises, an increasing number of migrants from sub-Saharan Africa have begun to remain in North African cities, such as Rabat, Tangiers, Tunis and Tripoli which were traditionally seen as gateways to Europe, and not the final destination (see map 2). These municipalities, therefore, now face new and increasing pressures to provide adequate services and to ensure security (Serageldin et al., 2014).

Map 2   **Transit cities - Africa**

Source: Adapted from the 2014 Mediterranean Transit Migration (MTM) Map on Mixed Migration Routes in the MTM Region (i-Map).

Note: The 2014 MTM Map is produced as an output of the project, 'Interactive Map on Migration in Africa, the Middle East and the Mediterranean Region (i-Map 2011-2014)' in the framework of the Dialogue on Mediterranean Transit Migration. International Centre for Migration Policy Development (ICMPD), Vienna. Available from www.imap-migration.org/index.php?id=470

In Morocco, migrants, who were unable to cross the border into Spain, are often to be found in Casablanca, Fes and Rabat and face challenges in terms of higher living costs, frequent identity checks, arrests and evictions from urban centres. Local and international non-governmental organizations are left to fill gaps in service provision for migrants, particularly the most vulnerable, living in urban settings (Serageldin et al., 2014). This situation has prompted the recent development of a national policy in Morocco that includes the regularization of some migrant groups and measures to provide for their basic needs. Effective policies need to be coordinated among sending, transit and receiving countries in order to turn this migratory trend toward local development in the countries of origin. The current focus on stemming the migratory trend towards ultimate destination countries in Europe is putting more pressure on Maghrebi central and local authorities in North Africa to acquire sufficient resources to govern, integrate and serve this growing population (EMHRN, 2014).

A similar situation can be found in the route to the United States. There are three main migrant land corridors used by Central Americans and Mexicans in transit through Mexico towards the United States. One starts in Tapachula, one in Tenosique and one in Chetumal. These three corridors divide into several other routes further north, the principal ones ending in the proximity of Brownsville, McAllen, Laredo, El Paso, Nogales, Calexico and San Diego (see map 3). Migrant movement along these paths leaves significant impacts as these "transit" migrants in many cases settle temporarily in shacks and shelters in slums and shanty towns. They are predominantly low-income workers living in the streets or in poor housing conditions, segregated from urban infrastructure services and vulnerable to abusive conditions and to criminality. Depending on migratory policies, border controls and available personal resources, these groups may reach the United States or remain stranded in poor living conditions en route. The permeability of the frontier between Guatemala, Belize, Mexico and the USA fluctuates which in turn influences the shape of migrant corridors and the demographic profiles of Mexican frontier cities. Text box 5 describes some efforts in a border town in Mexico to support migrants in transit and returned migrants.

Map 3   **Transit cities - Central America and Mexico**

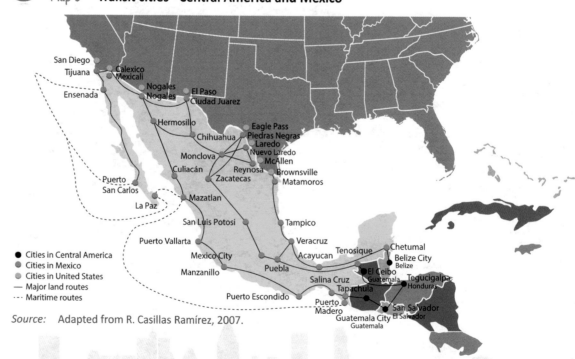

Source: Adapted from R. Casillas Ramírez, 2007.

Text box 5

A city where returning migrants and migrants in transit are offered assistance: Tijuana, Mexico

Tijuana, Mexico, the so-called "city without borders" located on the border with the United States with the Pacific Ocean to the West, is one of the major reception areas of migrants in transit and returning migrants from the United States. It is said that Tijuana receives 80 per cent of all migrants returning to the State of Baja California, Mexico. In 2014, it received around 60,000 returned migrants, more than a 30 per cent decline from the previous year (96,000). Tijuana also attracts a significant flow of internal migrants as it is the primary exporter of flat screen televisions in the world and is host to numerous "maquiladoras" (manufacturing operations in a free trade zone). These population movements make Tijuana a truly diverse city, yet its infrastructure has not kept up with the demands to meet the fast urban expansion and population growth.

Against this background, the State Council for the Attention of Migrants (Consejo Estatal de Atención al Migrante) came into being on 18 December 2013. The former Mayor of Tijuana and the current Governor of the State of Baja California, Francisco Vega de Lamadrid, was the most active promoter of this initiative that has already improved the well-being of many Mexican returnees.

The Council comprises 60 organizations and institutions, of which 30 are local delegations of Federal-level institutions, State-level institutions (including representatives from the Secretariats of Public Security, External Relations and Migration) and Municipalities (two representatives per city). The 30 remaining members consist of civil society organizations that assist migrants in Baja California.

The Council aims to create public policies to improve migrants' well-being, to carry out and coordinate activities for migrants, and to ensure the compliance by all State institutions of the obligations established by the Law for the Protection of the Rights and the Support of the Migrants of Baja California, which was approved in August 2014. The Council member organizations provide support to Mexican returnees from the United States, including travel assistance to their communities of origin, counselling, and cultural orientation as most of them have passed many decades abroad. Temporary shelter and free meals up to 90 days upon return are also provided.

The Council also runs the programme for migrant employment. For example, many returnees are hired by call centres given their English language proficiency gained during their time abroad. However, the retention of these returnees, and prevention of their re-emigration, is a challenge as their wages are rather low compared to the earnings they had in the United States. The Council has organized three job fairs where 3,000 positions were offered to returnees. Five hundred migrant returnees were successfully employed through the Council's labour reinsertion programme. Legal and administrative assistance is also available for returnees to obtain identity documents.

Recently, the Council has started an initiative to establish a Migrant Fund which will be used to provide assistance to vulnerable groups among the migrant returnees. The Council and the Government of Baja California plans a programme to quickly address the precarious situation in El Gordo, a settlement on the border with the United States.

Interview with Carlos Mora Álvarez, Executive President of the State Council for the Attention of Migrants, 16 January 2015.

2.3

PATTERNS OF MIGRATION

2.3.1. Internal migration

Internal migration interacts with urban environments in multiple ways. In a number of countries of the South, circular migration patterns are common with migrants relocating from rural to urban areas on a temporary basis. In some places, the main transition of migrants is from one urban area to another; elsewhere, rural–rural migration remains pre-eminent.

Internal migration is shaping urban growth and diversity around the world in different ways. In Asia, for example, about 47 per cent of its population now lives in urban areas. This number has almost doubled since 1970 and represents a profound change in the way people live, work and interact (Gross, Ye and Legates, 2014). The way internal migration to cities is managed will be critical to the economic and political development of the region. Internal migrants in India account for some 30 per cent of the total population, with estimates ranging from 309 million (2001 census) to 326 million according to the National Sample Survey 2007–2008 (Srivastrava, 2012). China has more than 220 million internal migrant workers (one sixth of its population) according to the 2010 census. The process of urban development is more complex than a simple redistribution of people and involves new mobility strategies of different groups of migrants (Hugo, 2014).

Circular migration to urban areas

Millions of people in China are circular migrants or commuters; they spend much of their time earning a living in large cities whilst leaving family members, especially children, behind in rural areas or small towns. Such mobility patterns and the resulting urban growth has become a new focus among urban scholars and practitioners centring on Asia who estimate that some 119 million people are expected to be added to the peri-urban areas of Asian countries over the next 15 years (Gross, Ye and Legates, 2014).

Urban–urban migration[4]

In Mexico, the most significant migration flow is internal urban-to-urban migration to cities of all sizes. Urban–urban population movements have increased from 65 per cent between 1995 and 2000 to 68 per cent between 2005 and 2010

---

4   Based on "Background Notes on Migrants and Cities in Mexico" provided by Salvador Gutierrez, IOM Regional Office for Central and North America and the Caribbean, San José, Costa Rica.

(INEGI, 2001 and 2011). In the meantime, rural to urban flows and international emigration are both on the decline. Net gain areas are located near the border with the United States where cities, such as Tijuana, Chihuahua and Tamaulipas, continue to draw low-skilled migrant workers particularly for the manufacturing and service industries. Newer and more recent net gain metropolitan areas, such as Cancun, Puerto Vallarta and Los Cabos, are located near the coast and the growing tourism industry. People are also attracted to cities due to special advantages such as access to education (Sobrino, 2010). Conversely, the Mexico City Metropolitan Zone, once the principal receiving city of internal migrants, recorded the largest negative population growth according to the 2010 census, due to high living costs and other factors. Veracruz and Acapulco also experienced a net population loss as economic activities declined in their respective industries of oil and tourism.

Rural–rural migration

India has low urbanization levels relative to the rest of the world; 31 per cent of its population was living in urban areas according to the 2011 census compared to 51 per cent globally in the same period (UN DESA, 2012). However, the urbanization rate at 1.1. per cent is higher than the global average (0.9%); its urban population is likely to reach 410 million in 2014 and then double to 814 million by 2050.

India has 25 of the 100 fastest-growing cities in the world and cities like Mumbai, Delhi and Kolkata are among the ten most populous urban areas on the planet. A significant source of this growth is rural-to-urban migration as people move in search of economic opportunities. The proportion of in-migrants among these fastest-growing cities varies from less than 15 per cent in Allahabad and Agra to 55 per cent and over in Surat, Ludhiana and Faridabad. About 45 per cent of the population of Mumbai and of Delhi was comprised of migrants in 2001. The proportion of migrants across these cities is closely related to the economic position and vibrancy of these cities.

Figure 3   **Percentage of migrants in selected urban agglomerations in India**

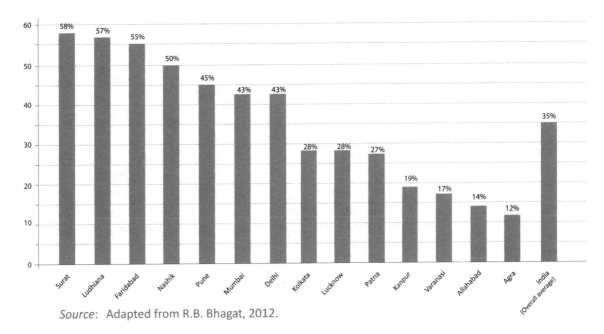

Source: Adapted from R.B. Bhagat, 2012.

Nevertheless, while urbanization is increasing, the rural segment will continue to be substantial for many more decades beyond the middle of the twenty-first century when India is likely to achieve population stabilization. Currently, more than two-thirds (69%) of India's 1.21 billion people live in rural areas, according to the 2011 Census of India. The rural population is expected to reach 857 million by 2050 (UN DESA, 2014).

The predominant mobility pattern in India is rural-to-rural movement for short distances and short durations. Internal migration in India is predominantly an internal state phenomenon (26%, 268 million), as opposed to inter-state, long-distance migration (4%, 41 million), according to the 2001 Census. Within states, the intra-district movement comprised about 53 per cent of all movements in 2007–2008, representing the largest share of internal migration, although it has since been showing a declining trend (Bhagat, 2014).

While some may migrate permanently, semi-permanent or long-term circular migration is common when people migrate leaving their families, and their land and property in the area of origin. This is especially the case when jobs in the destination areas are precarious or if the cost of permanent relocation is too high. There are also seasonal migrants. One of the main lacunae in both the Censuses and the National Sample Surveys is their failure to adequately capture seasonal and/or short-term circular migration (Srivastrava, 2012).

Internal migrants have widely varying degrees of education, income levels and skills, as well as varying profiles in terms of caste, religion, family composition, age and other characteristics. National-level data identifying trends in these characteristics are not available. However, microsurveys suggest that most migrants are between the ages of 16 and 40, particularly among semi-permanent and temporary migrants, whose duration of stay may vary from 60 days to one year. Lowest-income Indians are over-represented in short-term migration flows. Most labour migrants are employed in a few key subsectors, including construction, domestic work, textile and brick manufacturing, transportation, mining and quarrying, and agriculture (Rameez and Varma, 2014). Overall, India's internal migration of over 300 million (Srivastrava, 2012) far exceeds the number of Indian emigrants estimated at 11.4 million (UNESCO and UNICEF, 2012).

2.3.2. International migration

Much urban growth is taking place in low- and middle-income countries, particularly in Asia and Africa. Key urban centres in Asia include Singapore and Kuala Lumpur with migration driven by professional expatriates, international students and low-skilled migrant workers. Relatively homogeneous societies, previously unused to such diversity, are having to deal with it for the first time. African cities are increasingly part of a complex web of migration between countries of the Global South. They may be destination places, for instance Lubumbashi in the Democratic Republic of the Congo, Fes in Morocco, Accra in Ghana and Lagos in Nigeria. At the same time, Africa is a source of migration to other emerging economies, such as Guangzhou in China.

Most of the growth in city populations is taking place in low- and middle-income countries, where as many as 66 million people migrate to urban areas each year (UN DESA, 2014). The pattern of urban spread varies widely, yet almost 90 per cent is likely to occur in Africa and Asia, with China and India accounting for more than one-third of the global urban growth in the next 35–40 years. In contrast, the weakest urban population growth will be in Europe (ibid.). Much of this growth is due to internal migration as discussed above. However, international migration from both the Global North and South is a significant factor. For instance, the number of the foreign-born population in Mexican cities has doubled since 2000 to reach 961,121 in 2010. The majority of immigrants constitute North–South migration with 77 per cent being from the United States. They tend to be found in large cities; almost 57 per cent of the foreign-born population are under the age of 14 and of Mexican heritage and living in their parental communities of origin (INEGI, 2001 and 2011).

The rest of this section focuses on international migration dynamics and the growth of Asian and African cities.

Dynamic centres in Asia

International migration is on the increase to some of the dynamic centres in Asia which play a "gateway" role for international migrants. So far international migration has not been anywhere near as substantial a factor in contemporary population growth in Asia as it has been in North America and Europe. This is due to restrictive policies in Asian countries on the permanent settlement of overseas migrants. However, the picture is starting to change as economic and political cooperation among nations in the region is increasing through the Association of Southeast Asian Nations (ASEAN) and the Asia Pacific Economic Community (APEC) and is serving to remove barriers to movement.

Table 2 sets out the percentage of the foreign-born population living in major cities in the Asia–Pacific region. Singapore has the highest proportion with 34.7 per cent of the work force foreign-born (Singapore Foreign Workers Dormitory Guide, n.d.) and 38 per cent of the resident population (Singapore National Population and Talent Division, 2013). Other statistics show that rates are increasing; for instance, the number of foreign residents in Seoul, Republic of Korea, has doubled in the last ten years from 114,685 in 2004 to 263,678 in 2014 (Seoul Metropolitan Government, 2014). Japan has over 2.1 million foreign nationals residing in the nation's urban areas (Japan Ministry of Justice, 2011) and cities like Kuala Lumpur and Bangkok are home to significant numbers of foreign nationals.

In China, the size of the foreign-born population is still relatively very small but is growing as multinational corporations relocate to cities and transfer their multinational workers in and out of China. Between 2000 and 2013, China's overall international migrant stock increased by more than fifty per cent (Hugo, 2014) as its fast-growing economy attracts foreign professionals. Chinese expatriates are also drawn back as its cities grow and provide better living and work prospects, and opportunities for investment, entrepreneurship and careers with multinational companies. Chinese cities are also competing among themselves to attract overseas Chinese talents with various incentives (Zweig, 2006).

Table 2

Foreign-born population in major cities and countries in the Asia-Pacific Region (%)

City	Foreign-born (%)	Country	Foreign-born (%)
Beijing	0.5	China	0.05
Kuala Lumpur	9.0	Malaysia	8.40
Mumbai	1.4	India	0.50
Seoul	3.7	Republic of Korea	2.80
Singapore	38.0	Singapore	38.00
Sydney	39.0	Australia	28.00
Tokyo	3.0	Japan	1.60

Source: See list of sources at the end of the References section.

The international migrants to high-income Asian cities such as Singapore, Kuala Lumpur, Hong Kong SAR and Bangkok fall into three main categories:

- Professional and managerial expatriates, especially from India and the Philippines, as well as from Europe, North America, Japan, Republic of Korea, Australia and New Zealand. The recent global economic crisis has resulted in substantial numbers of European professionals from Spain, Greece, Italy and Ireland seeking work in the dynamic Asian economies. The increase in direct foreign investment in some Asian cities and the local demand arising from rapidly growing and restructuring economies has led to increased opportunities for international migrants.

- International students. They are becoming steadily more mobile within the Asia region, which is increasingly becoming home to globally renowned and competitive universities. For example, 20 per cent of Singapore's university students are foreign. There also have been large student migrations to Malaysia, China, Japan and the Republic of Korea (ADB Institute, OECD and ILO, 2014).

- Low-skilled migrant workers. They form the largest number of intraregional migrants and come from other Asian labour-surplus economies. As the demographic and development differences among Asian countries continue to grow, this will fuel further intraregional migration to fast growing cities in the region (Hugo, 2014). These migrant workers are often found in the construction sites of large cities such as Singapore, Kuala Lumpur and Bangkok. In several of such cities, foreign workers, many of them undocumented, have become an important part of the informal sector often after having first entered the country as a worker in designated occupations like construction, manufacturing or domestic work. There is a substantial influx of female domestic workers, especially to cities in the Taiwan Province of China, Hong Kong Special Administrative Region, Singapore, Brunei Darussalam and Malaysia. They mainly come from Indonesia, the Philippines and Sri Lanka and are estimated to number more than two million in the Asia region (Huang, Yeoh and Rahman, 2005).

These migratory flows are bringing the issue of diversity to the fore and cities like Seoul in the Republic of Korea and Tokyo in Japan are trying to grapple with these emerging trends (see text box 6 which describes the efforts made in Hamamatsu City, Japan). For example, in response to the influx of marriage migrants over the past two decades, the Republic of Korea has launched a series of strategies to embrace "multiculturalism" in family policies, to develop programmes to enhance integration of the increasingly diverse migrant population groups, and to diversify visa categories to meet demands especially for skilled migrant workers. Due to the lack of an overarching migrant integration policy and the restrictive permanent residency policy at the national level, cities of both the Republic of Korea and Japan face challenges in developing effective local inclusion policies to address the "multicultural" realities on the ground. International migration and diversity do not yet feature importantly in the public debate in these countries. Political leaders and mayors have not yet seriously engaged much in discussions on how to transform urban diversity into social and economic advantages.

Text box 6

Migration and localities in Japan: The Committee for Localities with a Concentrated Foreign Population

Japanese society is confronted with the unprecedented challenge of diversity due to an increase in the migrant population over the past two decades, mainly comprised of low-skilled workers from Latin America (mostly of Japanese descent) and Asia. The restrictive national policies on immigration do not officially accept low-skilled migrant workers and are consequently out of step with the needs of Japanese society for more workers and better integration. Furthermore, drastic national policy reform is required in order to eliminate the structural inequality experienced by migrants. This led to the formation of the Committee for Localities with a Concentrated Foreign Population (the Committee) in 2001.

The Committee promotes migrant integration based on the policy concept of *tabunka-kyōsei* (multicultural symbiosis). The Committee's first "Hamamatsu Declaration" called for "the establishment of a truly symbiotic society based on the respect of rights and fulfilment of duties that are mandatory for healthy urban life, amid deepening of mutual understanding and respect for each other's cultures and values between Japanese and foreign residents". Furthermore, the Committee advocated that the Government reform its education, social security, alien registration and labour systems at the national level.

Currently, the Committee has twenty-six member municipalities which have prosperous manufacturing industries, including TOYOTA in Toyota, SUZUKI in Hamamatsu and SUBARU in Ota. The average ratio of the foreign population among member cities is 3.3 per cent compared to the 1.6 per cent national average.[5] Hamamatsu has the largest number of foreigners with a total of 21,157 and Aisho has the smallest at 697. In

---

5   "Population and the Number of Households", based on the Basic Resident Registration as of 1 January 2014 and communications between the contributor and the Ministry of Internal Affairs, Japan.

general, Brazilians make up the largest foreign population followed by the Chinese and Filipinos.

The Committee's annual summit is attended by mayors and officials from member cities, officials of relevant national ministries such as Foreign Affairs, Home Affairs, Health, Labour and Welfare, and Education, as well as academics and non-profit organizations. Each summit adopts a resolution addressing specific aspects of migrant integration.

The Committee has developed a set of policy and programme responses to tackle common challenges facing member cities such as insecure employment and inadequate language skills among migrants, the difficulties in providing education to migrant children and cultural misunderstandings between migrants and residents. Proposed measures include intensified public employment security with the help of the Ministry of Health, Labour and Welfare; community language classes in Japanese for foreign residents provided by non-profit organizations; special language classes in municipal schools for foreign children; and reinforced consultation facilities at municipal offices. These efforts led the Government to establish a specific section within the Cabinet Office for promoting the equal treatment of migrants in the municipal resident registration system and the management of programmes to help foreigners who suffered from the financial crisis in 2008.

Contributed by Yasuyuki Kitawaki, Mayor of Hamamatsu City (1999–2007)

African cities and global connections

There are rich patterns of mobility to and from urban areas across Africa, especially in West Africa which has the heaviest concentration of expanding cities, followed by Southern Africa and East Africa (UN-Habitat and UNEP, 2010). Intraregional migration is becoming an important trend with 63 per cent of movements taking place in the region (73% in the Economic Community of West African States). These movements are driven by various economic, social and political factors and facilitated by the implementation of protocols for the free movement of people. They challenge the prevailing view underlying much migration literature about Africa that it is a place of out-migration. A recent study, 'African Perspectives on Human Mobility' which examined migration and mobility in five African cities (Lubumbashi, Democratic Republic of the Congo; Fes, Morocco; Accra and Kumasi, Ghana; and Lagos, Nigeria), found that African cities are not static spaces with limited links to rural hinterlands, nor simply departure points for migrants heading overseas or elsewhere for permanent settlement. They have themselves become significantly attractive spaces for migrants and transient traders.

African migrants and African cities are increasingly becoming inter-connected with many non-African cities in the Middle East, North Africa, Europe, China and other parts of Asia through links that are predominantly forged and maintained by migrants, their associations and diaspora communities. Economic growth in the Global South is one of the drivers behind these migration flows and when managed effectively global South–South migration can contribute significantly to the well-being of migrants, to their communities at home and their host cities.

It can act as a major poverty reduction tool for many countries in the South. Diasporas have a strategic role in making these connections (IOM, 2014).

For instance, African private traders and migrants in Guangzhou, China, and elsewhere are playing a significant part in changing African economies and societies and creating new interactions with Chinese cities. Bilateral trade has grown rapidly since the late 1980s when China adopted the "Open Door" policy which allowed foreign investment and encouraged the development of a market economy and private sector. This trade has endured through not only a period of booming international trade but also a fuel crisis and a world financial crisis in 2008 (Lyons, Brown and Zhigang, 2012). This diversification of migration flows to China emerges as a feasible alternative as Europe and North America tighten their immigration restrictions on people from Africa.

Connections between cities can be formal or informal. Various economic and non-economic activities and diaspora connections have helped African cities enjoy growing links with cities elsewhere, for instance, Lagos and London, Bamako and Paris, Addis Ababa and Beijing, and Nairobi and Delhi. City-twinning is a more formal way by which high- and low-income countries can be conjoined. For example, twinning arrangements between Moroccan cities and those in the US (including Chicago, Oakland and Los Angeles) involve the implementation of cultural exchanges in education, arts, music, sports and business at the municipal and community level and the strengthening of bilateral and multilateral relations at national level. Migrant involvement is implied but not highlighted in these types of city twinning arrangements.

2.4
DIVERSITY WITHIN CITIES

Increasing diversity within cities is another feature of modern day trends in migration and urban growth. The major cities of the industrialized world in particular have very diverse populations living side by side. In developing countries too, the ethnic and racial mix can be considerable as migrants are drawn from nearby countries and across the region. Managing diversity effectively poses a challenge for governments.

Developed world

The emergence of new forms of migration, mobility, networking and social media across national borders has led to a rapid change in the population structure and interactions between individuals and social groups in cities. Urban life in many cities today is therefore characterized by the presence of immigrant groups or longstanding ethnic and racial differentiations, often accompanied by inequality and segregation (Fincher et al., 2014). The presence of smaller, less organized, legally differentiated and non-citizen immigrant groups in some cities of developed countries is known as "super-diversity" (Vertovec, 2007 and 2011; Stren, 2010) which questions the validity of the existence of a sociocultural homogeneous "majority society" as opposed to "migrant others" (Özbabacan, 2012). Figure 4 shows the scale of diversity in London today.

Figure 4   **Foreign-born population in London (2011)**

Total foreign-born population: 2,998,264
Foreign-born population (%): 37

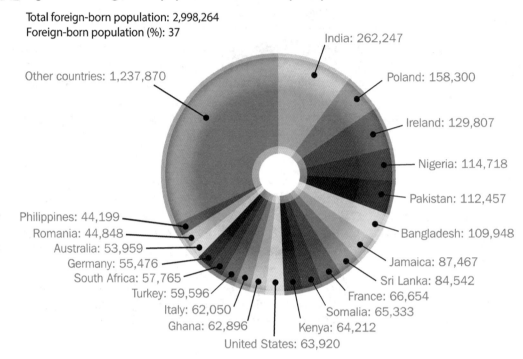

India: 262,247

Other countries: 1,237,870

Poland: 158,300

Ireland: 129,807

Nigeria: 114,718

Pakistan: 112,457

Philippines: 44,199
Romania: 44,848
Australia: 53,959
Germany: 55,476
South Africa: 57,765
Turkey: 59,596
Italy: 62,050
Ghana: 62,896
United States: 63,920
Kenya: 64,212
Somalia: 65,333
France: 66,654
Sri Lanka: 84,542
Jamaica: 87,467
Bangladesh: 109,948

Source: Based on 'Population by country of birth', London Data Store, Greater London Authority.
Note: See: http://data.london.gov.uk/dataset/population-country-birth/resource/d0f17333-0205-47b6-b90e-c3d0493e1f42 (accessed 22 May 2015).

Academic studies of urban diversity have so far been confined to a limited number of countries, which are mostly developed economies and members of the Organization for Economic Co-operation and Development (OECD) (Spoonley, 2014). Urban diversities will unfold differently in cities where the welfare state is absent and where there is a lack of formal employment, decent housing or social protection which affects both migrants and local residents alike.

Text box 7

Diversity in London, United Kingdom[6]

On Rye Lane, a shopping street in Peckham, South London, one of the most diverse neighbourhoods in London but also one of the most deprived areas in the United Kingdom, shop proprietors come from over twenty countries of origin. The high concentration of diverse countries of origin among the proprietors on this single street is accompanied by remarkable intercultural proficiencies. Almost a third of the proprietors on Rye Lane are able to converse in four languages or more. It is a place of reception in the city where migrants arrive and share space with established residents.

6   Taken from S. Hall, 2013, Super-diverse street: a 'trans-ethnography' across migrant localities. *Ethnic and Racial Studies,* 2015 38(1):22-37. DOI: 10.1080/01419870.2013.858175. Available from: www.tandfonline.com/doi/full/10.1080/01419870.2013.858175#preview

Growing diversity brings challenges, such as residential segregation when certain ethnicities, nationalities or a socioeconomic status concentrate in particular neighbourhoods of a city or metropolitan area (Iceland, 2014).

Although European cities are in general spatially less segregated than American cities, population groups are spatially unequally divided within many European cities: some neighbourhoods contain an overwhelming majority of a particular group (usually low-income households or specific minority ethnic groups), while other neighbourhoods may show a considerable mix between groups in a social, socioeconomic, ethnic and cultural sense (Tasan-Kok et al., 2013).

Moving to neighbourhoods with a high concentration of their own ethnic group may be attractive to migrants, with newcomers choosing to settle in ethnic enclaves where there is a support network. Yet, residential segregation is problematic when it becomes permanent and leads to intergenerational inequalities. Long-term segregation can limit residential choices; reduce economic and educational opportunities by restricting people's access to good jobs and schools; concentrate poverty in disadvantaged neighbourhoods, and contribute to social exclusion and alienation (Collet and Petrovic, 2014).

Reasons for segregation may include discrimination in the housing market or minority self-segregation, as well as the departure of members of the ethnic or national majority from the neighbourhood. In the United States and European context, this is often termed as 'white flight'. It is important to note that segregation patterns differ across countries and reflect social and economic exclusion in particular contexts rather than being inherent to certain ethnic minorities.

Many cities try and combat residential segregation either by implementing policies that directly tackle segregation or by more indirect integration policies. In addition to anti-discrimination legislation specifically aimed at the housing market, direct policies include the distribution of public housing across a wide range of neighbourhoods; providing rental subsidies and vouchers, and introducing quotas to prevent ethnic minorities from settling in neighbourhoods where they are already overrepresented. These policies, however, do not seem to reduce segregation as native-born majority-group members still tend to avoid neighbourhoods with ethnic concentrations. Indirect policies address the underlying causes of segregation, such as access to full citizenship, labour market integration and inter-group relations.

Urban policymakers tend to overlook evidence of the positive effects of ethnic clustering on migrants and other minorities. As highlighted before, migrants may benefit from living in ethnic enclaves. It should be acknowledged that migrant strategies of integration and inclusion in cities are tactical – dependent on individual or household needs, the context in which these occur and the responsibilities they demand (Kihato et al., 2010).

Given the strong socioeconomic structure in many ethnic enclaves in the cities of developed countries, which are facilitated by transnational (business) connections, telecommunication and transport technologies, migrant middle classes might be less driven to integrate into the mainstream. There is a need for policymakers to reconsider the incentive structures of integration in highly diverse societies that include strong migrant enclaves (Duncan, 2010).

Developing world

Multi-ethnic make-up is the normal condition of many cities in the less developed world. Due to cross-border cultural and linguistic ties and loose immigration controls, most migrants move to neighbouring countries. Emigrants from 45 out of 63 low- and middle-income countries (approximately 70%) are first destined for a bordering country which has a similar economic status to their origin country (OECD, 2011). Migrants will find themselves in a similar culture but nevertheless the variety of populations arriving in cities still results in a degree of multi-ethnicity. High population density in migrant-receiving areas and mixed migration flows, with a particularly high concentration of displaced persons and migrants stranded in transit, add to the complexity of urban societies.

In cities in the less developed world, urban residents and migrants alike acquire various strategies to secure basic needs, for example, through simultaneous participation in formal and informal economies, maintaining the household within different localities across the urban–rural divides and diversifying sources of assistance (Simone, 2008). Because of the ways many migrants enter the country or the city, the sectors they work in and the low administrative capacity of the destination country to properly register them, migrants are disproportionately represented in the informal sector (Hoang, Truong and Dinh, 2013).

In this context, migrants become vulnerable as they experience various barriers to accessing resources, though migration to urban areas is a strategy to improve livelihood and to reduce vulnerability due to the greater availability of services, easier access to infrastructure and more income-generating opportunities. Worse yet, cities, particularly the informal settlements in urban centres or peri-urban areas, also often host large populations of involuntary or humanitarian migrants who have fled conflict, crises, climate change and other shocks (See text box 8). Management of disaster-induced displacement becomes a main priority for local governments.

Mitigating risks linked to migration to urban areas, particularly by reducing drivers of forced migration and ensuring access to resources that help build resilience is essential in urban migration governance. Such urban governance would recognize the role migrants play in building the resilience of home and host communities, through remittances and other resources, and the need to design and implement mobility management policies in a way that does not create further vulnerabilities.

In general, migrant inclusion is not high on the agenda of many national and urban policymakers in the less developed world. The hostile stance of many local governments against migrants, the urban poor and the informal sector, as well as scapegoating of migrants especially during times of economic difficulties, leads to the extreme poverty among migrants. Lack of inclusion practices is often reinforced by discriminatory practices, both official and de facto. In many poor cities, local governments crack down on informal street traders and informal housing on a regular basis. Migrants still find protection and income opportunities in the informal settlements in spite of their lack of basic services such as sanitation, health care and education.

Text box 8

Migrants in Accra, Ghana[7]

In Accra, the 'migrant neighbourhoods' of Nima and Old Fadama are home to many people who were born there and have never lived anywhere else, yet are considered migrants because their parents or grandparents migrated from the north in the 1980s and 1990s.

- Nima, a poor neighbourhood which emerged in the 1940s, is a melting pot of ethnic groups and nationalities, especially from northern Ghana and the West Africa Sahelian countries of Mali, Niger and Burkina Faso.

- Old Fadama is a more recent poor migrant community, which dates back to the mid-1990s, and, in spite of its notoriously harsh and poor living conditions, is home to many of the poor, including female head porters, *kayaye*, who make their living in the markets.

Various factors drive migrants to accumulate in particular areas of the city, including social networks, exclusion from housing or employment in indigenous neighbourhoods, xenophobia and protection in numbers, and in order to claim land to farm.

2.5

CONCLUDING REMARKS

Urban development around the world is manifesting itself in increasingly diverse forms, ranging from global cities on the one hand, as powerhouses of the international economy, to forgotten informal settlements on the other hand, where inhabitants struggle to meet the most basic of human needs. This urbanization is being shaped by ever-increasing migration movements of equal diversity and complexity, within and between countries, between rural and urban areas, between the Global North and South in all directions, and constituting varying degrees of permanency. The common theme across all these different examples is that the vast majority of this urban growth is organic and cities around the world are struggling with the challenge of putting in place adequate services and infrastructure to meet the needs of fast-growing populations.

---

7   Taken from M. Awumbila, G. Owusu and J.K. Teye, (2014) Can Rural-Urban Migration into Slums Reduce Poverty? Evidence from Ghana. Migration out of Poverty, Working Paper 13. See: http://migratingoutofpoverty.dfid.gov.uk/files/file.php?name=wp-13---awumbila-owusu-teye-2014-can-rural-urban-migration-into-slums-reduce-poverty-final.pdf&site=354

Migrant voices

Enjoying opportunities African cities can offer: Young mobile professional in Bujumbura

Maya is a 27-year-old South African currently living in Bujumbura, Burundi. She recently decided to move to Bujumbura to work as a technical assistant on modelling and monetary policy for the Banque de la République du Burundi, the country's central bank. Maya found a job by herself and did not resort to any public or private employment service. She enjoys her work and considers it allows her to afford a good standard of living in Bujumbura. She actually acknowledges that her financial situation has improved since moving to Burundi.

Having lived in several big cities in the past, she describes the Burundian capital as small, chaotic and friendly. She feels that Bujumbura has quite a diverse population composed of both foreigners and Burundians from other parts of the country. Being fluent in both French and English and currently learning Kirundi, Maya manages to communicate with most people in the Burundian capital, where Kirundi, Swahili, French and English are the predominant languages.

Maya decided to move into a shared house and has a formal tenancy agreement. The house is functional with running water, toilets, electricity, etc. and is located in a neighbourhood that she considers safe. She did not receive any assistance from public or non-governmental services regarding accommodation. She feels comfortable in her house and in Bujumbura and in fact says that she feels at home in the city. When it comes to health services, she has health insurance and can easily go to the hospital or the doctor if needed.

For the moment, Maya does not belong to any association and is not eligible to participate in municipal elections. As she recently arrived in Bujumbura, her knowledge of the city government is limited. Although she considers her neighborhood safe, she does not feel that the police are particularly trustworthy. Moreover, she still needs to learn what to do in case of natural disasters; Bujumbura is prone to floods and she does not know what safety measures to follow if this situation arises.

Maya is planning to stay in Burundi for the next two years while maintaining contact with her community back home. After her Burundian experience, she would like to move around Africa and work in the field of development economics.

REFERENCES

Anirudh, K., M.S. Sriram and P. Prakash
2014   "Slum types and adaptation strategies: identifying policy-relevant differences in Bangalore", *Environment and Urbanization*, 26(2): 568–585.

Asian Development Bank (ADB) Institute, Organization for Economic Co-operation and Development (OECD) and International Labour Organization (ILO)
2014   *Labour Migration, Skills and Student Mobility in Asia.* Asia Development Bank Institute, Tokyo.

Australian Bureau of Statistics
2014   Australian Social Trends: Where Do Migrants Live? ABS Census of Population and Housing 2011. Available from www.abs.gov.au/ausstats/abs@.nsf/Lookup/4102.0main+features102014
2015   Media Release: Overseas born Aussies hit a 120 year peak. January 2015. Available from http://www.abs.gov.au/ausstats/abs@.nsf/latestProducts/3412.0Media%20Release12013-14

Awumbila, M.
2014   Linkages between Urbanization, Rural-Urban Migration and Poverty Outcomes in Africa. Background Paper for the *World Migration Report 2015, Migrants and Cities: New Partnerships to Manage Mobility.* IOM, Geneva.

Awumbila, M., G. Owusu and J.K. Teye
2014   Can Rural-Urban Migration into Slums Reduce Poverty? Evidence from Ghana. Working Paper No 13. Migrating out of Poverty Consortium, University of Sussex, Brighton. Available from http://r4d.dfid.gov.uk/Output/196216/

Bakewell, O. and G. Jónsson
2011   *Migration, Mobility and the African City: Synthesis report on the African Perspectives on Human Mobility research programme.* International Migration Institute, University of Oxford, Oxford. Available from www.imi.ox.ac.uk/publications/migration-mobility-and-the-african-city

Bayona, J. and F. Gil-Alonso
2011   Foreign migration, urban growth and suburbanization dynamics in large Spanish metropolitan areas. Paper presented at the European Network for Housing Research Conference. 5–8 July 2011. University Toulouse II-Le Mirail, Toulouse. Available from www.enhr2011.com/sites/default/files/Paper-BAYONA_GIL-WS04.pdf

Bhagat, R.B.
2012   Migrants (Denied) Right to the City. National Workshop on Internal Migration and Human Development, 6-7 December 2011. Workshop Compendium, Vol. II, Workshop Papers. UNESCO and UNICEF, New Delhi, pp. 86–99. Available from www.unesco.org/new/fileadmin/MULTIMEDIA/FIELD/New_Delhi/pdf/Internal_Migration_Workshop_-_Vol_2_07.pdf

2014   Urban Migration Trends, Challenges and Opportunities in India. Background Paper for the *World Migration Report 2015: Migrants and Cities: New Partnerships to Manage Mobility*. IOM, Geneva.

Brown, D.
2012   Migration and rural population change: Comparative views in more developed nations". In: *International Handbook of Rural Demography* (L.J. Kulcsar and K.J. Curtis, eds.). Springer, Dordrecht, pp. 35–49.

Çağlar, A.
2014   Urban Migration Trends, Challenges and Opportunities, Background Paper for the *World Migration Report 2015:Migrants and Cities: New Partnerships to Manage Mobility*, International Organization for Migration (IOM), Geneva, Switzerland.

Casillas Ramírez, R.
2007   *Una vida discreta, fugaz y anónima: los centroamericanos transmigrantes en México.* Comisión Nacional de los Derechos Humanos (CNDH) y la Organización Internacional para las Migraciones (OIM), México.

Collett, E. and M. Petrovic
2014   *The Future of Immigrant Integration in Europe: Mainstreaming Approaches for Inclusion*. Migration Policy Institute Europe, Brussels. Available from www.migrationpolicy.org/research/future-immigrant-integration-europe-mainstreaming-approaches-inclusion

Duncan, H.
2010   Some modern challenges to social inclusion in highly diverse cities. In: *How to Enhance Inclusiveness for International Migrants in Our Cities: Various Stakeholders' Views.* UNESCO, Paris, pp. 136–143. Available from http://zunia.org/post/how-to-enhance-inclusiveness-for-international-migrants-in-our-cities-various-stakeholders%E2%80%99-vie

Esipova, N., A. Pugliese and J. Ray
2013   The demographics of global internal migration. *Migration Policy Practice* 3(2): 3-5. IOM, Geneva. Available from http://publications.iom.int/bookstore/free/MigrationPolicyPracticeJournal10_15May2013.pdf

Euro-Mediterranean Human Rights Network (EMHRN)
2014   *Analysis of the Mobility Partnership signed between the Kingdom of Morocco, the European Union and nine Member States on 7 June 2013.* EMHRN, Copenhagen. Available from http://euromedrights.org/wp-content/uploads/2015/03/PM-Morocco_Final-Version-EN.pdf

Fahmi, F. et al.
2014   Extended Urbanization in Small and Medium-Sized Cities: The Case of Cirebon, Indonesia. *Habitat International*, 42: 1–10.

Federation of Canadian Municipalities (FCM)
2009   *Immigration and diversity in Canadian Cities and Communities*. FCM, Ottawa. Available from www.fcm.ca/Documents/backgrounders/Immigration_and_Diversity_in_Canadian_Cities_and_Communities_EN.pdf

Fincher, R. et al.
2014   Planning in the multicultural city: Celebrating diversity or reinforcing
            difference? *Progress in Planning*, 92: 1–55.

Florida, R.
2014   Two Very Different Types of Migrations Are Driving Growth in U.S.
            Cities. *Citylab*. 21 April 2014. Available from www.citylab.com/
            politics/2014/04/2-very-different-migration-driving-growth-us-
            cities/8873/

Glick Schiller, N. and A. Çağlar
2011   Downscaled cities and migrant pathways: locality and agency without
            an ethnic lens. In: *Locating Migration: Rescaling Cities and Migrants*
            (N. Glick Schiller and A. Çağlar, eds.). Cornell University Press, Ithaca
            and London, pp. 190–211.

Gross, J., L. Ye and R. Legates
2014   Asia and the Pacific Rim: The New Peri-Urbanization and Urban
            Theory. *Journal of Urban Affairs,* 36(S1):309–314.

Hoang, X.T., T.A. Truong and T.T.P. Dinh
2013   Urban poverty in Vietnam – a view from complementary assessments.
            Human Settlements Working Paper, Poverty Reduction in Urban Areas
            - 40. International Institute for Environment and Development (IIED),
            London. Available from http://pubs.iied.org/pdfs/10633IIED.pdf

Huang, S., B. Yeoh and N. Rahman, eds.
2005   *Asian Women as Transnational Domestic Workers*, Marshall
            Cavendish, Singapore.

Hugo, G.
2014   Urban Migration Trends, Challenges, Responses and Policy in the
            Asia-Pacific. Background Paper for the *World Migration Report 2015:
            Migrants and Cities: New Partnerships to Manage Mobility*. IOM,
            Geneva.

Iceland, J.
2014   Residential Segregation: A Transatlantic Analysis. Migration Policy
            Institute, Washington, D.C. Available from www.migrationpolicy.org/
            research/residential-segregation-transatlantic-analysis

Instituto Nacional de Estadística, Geografía e Informática (INEGI), México
2001   XII Censo General de Población y Vivienda 2000. INEGI, Aguascalientes.
            Available   from   www.inegi.org.mx/sistemas/olap/proyectos/bd/
            consulta.asp?c=10252&p=14048&s=est#
2011   XIII Censo General de Población y Vivienda 2010. INEGI, Aguascalientes.
            Available   from   www.inegi.org.mx/est/contenidos/proyectos/ccpv/
            cpv2010/Default.aspx

International Organization for Migration (IOM)
2014   International Dialogue on Migration, South–South Migration:
            Partnering strategically for development. IOM, Geneva. Available
            from http://publications.iom.int/bookstore/index.php?main_page=
            product_info&cPath=55&products_id=1395

Japan, Ministry of Justice
2011   Immigration Bureau. Available from www.moj.go.jp/ENGLISH/IB/ib-
            01.html

Kasimis, C.
2010   Demographic trends in rural Europe and international migration to rural areas. *Agriregionieuropa,* 21: 1–6. Available from http://agriregionieuropa.univpm.it/content/article/31/21/demographic-trends-rural-europe-and-international-migration-rural-areas

Kihato, C.W. et al.
2010   Introduction: Exploring the contours of inclusion and exclusion in twenty-first-century cities. In: *Urban Diversity - Space, Culture, and Inclusive Pluralism in Cities Worldwide* (C. W. Kihato, et al., eds.). Woodrow Wilson Center Press, Washington, D.C., pp. 1–17.

Lyons, M., A. Brown and L. Zhigang
2012   In the Dragon's Den: African Traders in Guangzhou. *Journal of Ethnic and Migration Studies*, 38(5): 869–888.

Marconi, G.
2008   Transit cities in transit countries: steering the consequences of US an EU closed doors. International Workshop - Narratives of Migration Management and Cooperation with Countries of Origin and Transit. University of Sussex, Brighton. Available from www.sps.ed.ac.uk/__data/assets/word_doc/0014/20183/Giobanna.doc

Münz, R.
2014   The global race for talent: Europe's migration challenge. Bruegel Policy Brief No. 2. Bruegel, Brussels. Available from www.bruegel.org/publications/publication-detail/publication/819-the-global-race-for-talent-europes-migration-challenge/

Murillo, F.
2014   Migration and urbanization paths: Emerging challenges of reshaping the human geography of Latin America. Background Paper for the *World Migration Report 2015: Migrants and Cities: New Partnerships to Manage Mobility*. IOM, Geneva.

Organization for Economic Cooperation and Development (OECD)
2011   *Tackling the Policy Challenges of Migration: Regulation, Integration, Development*. Development Centre Studies, OECD, Paris. Available from http://www.oecd-ilibrary.org/social-issues-migration-health/tackling-the-policy-challenges-of-migration_9789264126398-en

Ostanel, E.
2011   Citizenship in the making: Mozambicans in Johannesburg. Paper presented at the International Research Committee 21 conference: The struggle to belong: Dealing with diversity in 21st century urban settings. Amsterdam, 7–9 July 2011. International Sociological Association, Madrid. Available from www.rc21.org/conferences/amsterdam2011/edocs/Session%209/9-1-Ostanel.pdf

Özbabacan, A.
2012   European cities: From integration to diversity policies. *Migration Policy Practice* II(4): 11–14. IOM, Geneva. Available from http://publications.iom.int/bookstore/free/MigrationPolicyPracticeJournal_11Sept2012.pdf

Price, M.
2014   Cities Welcoming Immigrants: Local Strategies to Attract and Retain
            Immigrants in U.S. Metropolitan Areas. Background Paper for the
            *World Migration Report 2015: Migrants and Cities: New Partnerships
            to Manage Mobility*. IOM, Geneva.

Rameez, A. and D. Varma
2014   Internal Labor Migration in India Raises Integration Challenges
            for Migrants. *Migration Information Source*, March 2, 2014.
            Migration Policy Institute, Washington, D.C. Available from www.
            migrationpolicy.org/article/internal-labor-migration-india-raises-
            integration-challenges-migrants

Rienzo, C. and C. Vargas-Silva
2014   *Migrants in the UK: An Overview*. The Migration Observatory
            at the University of Oxford, Oxford. Available from www.
            migrationobservatory.ox.ac.uk/briefings/migrants-uk-overview

Rigg, J., T.A. Nguyen and T.T.H. Luong
2014   The Texture of Livelihoods: Migration and Making a Living in Hanoi,
            The Journal of Development Studies, 50 (3):368–382.

Sassen, S.
1991   *Global Cities: New York, London, Tokyo*. Princeton University Press,
            Princeton.

Seoul Metropolitan Government
2014   Data taken from the database of Seoul Metropolitan Government.
            Available from http://stat.seoul.go.kr/

Serageldin, M. et al.
2014   Urban Migration Trends in the MENA Region and the Challenge of
            Conflict Induced Displacement. Background Paper for the *World
            Migration Report 2015: Migrants and Cities: New Partnerships to
            Manage Mobility*. IOM, Geneva.

Simone, A.
2008   Moving Towards Uncertainty: Migration and the Turbulence of African
            Urban Life. In: *Immigration and Integration in Urban Communities:
            Renegotiating the City* (L. M. Hanley, B. A. Ruble and A. Garland, eds.).
            Woodrow Wilson Center Press with Johns Hopkins University Press,
            Washington, D.C., pp. 123–139.

Singapore Foreign Workers Dormitory Guide
n.d.   Foreign Workers Dormitories: Governmental policy about foreign
            workers' accommodation in Singapore. *Singapore Foreign Workers
            Dormitory Guide* (n.d.). Available from http://foreignworkerdormitory.
            com/statistics

Singapore, Prime Minister's Office
2013   Population in Brief 2013. National Population and Talent Division.
            Available from http://www.nptd.gov.sg/portals/0/news/population-
            in-brief-2013.pdf

Singer, A.
2013   Contemporary Immigrant Gateways in Historical Perspective.
            Daedulus 142(3): 76–91.

Skeldon, R.
2013   Global Migration: Demographic Aspects and Its Relevance for
            Development. UN DESA Technical paper 2013/6. Available
            from   www.un.org/esa/population/migration/documents/EGM.
            Skeldon_17.12.2013.pdf

Sobrino, J.
2010   Migración urbana. *La situación demográfica en México*. Consejo
            Nacional de Población, Mexico, D.F., pp. 155–170.

Spoonley, P.
2014   Superdiversity, social cohesion, and economic benefits. *IZA World of
            Labour article*, May 2014. Institute for the Study of Labor (IZA), Bonn.
            Available   from   http://wol.iza.org/articles/superdiversity-social-
            cohesion-and-economic-benefits.pdf

Srivastava, R.
2012   Internal Migration in India: An Overview of its features, trends
            and policy challenges. *National Workshop on Internal Migration
            and Human Development in India, 6-7 December 2011*. Workshop
            Compendium. Vol. II, Workshop Papers. UNICEF and UNESCO,
            New Delhi, pp.1–47.   Available from www.unesco.org/new/
            fileadmin/MULTIMEDIA/FIELD/New_Delhi/pdf/Internal_Migration_
            Workshop_-_Vol_2_07.pdf

Statistics Canada
2011   *National Household Survey 2011*. Available from www12.statcan.
            gc.ca/nhs-enm/index-eng.cfm

Stren, R.
2010   Diversity and Urban Governance. In: *Urban Diversity - Space, Culture,
            and Inclusive Pluralism in Cities Worldwide* (C. W. Kihato, et al., eds.).
            Woodrow Wilson Center Press, Washington, D.C., pp. 257–282.

Striffler, S.
2007   Neither Here Nor There: Mexican Immigrant Workers and the Search
            for Home. *American Ethnologist* 34(4):674–688.

Tacoli, C., G. McGranahan and D. Satterthwaite
2014   Urbanization, Rural-urban Migration and Urban Poverty. Background
            Paper for the *World Migration Report 2015: Migrants and Cities:
            New Partnerships to Manage Mobility*. International Organization for
            Migration, Geneva.

Tasan-Kok, T. et al.
2013   *Towards Hyper-Diversified European Cities: A Critical Literature
            Review*. Utrecht University, Faculty of Geosciences, Utrecht. Available
            from http://dspace.library.uu.nl/handle/1874/308523

The Canadian Press
2013   Canada's foreign-born population soars to 6.8 million. *The Canadian
            Press,* 8 May 2013. Available from www.cbc.ca/news/canada/canada-
            s-foreign-born-population-soars-to-6-8-million-1.1308179

The Demographia
2015   *Demographia World Urban Areas*. 11th Annual Edition. Demographia,
            Belleville, Illinois. Available from www.demographia.com/db-worldua.
            pdf

The Economist
2014   Special Report on China: Building the Dream. *The Economist,* 19 April.

Tobocman, S.
2014   *Revitalizing Detroit: Is There a Role for Immigration?* Migration Policy
            Institute, Washington D.C. Available from www.migrationpolicy.org/
            research/revitalizing-detroit-is-there-a-role-for-immigration

United Cities and Local Governments (UCLG)
2013   *Basic Services for All in an Urbanizing World: the Third Global Report
            on Local Democracy and Decentralization.* Routledge, London.

United Nations Department of Economic and Social Affairs (UN DESA)
2012   *World Urbanization Prospects: 2011 Revision.* United Nations, New
            York. Available from www.un.org/en/development/desa/population/
            publications/pdf/urbanization/WUP2011_Report.pdf
2014   *World Urbanization Prospects, The 2014 Revision: Highlights.* United
            Nations, New York. Available from http://esa.un.org/unpd/wup/
            Highlights/WUP2014-Highlights.pdf

United Nations Educational, Scientific and Cultural Organization (UNESCO) Chair
on the Social and Spatial Inclusion of International Migrants (UNESCO SSIIM)
n.d.   "PRIN Small size cities. Small-size cities and social cohesion: policies
            and practices for the social and spatial inclusion of international
            migrants", Research project description Available from www.
            unescochair-iuav.it/en/research/prin-small-size-cities/

United Nations Educational, Scientific and Cultural Organization (UNESCO) and
United Nations Children's Fund (UNICEF)
2012   Internal Migration in India Initiative: For a Better Inclusion of Internal
            Migrants in India – Policy Brief. UNESCO and UNICEF, New Delhi.
            Available   from   www.unesco.org/new/fileadmin/MULTIMEDIA/
            FIELD/New_Delhi/pdf/Policy_briefs_full_low_01.pdf

United Nations Human Settlements Programme (UN-Habitat)
2010   *The State of African Cities, Governance, Inequality and Urban Land
            Markets.* Nairobi. Available from http://mirror.unhabitat.org/pmss/
            getElectronicVersion.aspx?nr=3034&alt=1
2012   *State of Arab Cities – Challenges of Urban Transition.* UN-Habitat,
            Nairobi. Available from http://unhabitat.org/books/the-state-of-
            arab-cities-2012-challenges-of-urban-transition/
2013a   *Streets as Public Spaces and Drivers of Urban Prosperity.* UN-Habitat,
            Nairobi. Available from http://unhabitat.org/books/streets-as-public-
            spaces-and-drivers-of-urban-prosperity/
2013b   *State of the World's Cities 2012/2013 - Prosperity of Cities.* Routledge,
            New York. Available from http://unhabitat.org/books/prosperity-of-
            cities-state-of-the-worlds-cities-20122013/
2013c   *Urban Planning for City Leaders.* UN-Habitat, Nairobi. Available from
            http://unhabitat.org/books/urban-planning-for-city-leaders/
2014   *State of African Cities – Re-imagining Sustainable Urban Transitions.*
            UN-Habitat, Nairobi. Available from http://unhabitat.org/books/
            state-of-african-cities-2014-re-imagining-sustainable-urban-
            transitions/

United Nations Human Settlements Programme (UN-Habitat) and United Nations Environment Programme (UNEP)

2010   *State of African Cities – Governance, Inequality and Urban Land Markets.* UN-Habitat, Nairobi. Available from http://unhabitat.org/ books/state-of-african-cities-2010-governance-inequalities-and- urban-land-markets-2/

United States Census Bureau

2013   *County Totals: Vintage 2013.* Percentage Change in Population for Counties and Puerto Rico Municipios: July 1, 2012 to July 1, 2013. Available from www.census.gov/popest/data/counties/totals/2013/ index.html

Vertovec, S.

2007   Super-diversity and its implications. *Ethnic and Racial Studies* 30(6):1024–1054.

2011   Migration and New Diversities in the Global Cities: Comparatively Conceiving, Observing and Visualizing Diversification in Urban Public Spaces. MMG Working Paper WP 11-08. Max-Planck-Institute, Göttingen. Available from www.mmg.mpg.de/publications/working- papers/2011/wp-11-08/

Walton-Roberts, M.

2011   Immigration, the university, the welcoming second-tier city. *Journal of International Migration and Integration*, 12(4):453–473.

Zhu, Y.

2014   *In situ* urbanization in China Processes, Contributing Factors, and Policy Implications. Background Paper for the *World Migration Report 2015: Migrants and Cities: New Partnerships to Manage Mobility.* IOM, Geneva.

Zweig, D.

2006   Learning to Compete: China's Efforts to Encourage a Reverse Brain Drain. *International Labour Review*, 145(1):65–90.

List of sources for Figure 1 – Foreign-born population in major cities

Dubai

Dilenge, M.

2007   Dubai and Doha: Unparalleled Expansion. *Mobility*, October 2007. Worldwide ERC, Arlington.

United Arab Emirates, National Bureau of Statistics,

2005   2005 Census. Available from www.uaestatistics.gov.ae/EnglishHome/ tabid/96/Default.aspx

Brussels

Petrovic, M.

2012   Belgium: A Country of Permanent Immigration Migration. *Migration Policy Institute.* Available from www.migrationpolicy.org/article/ belgium-country-permanent-immigration

Toronto

Statistics Canada

2011   *National Household Survey 2011.* Available from www12.statcan.
        gc.ca/nhs-enm/2011/as-sa/99-010-x/99-010-x2011001-eng.cfm

Auckland

Statistics New Zealand

2013   2013 Census. Available from www.stats.govt.nz/Census/2013-
        census/profile-and-summary-reports/qstats-culture-identity-auck-
        mr.aspx

Sydney

Australian Bureau of Statistics

2014   *Australian Social Trends: Where Do Migrants Live?* ABS Census of
        Population and Housing 2011. Available from www.abs.gov.au/
        ausstats/abs@.nsf/Lookup/4102.0main+features102014

2015   *Media Release: Overseas born Aussies hit a 120 year peak.*
        January 2015. Available from www.abs.gov.au/ausstats/abs@.nsf/
        Latestproducts/3412.0Media%20Release12013-14?opendocument&
        tabname=Summary&prodno=3412.0&issue=2013-14&num=&view

Los Angeles

United States Census Bureau

2012   *Statistical Abstract of the United States: 2012.* Available from www.
        census.gov/compendia/statab/2012/tables/12s0038.pdf

Singapore

Singapore, Prime Minister's Office

2013   *Population in Brief 2013.* National Population and Talent Division.
        Available from www.nptd.gov.sg/portals/0/news/population-in-
        brief-2013.pdf

London

Rienzo, C. and C. Vargas-Silva

2014   *Migrants in the UK: An Overview.* The Migration Observatory
        at the University of Oxford, Oxford. Available from www.
        migrationobservatory.ox.ac.uk/briefings/migrants-uk-overview

New York City

United States Census Bureau

2012   *Statistical Abstract of the United States: 2012.* Available from www.
        census.gov/compendia/statab/2012/tables/12s0038.pdf

Melbourne

Australian Bureau of Statistics

2014   *Australian Social Trends: Where Do Migrants Live?* ABS Census of
        Population and Housing 2011. Available from www.abs.gov.au/
        ausstats/abs@.nsf/Lookup/4102.0main+features102014

2015   *Media Release: Overseas born Aussies hit a 120 year peak.*
             January 2015. Available from www.abs.gov.au/ausstats/abs@.nsf/
             Latestproducts/3412.0Media%20Release12013-14?opendocument&
             tabname=Summary&prodno=3412.0&issue=2013-14&num=&view

Amsterdam

Onderzoek, Informatie en Statistiek (OIS), Amsterdam
2014   Available from www.ois.amsterdam.nl/english/#

Frankfurt

Frankfurt-am-Main City Government
2013   *Statistical Portrait.* Available from www.frankfurt.de/sixcms/media.
             php/678/J2014K00_Statistisches_Portrait_2013.pdf

Paris

Eurostat
2015   Population by citizenship and country of birth –cities and greater
             cities. Available from http://ec.europa.eu/eurostat   (accessed May
             2015).

Stockholm

Eurostat
2015   Population by citizenship and country of birth- cites and greater cities.
             Available from http://ec.europa.eu/eurostat (accessed May 2015).

Montreal

Statistics Canada
2011   *National Household Survey 2011.* Available from www12.statcan.
             gc.ca/nhs-enm/2011/as-sa/99-010-x/99-010-x2011001-eng.cfm

Rotterdam

Juzwiak, T.
2014   A case study of Rotterdam, The Netherlands. *Migrant and Refugee
             Integration in Global Cities, the Role of Cities and Businesses* (T. Juzwiak,
             E. McGregor and M. Siegel, eds.). The Hague Process on Refugees and
             Migration, The Hague. Available from http://thehagueprocess.org/
             wordpress/wp-content/uploads/2014/05/THP_Rotterdam.pdf

Chicago

United States Census Bureau
2012   *Statistical Abstract of the United States: 2012.* Available from www.
             census.gov/compendia/statab/2012/tables/12s0038.pdf

Madrid

Eurostat
2015   Population by citizenship and country of birth- cites and greater cities.
             Available from http://ec.europa.eu/eurostat (accessed May 2015).

Milan: based on Comune di Milano data

Comune di Milano

2015   *Settore Statistica.* Comune di Milano (Municipality of Milan) http://
         mediagallery.comune.milano.it/cdm/objects/changeme:30351/
         datastreams/dataStream5691500898647946/content   (accessed
         December 2014)

List of sources for Table 2 – Foreign-born population in major cities and countries in the Asia–Pacific region

Australian Bureau of Statistics

2014   Australian Social Trends: *Where Do Migrants Live?* Available from
         www.abs.gov.au/ausstats/abs@.nsf/Lookup/4102.0main+features10
         2014#WHERE

2015   Media Release: *Overseas born Aussies hit a 120 year peak*, January
         2015, Cat. No. 3412.0. Available from www.abs.gov.au/ausstats/
         abs@.nsf/Latestproducts/3412.0Media%20Release12013-14?op
         endocument&tabname=Summary&prodno=3412.0&issue=2013-
         14&num=&view

Japan, Ministry of Internal Affairs and Communications

2015   *Japan Statistical Year Book*, Statistics Bureau. Available from www.
         stat.go.jp/english/data/nenkan/1431-02.htm

Japan, Ministry of Justice

2011   Immigration Bureau, Tokyo. Available from www.moj.go.jp/ENGLISH/
         IB/ib-01.html

Malaysia, Department of Statistics

2010   Migration and Population Distribution Available from www.statistics.
         gov.my/

Republic of Korea, Ministry of Government Administration and Home Affairs

2014   Statistical Year Book. Available (in Korean only) at www.mogaha.
         go.kr/frt/bbs/type001/commonSelectBoardArticle.do?bbsId=BBSMS
         TR_000000000013&nttId=42584 (for Seoul)
         English website: www.mogaha.go.kr/eng/a01/engMain.do

Singapore, Prime Minister's Office

2013   *Population in Brief 2013*, National Population and Talent Division.
         Available from www.nptd.gov.sg/portals/0/news/population-in-
         brief-2013.pdf

World Cities Culture Forum

2001   Mumbai. Available from www.worldcitiescultureforum.com/indica-
         tors/foreign-born-population and www.worldcitiescultureforum.
         com/cities/mumbai

2005   India. Available from www.worldcitiescultureforum.com/indicators/
         foreign-born-population

World Population Review

2014   Kuala Lumpur. Available from http://worldpopulationreview.com/
         world-cities/kuala-lumpur-population/

Urban migrants, vulnerability and resilience

CHAPTER 3

Lorenzo Guadagno

HIGHLIGHTS

- Cities offer potential access to a variety of resources, services and opportunities that are essential for people's well-being and resilience. Therefore, for most migrants, moving to a city is a sound decision that is likely to benefit their well-being and strengthen their resilience to adversity.

- However, when inadequately managed, migration can actually result in conditions of exclusion and vulnerability for the individuals who are moving, as well as for host communities. Migrants are often faced with legal, cultural and social barriers and obstacles to accessing formal housing, employment, education, health and other social services. These barriers may force them to live in conditions of exclusion, segregation and vulnerability.

- Vulnerability can be particularly acute for specific migrant groups. Migrant women, for instance, are more likely to work in low-paid, irregular, and potentially exploitive jobs, often in the informal sector. However, cities also present potential opportunities, such as increased economic independence and capacity to challenge rigid gender norms.

- Migrants' health vulnerability is of special concern in urban settings, as the conditions in which many migrants travel, live and work make them particularly vulnerable to infectious and non-communicable diseases, as well as accidents, violence and abuse, and can adversely affect their mental and psychosocial well-being. At the same time inequalities in access to health care between migrant and non-migrant populations exist in many urban locations which affect the individual and public health of urban communities.

- Managing and addressing urban population displacement as a result of natural disasters, conflict or violence creates particular challenges to relevant actors and can result in increased conditions of long-term vulnerability for both the displaced and their host communities.

- Local level coordination, especially among different government and non-government stakeholders working in local disaster response, immigration, health, labour, social development and inclusion of migrants, is essential in building the resilience of migrants in the face of everyday stresses, as well as specific shocks. Migrants themselves can play a key role in building resilience. Migrant associations can deliver basic services and give voice to migrant concerns through political representation. It is also essential to involve migrants in disaster preparedness planning.

This chapter examines the causes and patterns of vulnerability that are specific to migrant groups in urban areas, looking at the barriers migrants face when accessing resources and opportunities and at how they result in different risk outcomes for different migrant groups, with specific consideration for migrant women and forced migrants. It also highlights the specific types and circumstances of vulnerability facing populations which move to cities. Finally it considers how partnerships among migrants, non-governmental organizations, and local governments can help build resilience to natural and man-made hazards.

3.1 INTRODUCTION

Urban migration and mobility includes a variety of population movements which take place for a range of reasons and for different durations. Most occur over short distances and within national borders. Whatever the nature of the movement, people move to urban areas in the hope of benefitting from the greater availability of services and accessing better infrastructure and income-generating opportunities, in order to establish improved and more secure livelihoods. When urban migration is well-managed, it can induce social and economic dynamics that enhance the capacity of urban migrants to cope with shocks and pressures. However, movement to cities can also bring social risks. Unmanaged urban migration can contribute to infrastructure, housing and service shortages, as well as aggravate financial problems and delivery challenges for the responsible local institutions. Whenever the capacity of urban authorities and markets are insufficient to provide adequate employment, water and sanitation, decent housing, efficient transportation, and quality health care, some segments of the urban populations will be marginalized and made ever more vulnerable.

3.2 PATTERNS OF VULNERABILITY

Cities offer potential access to a variety of resources, services and opportunities that are essential for well-being and resilience. Therefore, for most migrants, moving into a city is a sound decision which generates well-being and resilience. However, when inadequately managed, migration can actually result in conditions of exclusion and vulnerability for those moving, as well as for their host communities.

Population movements are a key dynamic to the evolution of urban areas. They contribute to shaping location, size, composition and characteristics of human communities, as well as the features of the environment where they live (Greiner and Sakdapolrak, 2012). Moving modifies the migrants' exposure to hazards and their access to resources to anticipate, cope with and recover from stresses (ibid.), but it also changes the risk patterns faced by urban dwellers in host communities. As people increasingly move towards, within or between urban areas, cities are today the main arena in which these risk dynamics unfold (ibid.).

Depending on the circumstances in which it takes place, however, urban migration can have widely diverse effects on the vulnerability and resilience of migrants and host communities. Migration to cities has traditionally offered people the opportunity to escape socioeconomic and other pressures in their areas of origin, and to diversify livelihoods in ways that make their households less vulnerable to the impacts of rural hazards. Cities provide centralized, reliable services, and a variety of economic opportunities that continue to be available in times of hardship (ibid.). Rural inhabitants typically undertake short- and long-term labour migration to urban areas in an attempt to diversify their sources of income during the off-farm season or in response to drought and floods (ibid.). Similarly, flight to the relative safety of cities has been a traditional response to rural conflicts and violence (Brookings Institution, 2013).

However, migrating to cities can result in increased vulnerability, especially if formal employment, decent housing, and the basic services needed for a decent life, are lacking. This can force people into making trade-offs between meeting their immediate needs and achieving long-term well-being and security (Cannon,

2008; Gaillard et al., 2010). This typically creates patterns of spatial segregation and marginalization, with people settling in informal or poorly planned areas where they face a number of natural and man-made hazards such as floods and disease (see text box 10), or violence (see text box 9).

Text box 9

Urban migration and different forms of urban violence

The city may be a refuge from violence, but, as the world's population has become predominantly urban, the city has also become the site of more and more violent activity. Urban population dynamics have drawn intensified interest in the linkage between urbanization and violence. Over two-thirds of refugees in the world, for instance, live in urban areas. The anonymity, density of populations and concentration of resources associated with urban living offer options for escaping violence and remaking lives that are much harder to find in rural areas.

Where rapid urbanization coincides with a significant rise in urban violence, migrants are often blamed. However, newcomers are over represented amongst poor and marginalized groups who typically suffer the most serious consequences of violence – they are much more likely to be victims of violence than perpetrators. Urban migrants may experience violence, both in the form of direct and indirect threats to their lives, integrity and freedom of choice in three main ways: violence as a reason for moving to cities, violence as a reason for displacement within cities and violence as a factor worsening the living conditions of migrants in cities.

According to the UN's 2009 World Population Policies report, 72 per cent of developing country governments see rural-to-urban migration as a problem. Resulting restrictions may involve the threat or use of force, typically related to relocation of unwanted groups. Even where no direct force is used to relocate people, such processes can disrupt local livelihoods and reduce access to public services. The engagement of target communities in planning relocation or better in situ development offers an opportunity to reduce or eliminate these forms of institutional violence.

Since urban areas experience higher levels of direct violence than rural areas, migration to urban areas results in more frequent experiences of violence. Low-income migrants will typically have little choice but to move to areas of cities where direct violence is more common. The Safe and Inclusive Cities project, exploring involuntary displacement in Sri Lanka and Southern India, found that when forced, intra-urban population movements are more likely to result in increased exposure to low level, criminal violence. This is most likely the result of the disintegration of established community dynamics that provide a degree of control over crimes such as burglary and aggression.

Reductions in violence experienced by migrants can only be achieved through careful community engagement policies. Trust in public authorities, especially police forces, will inevitably be disrupted by experiences of systematic urban violence. This trust may take time to develop but this is an essential element in any attempt to reduce further violence. In the longer term, violence reduction may take place through planning processes. Inclusive cities are settlements in which equal access to opportunities and safety is actively promoted.

There is no straightforward relationship between migration to cities and violence. The city may be a refuge from violence, but as the world's population has become predominantly urban, the city is also the location of more and more violent activity. The rise in urbanization has coincided with a shift in the nature and function of organized violence: wars have become increasingly internal to states; non-state actors have become increasingly significant perpetrators of violence and civilians do not simply account for a vastly disproportionate share of the victims of violence but increasingly form the explicit target of violent activities. All these trends highlight the growing concentration of organized violence in urban areas.

Contributed by Michael Collyer, Reader in Geography, Sussex Centre for Migration Research, University of Sussex, Brighton, United Kingdom.

Urban mobility in itself does not lead to vulnerability (Donner and Rodriguez, 2008). It is only when population pressures on urban labour and housing markets, health and education systems as well as water supply, sanitation and waste management infrastructures are unmanaged, that conditions of marginalization, exclusion and risk are produced. Unmanaged pressures on natural resources, including land, can also lead to other hazards arising from environmental degradation, or affect food and water security of both newcomers and host communities (de Sherbinin et al., 2012; Eswaran et al., 2011).

Such marginalization in cities is not unique to migrants. It tends to more heavily affect the weakest social groups, which often include women, youth and the elderly (UNDP, 2009). Migrants, and in particular recent migrants, however, tend to be disproportionately represented among the poor and vulnerable of urban populations in both developed and developing countries. Urban migrants are likely to live in the cities' most marginal and least safe locations, forced to make a living from informal income opportunities and to rely on basic service provision (see text box 10). Understanding the conditions of migrants in urban contexts is key to success in reducing risks in increasingly diverse cities (IOM, 2008; Juzwiak, McGregor and Siegel, 2014).

Text box 10

Migration and risk in Jakarta's informal *Kampungs*, Indonesia

The Jakarta metropolitan area is the major migration hub in Indonesia. Over the last few decades, millions of internal migrants have moved into the city, and as of 2000, 42.4 per cent of the city's population had been born outside Jakarta. Most moved to the city through informal channels and in violation of existing administrative procedures. Limited income opportunities within the city have resulted in high unemployment and poverty rates.

Lacking formal livelihood, land tenure and housing options, many migrants have settled in informal neighbourhoods (so-called *Kampungs*) in flood-prone areas. In some Kampungs, the percentage of people born outside Jakarta is well over 90 per cent. About half of those living in such neighbourhoods are undocumented migrants, 60 per cent have little or no education; only about 20 per cent have stable employment and most earn less than USD 1 per day. Most live in zones where constructions are not allowed, which have no formal access to water provision networks and official rubbish collection.

These constraints force people to make hazardous choices, in terms of building construction, inadequate measures to prevent water- and vector-borne diseases, utilizing unsafe drinking water, and throwing waste in waterways. Precarious tenure rights and the need to protect their own possessions have also led informal settlers to refuse to evacuate when floods have occurred in the past, or to return back home prematurely in the immediate aftermath of a flood which increases exposure to flood-related hazards.

Undocumented migrants tend to be insufficiently accounted for at the political level and in risk management systems. Formal support systems exist for enhancing the food security and access to health care for the urban poor; however, they are not accessible to unregistered migrant households. Lack of status also prevents them from accessing support in the aftermath of disasters. Pre-disaster efforts, instead, tend to focus on awareness-raising and do not address the structural factors which push people into situations of vulnerability. Consequently such awareness-raising has limited effect on people's behaviour and exposure to hazards. In addition, ever since the 1980s, risk management measures have favoured the establishment of no-build green areas along all waterways, resulting in evictions and relocations into low-cost urban neighbourhoods. This has often disrupted people's access to opportunities and social support systems, and forced them into unaffordable public housing, which is not adapted to their needs and living situation. As a consequence, many relocated individuals have gone back to flood-prone areas. More recently, however, policies have started providing livelihood options to relocated households in neighbourhoods of destination.

Migrant groups often mobilize capacities and resources within themselves to address these factors of vulnerability. Local networks are an essential form of support in times of hardship, due to economic factors, for instance, throughout the period of the Asian "Tiger" financial crisis of 1997, or to natural hazards, such as the 2007 floods. Neighbourhood-level connections are essential for disseminating flood alerts, facilitating the construction of housing and infrastructure, delivering basic services (e.g. rubbish collection), removing post-disaster rubble, and providing recovery assistance.

Local connections therefore determine migrant settlement choices within Jakarta, explaining why *Kampungs* tend to consolidate and resist official efforts at upgrading or regularizing settlement dwellers. Bonds with households and communities of origin, instead, are what push migrants to endure conditions of risk in order to achieve improvements in social and economic status.

Contributed by Pauline Texier, Senior Lecturer, Jean Moulin University Lyon III, Lyon, France.[1]

1   P. Texier, *Vulnérabilité et réduction des risques liés à l'eau dans les quartiers informels de Jakarta, Indonésie – Réponses sociales, institutionnelles et non institutionnelles*. PhD, Université Paris Diderot (2009).

3.3

BARRIERS TO ACCESSING RESOURCES AND OPPORTUNITIES

Migrants are often faced with legal, cultural and social barriers, and obstacles to accessing the full range of resources, services and opportunities that cities can offer, including formal housing, employment, health care, education and social support systems. As a consequence, they are often forced to live in conditions of exclusion, segregation and vulnerability.

The limited access of migrants to essential resources and opportunities is linked to socioeconomic, cultural and political barriers that are created by the interplay between policies, institutions and markets of the destination area and individual profiles, experiences and sensitivities of the migrants themselves. The most recurrent barriers are the following:

Linguistic barriers: Lack of linguistic skills can impede access to local markets (in particular the labour market), information (including disaster preparedness warnings), health care and education, and hinder an understanding of administrative procedures that are key to daily life. Linguistic barriers transcend internal and international migration; they may be present in countries where more than one language is spoken, or not apply in the case of international migration between two countries speaking the same language.

Legal and administrative barriers: Laws and regulations can exclude all or some specific groups of migrants from formal access to housing, employment, health care, education, and response and recovery assistance in the case of disasters. While such situations are often the result of policies regulating immigration from abroad, they can also stem from registration requirements for internal urban migrants.

Reduced access to social networks: Moving away from the place of origin often disrupts family and community ties that help provide income, health and childcare and education, emotional support or additional resources to cope with hardship. Availability of these forms of social capital is usually reduced in urban areas of destination. However, social ties and connections both with people from areas of origin and with kin, origin or ethnicity-based networks in areas of destinations are a significant source of resilience for urban migrants, and often one of the key factors influencing their decision to move.

Reduced knowledge of the local environmental and social context: Moving out of a particular local context also means that site-specific knowledge is lost, and that it might not be replaced, at least in the short term, by an equal level of understanding of the context of destination. This may include insufficient awareness of local resources and opportunities (such as housing, health care, social support systems) and how to access them, as well as local hazards (for example, violence, illness, landslides, floods). Both can result in specific patterns of exclusion and risk for incoming populations.

Inadequacy of skills for urban labour market: Urban labour markets may require completely different skill sets from those in the areas of origin. As a consequence, people arriving in cities might face specific challenges in accessing income opportunities, and may have to deal with unemployment or deskilling. This is likely to be more relevant in the case of rural–urban than urban–urban movements. In some instances, a different skill set might also be an advantage when filling local skill gaps.

Lack of representation, discrimination and xenophobia: Lack of political representation results in a lack of recognition within decision-making processes of the needs and capacities of migrant communities. In some cases an outright hostile environment can lead to excluding migrants from the delivery of basic resources and services (such as housing, employment, health care) or to exposing them to risks linked with their migration status (for example, xenophobic violence).

These barriers can constrain the ability of urban migrants, displaced persons and refugees to access basic resources and opportunities or receive support from formal and informal systems and networks (IOM, 2013; Duong, Linh and Thao, 2011; Ku and Jewers, 2013; Sabates-Wheeler, 2009; Adams and van Hattum and English, 2009) (see Figure 5). Migrants may end up living in informal settlements and slums and forced to make a living working in the informal economy. These conditions push people into situations of limited personal, environmental and financial security (UN-Habitat, 2003).

These barriers may arise in the case of all kinds of mobility (internal or international migration, displacement and relocations). As a consequence, the type of population movement people are involved in is not necessarily the main determinant of their level of well-being and risk. It is rather the socioeconomic and institutional context in which the movement takes place that plays a bigger role in determining outcomes (De Haas, 2007). However, the situation of forced migrants in cities is highlighted in point 3.4.2. as it presents challenges to a number of actors (such as the humanitarian sector) that are not included in routine management of urban mobility.

Figure 5 **Challenges and opportunities for urban migrants**

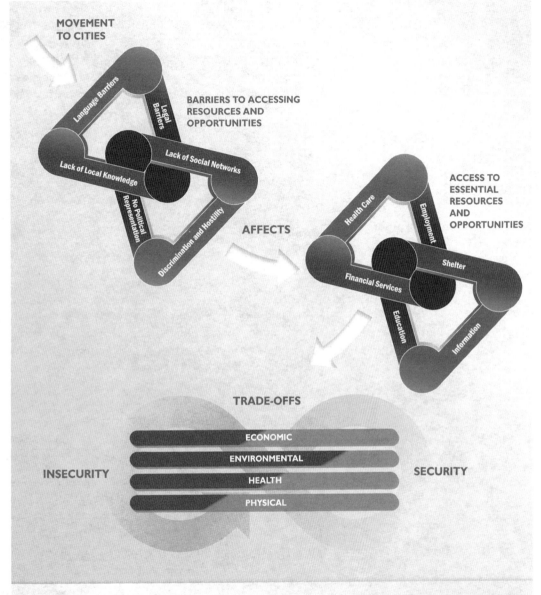

Migrants move to urban areas to gain increased access to resources and services essential for well-being. In doing so, they are often confronted with a specific set of barriers that constrain the options they can access. As a consequence, migrants often adopt trade-off solutions, as they need to consider and compromise between different types of risks and rewards, such as economic, environmental, and physical (in-)security. Access to resources and opportunities and risks/rewards resulting from concrete decisions are interconnected: for example, in order to have adequate access to housing options, employment opportunities or social support systems that offer a basic degree of economic and personal security, migrants may end up living in hazard-prone areas. In this case, disaster risk resulting from living in an unsafe location represents the trade-off to earning an income and the opportunity to create a better life.

The passage of time tends to positively influence the level of establishment and inclusion of migrants in host cities. It is common to observe urban segregation patterns following the chronology of the arrival of different migrant groups (Metcalfe, Haysom and Martin, 2012; UNDP, 2009). Other distinguishing characteristics such as gender, age, education, occupational skills and ethnicity may affect the migrant experience of exclusion or vulnerability (see text box 11).

Vulnerabilities of migrant women in urban settings

Gender is an important dimension of migrant vulnerability in the cities as women migrate to urban centres in increasing numbers, especially to low- and middle- income countries, given that the proportion of female-headed households is typically higher in urban areas. The move is often motivated as much by the income opportunities as by discrimination against women in areas of origin. For instance, widowed or separated women move to urban areas of Honduras, the United Republic of Tanzania and Ethiopia, with their families as their claim to rural land and inheritance is denied. Urban migration usually means greater independence for women, with better opportunities for employment, better access to services and lower fertility rates, as well as less rigid social norms and cultural constraints. While migration and urbanization involve often profound changes in gender relations, benefits can be minimal for the large number of women living in low-income settlements and working in low-paid, insecure jobs. Women are more likely than men to be employed in the urban informal sector.

In sub-Saharan Africa, 74 per cent of female non-agricultural workers are informally employed compared to 61 per cent of men, while this proportion is 54 per cent of women and 48 per cent of men in Latin America. In urban China, women account for 36 per cent of informal sector workers, compared to 30 per cent of men. While easily available, employment in the informal sector is low-paid, often on a daily basis, in dangerous working conditions, that can result in injury and exposure to additional financial insecurity, and to the costs of health treatment.

Domestic service is the other major informal employment for women in urban areas in low- and middle-income countries. In South Africa, domestic service was the second-largest sector of employment for black women in the early 2000s and employing some 755,000 workers, a large proportion of them internal migrants from rural areas. Work in private households is also a major source of employment for rural–urban migrant women in Viet Nam and in the United Republic of Tanzania. In Latin America, an estimated 7.6 million people are employed as domestic workers, the majority migrant women. Wages are low, and while accommodation provided by employers makes it relatively attractive especially for migrants, long working hours, potential abuse by employers and social isolation increase workers' vulnerability. Outside of employment, women's primary responsibility for unpaid care work in the family life is an additional and considerable burden, and significantly increases the vulnerability of recent migrants who do not have the support of family and friends or access to national and municipal support services.

Based on C. Tacoli, G. McGranahan and D. Satterthwaite, Urbanization, Rural-urban Migration and Urban Poverty, 2014. Background paper for the *World Migration Report 2015: Migrants and Cities: New Partnerships to Manage Mobility*, International Organization for Migration, Geneva.

3.4 SPECIFIC TYPES AND CIRCUMSTANCES OF VULNERABILITY

3.4.1. Health[2]

Vulnerability to ill-health is a particular issue facing migrant populations in urban areas. While opportunities for better health services are available in urban areas, migrants often have little choice but to live and work in unsafe conditions that result in exposure to infectious and non-communicable diseases, as well as accidents, violence and abuse, which in turn have an adverse effect on their mental and psychosocial well-being. Vulnerabilities are influenced by age, gender, overcrowding, air pollution, and lack of quality health care, amongst others. Migrants' ill-health carries negative social and economic consequences for the individual, the family and society at large leading to lower socioeconomic development outcomes. At the same time, migrants are often left out of public health services. The most vulnerable among urban migrant populations are those who do not have a regular residence status, and those with specific health needs, such as women, children and the elderly.

Rapid urbanization processes pose severe challenges, in particular for public health authorities. The World Health Organization (WHO) and UN-Habitat (2010) have identified a "triple threat" to describe the main drivers of health outcomes in urban areas. This "triple threat" consists of infectious diseases that thrive in poor and overcrowded urban environments; non-communicable diseases which are exacerbated by unhealthy lifestyles accessible in urban areas and taken up in the course of settling in cities; and injuries and violence that stem from dangerous road traffic and unsafe working and living conditions (WHO and UN-Habitat, 2010: 14).

Social determinants of health

The state of a person's health is shaped not only by his or her access to health services, but by a multitude of factors, which have been coined as the social determinants of health. These are the conditions in which people are born, grow, live, work and age, and which are mainly responsible for persisting health inequities within and across countries – and cities. These conditions result mainly from inadequate or non-existing social policies or unfavourable political and economic structures (WHO, 2008).

In urban settings, specific social determinants for health interact and mutually define an individual's vulnerability to disease (Alirol et al., 2010). As described in a joint global report by WHO and UN-Habitat (2010), *"[c]ities offer both the best and the worst environments for health and well-being."* Of the factors that determine health in urban settings, the report identified the following: population characteristics, urban governance, the natural and built environment, the social and economic environment, food security and quality, and services and health emergency management. Other research (Ompad et al., 2007) provides a similar list of social determinants of health for urban dwellers, including the place of residence within the city, race and ethnicity, gender, socioeconomic status and education (Alirol et al., 2010). From this list, it is possible to deduce that urban migrants might be especially vulnerable to ill health. As stated in the above-

---

2   This section is based on C. Schultz, Migration, Health and Urbanization: Interrelated Challenges, 2014. Background Paper for the *World Migration Report 2015: Migrants and Cities: New Partnerships to Manage Mobility*, IOM, Geneva.

mentioned report, *"[t]hose who migrate to escape difficult circumstances often experience a double jeopardy in cities: pre-existing vulnerabilities combined with greater exposure to migration-associated stressors. A social and economic gap often emerges between long-time urban residents and migrants"* (WHO and UN-Habitat, 2010). Hence, both migration and urbanization determine the health of urban migrants.

The conditions in which migrants travel, live and work often carry exceptional risks to their physical and mental well-being, and migration can therefore be regarded as a social determinant of health for migrants. This link has been acknowledged by the World Health Assembly (WHA), which adopted Resolution 61.17 on the "Health of Migrants" in 2008,[3] in which Member States *"recogniz[ed] that health outcomes can be influenced by the multiple dimensions of migration"*. These include restrictive immigration, employment, social protection and housing policies, namely the reasons for which migrants often have to travel, live and work in unsafe and unhealthy conditions. Text box 12 lists some specific barriers to quality health care for urban migrants.

Text box 12

Barriers to quality health care for urban migrants

Migrants and their families often lack access to health care because of a lack of regular legal status. Even if migrants have access to health services, they tend to avoid them due to fear of deportation, xenophobic and discriminatory attitudes, and other linguistic, cultural and economic barriers.

Specific impediments to accessing optimal health services in urban areas are as follows:

Language - Communication and language barriers can negatively impact diagnostics, medication, medical follow-up, hospital visits and admission, as well as the adherence of patients to treatment protocols.

Law and administration - Often migrants are formally excluded from national or city-level health systems. Even when relevant laws and regulations are in place, in practice migrants are often denied access to health care. In China, with the *hukou* system of household registration, millions of internal rural-to-urban migrants lack official documentation and are excluded from urban services, including health care (Hu, Cook and Salazar, 2008). In some places such as South Africa and Argentina, migrants in practice are reported to be excluded from services despite an official policy of inclusion (Mberu et al., forthcoming). A widespread lack of health insurance coverage coupled with prohibitively high costs of paid health services constitutes one of the most common barriers preventing poor migrants and displaced persons from accessing medical services (IOM, WHO and OHCHR, 2013).

Knowledge - People's knowledge about healthy behaviours and disease prevention are potentially higher in urban than in rural settings, as urban residents can be more easily reached via mass media and health and disease prevention campaigns. However, striking intra-urban health literacy

---

3   http://apps.who.int/gb/ebwha/pdf_files/A61/A61_R17-en.pdf

disparities remain, with health literacy and immunization coverage being much lower in slum residents, sometimes even lower than in rural areas (Alirol et al., 2010).

Discrimination, victimization, and stigmatization - Negative or even abusive attitudes of health staff towards migrant patients have been reported, for instance in South African cities (IOM, WHO and OHCHR, 2013). In China, migrant patients with tuberculosis said they were dismissed by their employers or generally avoided after having the disease (Wei et al., 2009).

Migrants' susceptibility to particular diseases and illnesses

Infectious diseases: In an increasingly mobile world, resource-poor urban agglomerations become catalysts for the transmission of infectious diseases (Alirol et al., 2010). Rural-to-urban migrants may acquire communicable diseases in their host locations and then transmit them when returning to their areas of origin or, vice versa, they might get infected by their partners upon return.

HIV/AIDS, still the most widely diffused deadly infectious disease, is largely an urban phenomenon. In Latin America and the Caribbean, it is most prevalent in cities, in particular, in commercial hubs and ports (UNAIDS, 2014: 84). Migrants are particularly susceptible to contracting HIV/AIDS, especially in urban settings. In India, HIV prevalence among rural-to-urban migrants is estimated at 0.9 per cent, which is almost four times the national prevalence rate (ibid.). Among the 56,000 slum residents of Nairobi, Kenya, many of whom are migrants, HIV/AIDS and tuberculosis (TB) account for about half of the deaths in people over five years of age (Kyobutungi et al., 2008).

Moreover, migration has been associated with increased risk of tuberculosis infection (WHO and IOM, 2014). In South Africa, for instance, TB rates are higher for international migrants and mobile people than in the non-migrant population; the high TB prevalence among migrants is at least partly associated with migrant workers being exposed to high levels of silica dust in mines (Mberu et al., forthcoming; Mosca, Rijks and Schultz, 2013). In the cities of Shanghai and Beijing in China, new TB cases are recorded to disproportionately occur among rural-to-urban migrant workers, while treatment outcomes are worse for migrant patients compared to the general population (Wei et al., 2009). In many high-income countries of destination, illnesses such as TB and HIV are primarily observed in the immigrant population[4] (ECDC and WHO, 2014).

The recent outbreak of Ebola in West Africa has shown the critical role of high population mobility in the spread of the disease across porous borders (WHO, 2015). To a large extent, poverty drives this mobility as people travel daily looking for work or food. Many extended West African families have relatives living in different countries. Population mobility created two significant impediments to control. First, cross-border contact-tracing is difficult. Populations readily cross

---

4   For instance, in the United States, "[t]he TB incidence rate among foreign-born persons in 2013 was approximately 13 times greater than the incidence rate among US-born persons, and the proportion of TB cases occurring in foreign-born persons continues to increase, reaching 64.6% in 2013". (Alami et al., 2014)

porous borders but outbreak responders do not. Second, as the situation in one country began to improve, it attracted patients from neighbouring countries seeking unoccupied beds for treatment, thus reigniting transmission chains. In other words, as long as one country experienced intense transmission other countries remained at risk, no matter how strong their own response measures were. The traditional custom of returning, often over long distances, to a native village to die and be buried near ancestors is another dimension of population movement that carries an especially high transmission risk. In past outbreaks, Ebola was largely confined to remote rural areas, with just a few scattered cases detected in cities. In West Africa, cities – including the capitals of the three main Ebola affected countries, Liberia, Guinea and Sierra Leone – have been epicentres of intense virus transmission. The Ebola outbreaks in West Africa demonstrated how swiftly the virus could move once it reached urban settings and densely populated slums.

Non-communicable diseases: The four main groups of non-communicable diseases (NCDs) are heart disease, cancer, chronic respiratory ailments (asthma) and diabetes. Migrants are more vulnerable to NCDs than the local population at all levels of society. This is due to their experiencing socioeconomic inequalities and related stress, which increases exposure to NCD risk factors, such as poor diet, lack of exercise, drinking and smoking (Davies, Blake and Dhavan, 2011).

Psychosocial vulnerabilities: Migration can create specific psychosocial vulnerabilities. Forced movements as a result of war, conflict, insecurity or natural disaster usually pose higher threats to the mental and psychosocial health and well-being of migrants. However, even in the case of voluntary, well-planned migration, the separation from families and friends and the risk of exploitation, discrimination, xenophobia or sexual and gender-based violence in countries of transit and destination can heighten the vulnerability of migrants to psychological illnesses.

Improving migrants' health in cities

Migrant inclusive health systems

There are striking inequities between migrants and non-migrants within cities across the world, both with regard their state of health and the accessibility to quality health-care services. There is generally very little effort on the part of local and national governments to improve the health of urban migrants. In many countries and cities they remain excluded from the health system and, even if formal policies of inclusion have been set up, they are often not implemented or respected by health and migration authorities. Outreach systems and referral systems are often weak (Shetty, 2011). There are some good examples from different parts of the urban world where partnerships have been formed between government NGOs, International organizations and private actors to take responsibility for improving the health of migrants (see text box 13).

Text box 13

Examples of effective partnerships in health care

Good Practice Example: Access to health care for undocumented migrants, Seoul, Republic of Korea[5]

The Municipal Government of Seoul, Republic of Korea, introduced medical aid for undocumented and uninsured foreign workers, their foreign spouses as well as undocumented migrant children and refugees in 2012. Formerly, these groups had not been entitled to receive any health benefits. In addition to fully covering surgery costs and hospital charges of up to a threshold of five million won (USD 4,400) and partially for charges above this amount, interpretation and nursing services are provided. These benefits are available at eight designated hospitals. Officials from the municipality assured that the workers will not be in danger of deportation after receiving health benefits. In the capital city of the Republic of Korea, home to almost 10 million people, the number of foreign undocumented workers is estimated at about 280,000. Most of them entered the country legally but then stayed on after their visas expired.

Networks of voluntary doctors providing health services in German cities[6]

In many cities in the Global North, it is voluntary health workers who offer health services for free and anonymously for marginalized populations such as irregular migrants and asylum-seekers, the latter being often only entitled to minimal care in receiving countries. The Malteser Migranten Medizin (MMM) constitutes an example of this. Under the umbrella of Malteser International, the Order of Malta's relief agency for humanitarian aid, MMM offers support in several German cities to all people without health insurance, including undocumented residents. They provide help through medical examinations and counselling, emergency treatment in case of acute illness, referral to specialized physicians if necessary, care during pregnancy and delivery, and referral to services for social and legal counselling. Anonymity is assured to all beneficiaries, who often fear to seek help from an ordinary doctor's practice or hospital. MMM's first office was opened in 2001 in Berlin and, since then, twelve more offices have been opened in cities throughout Germany. Both health professionals and administrative staff work voluntarily, without any remuneration. Medical equipment and medicine are funded by financial and in-kind donations. MMM works in cooperation with a network of voluntary health professionals and also with churches, NGOs and associations. It has supported more than 40,000 patients in the past ten years. Frequent reasons for seeking help at MMM are pregnancy, injuries, acute dental conditions, tumours and communicable diseases.

---

5   *Source*: Medical support set for undocumented migrants. Lee Woo-young, *The Korea Herald*, Seoul, 7 March 2012: www.koreaherald.com/view.php?ud=20120307001296

6   *Source* : Malteser Migranten Medizin, 2014 - http://www.malteser-migranten-medizin.de

Community Health Centre, Nairobi, Kenya[7]

The city of Nairobi in Kenya has made significant progress in providing health care for migrants and refugees. For example, in 2002 the City Council's health department established a community health centre in Eastleigh, a neighbourhood with the highest concentration of migrant residents. The Eastleigh Community Health Centre is supported by effective collaboration between the city government and IOM for the purpose of integrating migrants into the health-care system. It brings health care to the place where the most vulnerable migrant populations reside, thereby eliminating a significant barrier to health-care access, that is, the danger and difficulty of travelling long distances in the city. The free and non-discriminatory clinic also eliminates the problem of refugees foregoing health care due to insufficient means or fear of persecution.

3.4.2. Mass displacement to and in urban areas

Managing and addressing urban population displacement as a result of disasters, conflict or violence creates particular challenges for relevant actors and can result in increased conditions of long-term vulnerability for both the displaced and their host communities.

Of the 72 million displaced persons in the world, about half are thought to live in urban areas, mostly in less developed countries (IFRC, 2012). People affected by crises – both natural and man-made – move to cities that might at least offer basic services, income opportunities and markets that can continue to provide food and shelter. At the same time, as the world becomes more and more urbanized, crises and related displacement tend to more often affect urban areas: as people and assets concentrate in hazard-prone areas, the risk of disaster becomes increasingly urban (IDMC, 2014), and conflicts and violence increasingly affect urban centres and undermine their ability to be "safe havens" (Jacobsen and Howe, 2008).

Managing population displacement in urban areas

Mass displacement creates specific vulnerabilities for the displaced population and poses unique challenges to those who need to respond, including local authorities and host communities. Identifying and registering intense population flows within complex urban communities is difficult. Urban displaced persons are often dispersed in a variety of settings, mostly outside official sites, and frequently circulate, within and outside cities, in the attempt to access basic resources, services and opportunities (Brookings Institution, 2013). In many contexts, urban IDPs face barriers to status recognition, and might refrain from accessing assistance for fear of arrest or deportation (Weiss Fagen, 2014).

As a consequence, traditional models based on dedicated delivery of assistance in homogeneous camp settings might not work as well in urban contexts. In fact, urban displaced persons tend to rely much more on local communities, markets and institutions for their survival and well-being than their rural counterparts (Ferris and Ferro-Ribeiro, 2012). However, markets and institutions might

---

7   Based on: T. Juzwiak, E. McGregor and M. Siegel, *Migrant and Refugee Integration in Global Cities, the Role of Cities and Business* (2014), The Hague Process on Refugees and Migration, The Hague.

not be ready to absorb the sudden, massive inflow of people and the lack of political representation, administrative obstacles and spatial segregation might further reduce the ability of displaced persons to access essential resources and opportunities. As a consequence, urban displaced persons often face food insecurity, malnutrition, personal insecurity, unmitigated psychosocial impacts, poverty and unemployment, and may end up living in informal settlements in areas at risk of disasters or where they are threatened by evictions or relocations (Haysom, 2013; Carrillo, 2009; Albuja and Ceballos, 2010).

Additional demographic pressures can also result in reduced availability of income opportunities, health care and education, and soaring prices for housing, food and essential resources, with long-lasting negative effects on the well-being of households and communities hosting the displaced. It is always the most vulnerable groups (namely, women, youth and unskilled workers) within the incoming and the host communities who are likely to confront the worst consequences (Zetter and Deikun, 2010; UNDP, 2009). Inter-communal tensions and xenophobic stances often arise as living conditions are made worse by the unmanaged inflow of IDPs and refugees into urban areas (MercyCorps, 2012). Such tensions might be further aggravated by the host communities' perceptions that displaced persons are receiving disproportionate assistance (Carrillo, 2009). In addition, stigma might be associated with the condition of displacement, which further worsens the situation of displaced people (Esnard and Sapat, 2014). Text box 14 describes the challenges of finding shelter for displaced persons in the city of Aleppo.

Text box 14

Aleppo, Syrian Arab Republic: Shelter options for internally displaced persons (IDPs)[8]

Before 2011, Aleppo was one of the most attractive destinations for Syrian Arab Republic's rural migrants and the largest city in the country, hosting about one quarter of its urban population. Over half of Aleppo's residents were displaced when turmoil reached the city in late 2012, though estimates report that 48 per cent of those displaced moved to other neighbourhoods in the city, largely following a trend of moving westward to more secure areas (UN-Habitat, 2014a). Many internally displaced persons from other parts of the country also sought shelter in Aleppo as they had relatives and social connections there.

The housing stock has suffered extensive damage and 52 per cent is no longer in use. Damage has been particularly concentrated in informal settlements, which accounted for 45 per cent of the housing stock before the crisis (ibid.). Nonetheless, informal construction in the more secure western neighbourhoods is accommodating a growing number of displaced persons from other parts of Aleppo and neighbouring towns and villages.

The solutions for providing shelter for the waves of displaced populations vary across Syrian cities and in the different parts of each city. Profiles carried out by UN-Habitat in selected Syrian cities in 2014 point to a great

8   Extracted from M. Serageldin, F. Vigier and M. Larsen. Urban Migration Trends in the MENA Region and the Challenge of Conflict Induced Displacement (2014). Background Paper for the *World Migration Report 2015: Migrants and Cities: New partnerships to manage mobility*. IOM, Geneva.

majority of internally displaced persons relying on relatives, friends, and property owners who allow them to settle in vacant units. Hosting is the preferred shelter solution sought by internally displaced persons in the cities of Aleppo, Dara'a, and Homs, for both economic and security reasons. Households that are hosted by relatives generally see this as a temporary solution before finding other accommodation in the future.

As much as 82 per cent of internally displaced persons in Lattakia, a secure city, are renting their dwellings. Rising rents in sought after neighbourhoods in each city have also led to collective renting, whereby multiple households rent one apartment. Collective shelters, however, accommodate no more than 10 per cent of IDPs in any of the cities surveyed (UN-Habitat, 2014b). In Homs, heavily damaged housing and a high rate of out-migration with a fairly limited number of returnees to date has resulted in collective shelters remaining a more common shelter solution for those displaced within the city.

Other shelter solutions adopted by Syrian internally displaced persons in urban areas include the occupation of unfinished or partially damaged buildings, squatting in empty but functional housing units, sheltering in low-income or informal neighbourhoods where the informal economy can provide a basic income. A large majority of the agreements made between those who abandon or rent their housing and the new occupants are unofficial or undocumented, which raises concerns about potential future tenure disputes and lengthy litigation.

Renting or being hosted in a house or apartment constitutes the most common shelter solutions for Syrian migrants and refugees in Lebanon, as well as in urban areas across Jordanian governorates, with cities in the Amman, Irbid and Zarqa governorates facing the greatest housing pressures (UNHCR, 2014a). Informal settlements in Lebanon currently accommodate an estimated 193,000 refugees (UNHRC, 2014b). While 20 per cent of refugees in Jordan live in the camps of Za'atari, Mrajeeb al-Fhood, Cyber City and Al-Azraq, the remainder live predominantly in the poorer urban areas in the northern part of the country.

Sustainable ways of addressing urban displacement

Ending displacement in urban contexts poses particular challenges. Most of those displaced in cities and towns look at integrating into their host communities, rather than returning to their places of origin, in the belief that they can find better opportunities in areas of destination - a feeling that only becomes stronger as displacement protracts (Majidi, 2011; Carrillo, 2009).

In addition, urban integration happens in dense contexts characterized by a wide diversity of situations of vulnerability, making it difficult to address the specific needs of incoming displaced persons without confronting marginalization and risk patterns for host communities. Such interventions, therefore, should look at needs rather than status. If they fail to address prevalent conditions of urban vulnerability, they are unlikely to produce the intended positive, long-term effects on target populations, but only modify or reinforce existing patterns of exclusion (Zetter and Deikun, 2010; Sherwood et al., 2014). However, if successful, such efforts can effectively support the well-being of urban communities in their entirety. Text box 15 gives an example of inclusion in Gaziantep, Turkey.

Access to formal options for livelihood opportunities and decent housing, for instance, are key to the long-term well-being of displaced persons but are also key challenges for urban development in normal times (Esnard and Sapat, 2014). The additional numbers of people needing support, in particular after disruptive events affecting urban areas, only makes their provision more difficult, which can further lead to situations of vulnerability. These longer-term interventions are further complicated by the fact that resources available for addressing displacement are limited and often only available in the immediacy of a crisis (Carrillo, 2009).

Text box 15

Gaziantep, Turkey: A story of inclusion

Social Support Program for Syrian Women and Children Refugees

Gaziantep is an industrial city of 1.3 million inhabitants in the southeast of Turkey. Strong kin and commercial ties exist between the local population and Syrian communities just across the border. According to the Government's Disaster and Emergency Management Presidency, the city is currently hosting 225,000 displaced Syrians, of whom only 33,000 live in camps. The rest have found accommodation and assistance through local networks and family or community members who had previously migrated to the city.

With the support of the local communities, whose acceptance of the displaced Syrians remains high, the city has adopted a comprehensive programme for those displaced by the conflict, to provide adequate assistance and integration support, without undermining the well-being of host communities. The programme provides for the immediate and longer-term needs of displaced persons, through the distribution of food and essential household items, the protection of specifically vulnerable groups and improved longer-term access to services and opportunities.

The local health system has assisted over 50,000 Syrians through free consultations and medicines, addressing health concerns linked with the living conditions of many of the displaced. Specific assistance has targeted children, who have benefited from targeted psychosocial support and vaccination campaigns, and women. Further efforts will be needed to raise awareness among the displaced of their right to assistance, as well as to improve accessibility of health care for those living in marginalized settlements.

Over the last two years, the municipality has opened two schools in order to address the education needs of the almost 10,000 minors who have arrived in the city. The curricula include targeted Turkish language courses and remedial classes to bring Syrian children up to speed within the Turkish education system. The municipality supports all costs associated with education.

The city has implemented a programme to assist Syrians living outside camps and support their access to the formal labour market. The Gaziantep Chamber of Commerce recommended that Syrians be given formal short-term work permits and access to vocational training and social security benefits. The plan was based on an assessment of the skills profile of Syrian workers and included quotas for local businesses to employ displaced Syrians. It also included the establishment of industrial zones close to the border, in which public-private ventures could employ Syrians to produce goods that could then be sold to the Syrian Arab Republic. The programme has been operational since October 2014, and has multiplied the opportunities for Syrian newcomers to access formal employment. These efforts have also resulted in an overall drop of the unemployment rate at the city level, despite the massive inflow of displaced persons.

A new approach to migration in Turkey

The practices of inclusion implemented by the city of Gaziantep are supported by a strong legal and policy framework at the national level. The Government established a Temporary Protection regime for Syrians seeking assistance in camps and non-camp settings, including urban areas, regardless of the duration of stay.

This is part of a new strategic approach built around the idea that well-managed migration can deliver benefits to all. With this aim, in 2013, Turkey adopted the Law on Foreigners and International Protection. The law explicitly recognizes the importance of integrating all types of migrants into Turkish society, and establishes a strong institutional framework for their inclusion into local contexts of destination. This has resulted in significant improvements in the legal and socioeconomic status of people moving in response to humanitarian crises, and has allowed Gaziantep, a city for which human mobility will be a key development issue in the decades to come, to invest in forward-thinking solutions that promote good, adaptive governance of urban migration.

Based on:

"Social Support Program for Syrian Women and Children Refugees" by Fatma Şahin, Mayor, Gaziantep Metropolitan Municipality, Turkey, and

"The New Approach to Migration in Turkey" by Atilla Toros, Director General, General Directorate of Migration Management, Ministry of the Interior, Turkey.

Coordination among different actors

Given the complexity of these interventions, the coordinated efforts of a variety of actors, well beyond those responsible for emergency responses, are needed. In urban contexts, a number of different actors, ranging from the international to the local level, are likely to be involved in efforts to assist and support displaced populations – each bringing capacities and resources, but also different priorities, and operational and political stances (Brookings Institution, 2013).

In particular, while the legal responsibility for assisting IDPs lies with national governments, it is local authorities that are usually in charge of implementing concrete measures that determine what resources and opportunities will be available to the displaced persons and their host communities. However, they are often too under-resourced to adequately respond to massive population movements. Lack of local leadership, clear mandates and responsibilities to manage and address displacement flows can be major obstacles to working in situations of urban displacement (Weiss Fagen, 2014).

In addition, cities host a variety of non-governmental, civil society and private sector actors, which play a role, often subsidiary or complementary to that of local administrations, in promoting access to essential services and opportunities and reducing people's vulnerability before, during and after disasters. Involvement of the whole range of local actors is necessary to better inform interventions to the specifics of the local context, and to make them better accepted by the local population and more sustainable (Zetter and Deikun, 2010).

Lastly, involvement of displaced persons themselves, as well as host communities, is essential to designing and implementing well-informed interventions that address the needs of the most vulnerable. In most cities, IDPs' confidence and participation in local decision-making is low, and informal, collective governance systems prevalent (Haysom, 2013). Coordination with the whole range of governmental and non-governmental actors relevant for planning, service provision, governance and resilience-building at the municipal and sub-municipal level requires efforts that emergency managers and humanitarian actors are not necessarily able to provide. Responding and addressing urban displacement, therefore, should be a priority for urban development efforts at large.

3.4.3. Natural hazards and disasters

Migrants often find themselves occupying marginal, unserviced land exposed to natural hazards such as landslides and floods. They also often inhabit unsafe buildings and lack access to the information and resources needed to prevent or cope with disasters when they occur. For these reasons, migrants may end up disproportionately suffering in disasters. Ensuring migrants are included in risk management plans which outline what needs to be done before, during and after disasters is critical.

Exposure to hazards

In both high- and low-income countries, disasters which hit cities with complex demography may disproportionally affect marginalized migrant communities. Newcomers to cities often have little choice but to settle in the most dangerous locations within urban "hazardscapes" (that is the existing and potential sources of hazards) (Bolin, 2006). They end up occupying marginal, unserviced land not claimed by formal activities and inadequately developed from the infrastructural point of view, often located on steep, unstable hill slopes or flood-prone riverbanks. In addition, increasing population pressures can induce land-use changes that result into localized natural hazards such as urban landslides and floods. Newcomers and migrant communities are often highly exposed to such hazards, and may end up suffering disproportionately in disasters (de Sherbinin et al., 2012; Seibert, 2014).

This can be seen in Rio de Janeiro's favelas with the inflow of rural–urban migrants from the Brazilian North-East. The Rocinha favela, in particular, has grown into an unplanned settlement hosting several hundred thousand inhabitants, about 80 per cent of whom are originally from Ceará and Paraíba States. Unsustainable land-use, soil degradation and increased overflow create the conditions for hydro-geological instability and recurrent, disastrous landslides and flash floods (Perlman, 2002). In an example from the Democratic Republic of the Congo, economic migration and inflow of displaced persons and refugees to the city of Goma, which has areas exposed to volcanic hazards, led to 147 deaths and widespread disruption following the Nyiragongo eruption of 2002 (Wisner, 2002a).

In addition, migrants often live in unsafe buildings, which might be particularly vulnerable to the impacts of natural hazards. When the 1995 earthquake struck Kobe, Japan, a disproportionate number of the local Korean minority were living and working in wooden buildings with heavy roof tiles that collapsed during the earthquake or burned down in the subsequent fires; this had very damaging repercussions on migrant lives, their health and economic prospects in the aftermath of the disaster (Wisner et al., 2004).

Migration status can be also linked to increased barriers to accessing and using resources, including information, to avoid, reduce or recover from the impacts of disasters (see text box 16 on Hurricane Sandy). In the recent 2011 floods that affected Bangkok and almost one fifth of the territory of Thailand, an estimated 600,000 Burmese migrant workers were trapped in affected areas, with very limited options for moving out to safer places due to restrictions on movement and very limited livelihood options in the reconstruction phase (Koser, 2014). During the 2011 Tohoku triple disaster in Japan, non-Japanese, and in particular refugees and asylum-seekers, faced additional challenges in accessing emergency information, and evacuation and recovery assistance (Koike, 2011; Crimella and Dagnan, 2012).

Disaster risk is increasingly urbanizing and cities are becoming progressively diverse as a consequence of internal and international population movements. The inclusion of urban migrants, displaced persons and refugees in disaster risk reduction is therefore a priority, to reduce the overall impacts of hazards on communities and societies. As other sections of this report deal with the structural factors of urban life that determine disaster vulnerability, the following section only focuses on barriers to the inclusion of migrants in disaster preparedness, emergency management, and reconstruction and recovery.

Before disasters

Accessing warning and information in time of disaster is critical in determining people's levels of disaster preparedness. Language barriers can hinder the capacity of migrants to access timely, high quality and complete information (Shepherd and van Vuuren, 2014; Benavides, 2013). Migrant preference for specific media – social networks or face-to-face contacts (as opposed to public media and broadcasting) or particular TV and radio channels or programmes – as well as lack of trust in governmental bodies, can influence the capacity of public authorities to reach out to them (Wang, Amati and Thomalla, 2011; Perry and Mushkatel, 2008; Phillips, 1993; Arlikatti, Taibah and Andrew, 2014). Remoteness and isolation of spatially segregated neighbourhoods might also hinder provision of information (as well as emergency assistance) before and during emergencies (Sabates-Wheeler and Macauslan, 2007).

Due to lack of knowledge and a differential understanding of local contexts, migrants tend to have different awareness and perception of environmental risks (Adeola, 2009; Lindell and Perry, 2004). They might not interpret the information they receive in the same way as native populations or exhibit different reactions and behaviours to the information they receive.

During disasters

Migration status can influence the effectiveness of evacuation and disaster risk management measures. Migrants' freedom of movement can be restricted by administrative regulations, which limit their capacity to move out to safer places in disaster situations (Koser, 2014). In particular, in the case of informally settled migrants, the need to stay behind to guard otherwise unprotected houses and belongings can also reduce their willingness to evacuate (see text box 10).

Migrants, particularly undocumented ones, might restrain from seeking help in disasters due to the lack of trust in aid workers and immigration officers and for fear of deportation (Enarson and Morrow, 2000). Inadequacy of assistance systems can result in migrants receiving unfair assistance, or refusing support when it is provided (Jones-DeWeever and Hartmann, 2006). In cases in which documentation is a prerequisite for receiving emergency and recovery assistance, undocumented migrants and migrants who have lost their documents in the disaster might face specific challenges in accessing aid (Donner and Rodríguez, 2008).

After disasters

Linguistic barriers, migration status and reduced knowledge of local administrative procedures can also hinder the capacity of migrants, displaced persons and refugees to receiving recovery assistance (Bolin, 2006). Due to their higher likelihood of being employed in the informal sector, in risky areas and with limited access to social safety networks, migrants are often disproportionately affected by business interruption or closure in the aftermath of disasters (Koser, 2014).

Migrant housing may be more prone to damage or destruction in disasters due to higher hazard exposure and structural fragility. In addition, migrants are more likely to be overlooked in reconstruction and recovery assistance efforts. Limited access to social networks can also reduce the options available to non-natives for informal accommodation with relatives and friends after disasters. As a consequence, they may be more likely to experience situations of protracted displacement (Phillips, 1993). In the aftermath of, and often as a result of, disasters, xenophobic stances and migrant scapegoating can also affect the personal security of migrants as well as their capacity to recover.

Text box 16

Latino migrants in New York before and after Hurricane Sandy[9]

Twenty per cent of the total population of Staten Island and Long Island, among the New York areas most heavily affected by Hurricane Sandy in 2012, was foreign-born at the time of the disaster. Migrants accounted for well over 50 per cent of the residents of specific neighbourhoods. The impact of the storm on their well-being was significant. Forty per cent of the migrants living in affected areas reported economic loss, one in three suffered from damage to home or property. In Staten Island, 60 per cent of the migrants reported damage and 40 per cent were displaced. However, only 22 per cent of those affected applied for relief, due to a lack of understanding of the system in the United States, and only 25 per cent of those who applied actually received assistance.

Language barriers, administrative requirements and lack of organization hindered migrant access to support by the Federal Emergency Management Agency and local charities. Many migrants avoided applying fearing the possibility of xenophobic incidents. "Non-qualified aliens", including some groups of documented migrants (such as those with a "Temporary Protected Status" in light of the situation of their country of origin), could not access cash assistance or unemployment benefits. Other migrants were eligible for benefits because their children were citizens of the United States, but did not apply for fear of arrest and deportation, despite statements from national and local authorities that no immigration enforcement initiatives would be conducted. This, in turn, resulted in a number of unassisted children.

Migrant communities were disproportionately affected by loss of income and livelihoods related to the physical destruction of homes and displacement: many migrants employed as domestic workers, for instance, no longer had a workplace. Reduced access to safety nets for migrant workers resulted in widespread unemployment (11% of the migrant community) and economic hardship. Thirty per cent of migrants reported falling back on the payment of rents, and there were reports of migrant tenants being abused by landlords (through retaining security deposits or being forced to repair their home in spite of contractual obligations). For the 53 per cent of migrants in the low-income groups, the 50 per cent increase in rents in disaster-affected areas had devastating consequences on the availability of affordable accommodation, and resulted in migrants being more likely to live in unsafe conditions and overcrowded dwellings in the aftermath of Sandy. This led to further suffering as a wave of cold weather followed the storm. One year after the storm, the media reported that many migrant residents were still waiting for aid, and that

9   *Sources:*
US Census 2010 – www.census.gov/2010census/
www.latintimes.com/latino-victims-sandy-neglected-hispanic-group-launches-official-complaint-132405
www.immigrantings.com/2013/02/immigrants-struggle-after-hurricane-sandy.html
www.buzzfeed.com/davidnoriega/the-undocumented-immigrants-who-rebuilt-new-york-after-sandy#.dwKz1weW0
Make the Road New York: 2013 Victories - www.maketheroad.org/report.php?ID=3276

non-English speakers were still receiving insufficient information on the recovery process. This sparked collective action and complaints with the State and the Government.

On the other hand, the continuity of migrant business and activities, accounting for 22.4 per cent of New York State's gross domestic product, was essential to the economic and social recovery of the whole region. Thousands of migrant workers were recruited by businesses and individuals to support early recovery activities, including rubble removal and infrastructure rehabilitation. Up to 75 per cent of these informal, day labourers were undocumented, and many ended up facing further hazards linked to unsafe working conditions and exploitation by employers in order to access the opportunities linked with reconstruction.

3.5

PARTNERSHIPS FOR BUILDING RESILIENCE

Wider coordination is needed in urban contexts beyond the usual actors to build resilience in migrant communities. Partnerships need to involve governments, NGOs, civil society, the private sector and migrants themselves. Migrant associations particularly have a key role to play in providing basic resources and support, in improving access to essential services and opportunities, in giving voice to migrant concerns through political representation and in preparing for and responding to disasters. The participation of migrants in institutional planning and disaster risk management needs to be fostered. Indeed, migrants can play a useful and practical role in risk reduction for urban communities as a whole.

3.5.1. Migrant-led resilience building in cities of destination

As migrants converge on cities, groups sharing a common origin, ethnicity or culture, can leverage common resources in order to tackle barriers experienced in cities of destination in a collective fashion. In particular where local institutions and markets do not provide sufficient formal resources and opportunities, this type of social capital can be essential for migrant survival and well-being. However, reliance on networks based on origin or ethnicity can result in spatial segregation by leading to the creation of socially homogeneous, isolated neighbourhoods (UN-Habitat, 2003; European Foundation for the Improvement of Living and Working Conditions, 2007). Collective action by migrants nonetheless often contributes to the resilience of home and host communities. Migrant groups and associations, for instance, can support development and risk reduction projects in areas of origin (such as food and water security, basic services, infrastructural interventions) through financial resources, technical expertise or political engagement (Orozco, 2008; Sall, 2005). They can also be actors of resilience in areas of destination, allowing for the mobilization of a variety of resources and capacities in normal times as well as before, during and after crises.

Basic services and opportunities

Associations of internal and international migrants, displaced persons and refugees are essential in providing basic services and opportunities, such as housing, employment, legal assistance and access to information, to both newcomers and more established urban dwellers. For example, migrant associations in Accra provide local networks through which Nigerian immigrants are supported in finding and paying for housing and accommodation, accessing the local labour market and financing family expenses and health care (Bosiakoh, 2011). Savings groups of Peruvian migrants in Buenos Aires assist fellow labour migrants with housing and household expenditure (Hardoy and Pandiella, 2009). In New York, an organization called Alianza Dominicana provides English classes, citizenship education and health-related services to Dominican migrants (Sommerville, Durana and Terrazas, 2008).

Civic engagement and participation

Associations provide social and emotional support and facilitate the perpetuation of culture and customs of places of origin (Owusu, 2000; Lyons and Snoxall, 2005). They are also key to promoting the civic engagement and political participation of migrants and their communities, improving their visibility and capacity to advocate for migrants with local authorities. Migrant groups can be engaged directly by local authorities in efforts aimed at developing and implementing more inclusive policies and planning, such as through a participated reform of the local education system or civil rights debates (Sommerville, Durana and Terrazas, 2008). Associations have also been critical in advocating for the implementation of risk reduction measures in the recovery phase after urban disasters, resulting in effective community-based disaster risk management systems and better preparedness for subsequent events (Hardoy, Pandiella and Velásquez Barrero, 2011).

Support before, during and after disasters

Migrant-led initiatives also play a key role in allowing migrants to better prevent, prepare for, respond to and recover from disasters. Prevention and preparedness information, including early warnings, are often efficiently transferred within minority groups, including migrants (Perry and Mushkatel, 2008). Key individuals within these groups might be in charge of gathering and adapting official warnings and information, and further disseminating them to their communities (as was the case, for instance, during the 2011 floods in Brisbane) (Shepherd and van Vuuren, 2014). Such groups can also help migrants and displaced persons access post-disaster information, psychosocial support and targeted advocacy. Following Hurricane Katrina, the New Orleans Vietnamese community's tight social bonds were essential in helping survivors find shelter, medical aid, administrative assistance and information (including through their own community-based radio stations), overcoming the lack of official preparedness and emergency communications available in Vietnamese (Li et al., 2008; Vu et al., 2009). Similarly, the Afghan refugee community drew on self-help mechanisms to recover efficiently from the 2011 earthquake in Canterbury, New Zealand (Marlowe, 2013).

3.5.2. Building the resilience of migrants through inclusion

Many of the decisions that influence the vulnerability of migrants, displaced persons and refugees are taken at the local level by institutional, non-governmental and private sector actors. Targeted local efforts toward the inclusion of incoming people are essential to reducing the risks migrants face, in particular as cities assume an increasing role in international policy on development and the environment.

WORLD MIGRATION
REPORT 2015
Migrants and Cities:
New Partnerships
to Manage Mobility

101

In most systems, local authorities are responsible for a number of activities that are key to the everyday life of urban dwellers, including land use planning, development of building codes and infrastructure, transportation and provision of social services. Planning processes can effectively promote migrant participation in public affairs, better addressing their needs through improved access to services and opportunities and leveraging their skills and capacities for the well-being of the whole community. For instance, the city of Portland in the United States has structures in place for inclusive neighbourhood-level development planning while many cities, including Amsterdam in the Netherlands, promote spatial diversification as a way of achieving social and economic inclusion (Eurofund, 2007).

Efforts by local authorities, often complemented by private sector and civil society actors, can effectively reduce many of the obstacles faced by newcomers, facilitating their access to economic initiative and income opportunities, health care and education, and promote harmonious communities (Juzwiak, McGregor and Siegel, 2014). A number of cases even exist of local authorities that have looked at fostering participation of migrants in host communities by involving them in development programmes which targeted their communities of origin (Sall, 2005; Østergaard-Nielsen, 2011).

Text box 17

Los Pinos: Evolution of an informal settlement in the metropolitan area of Buenos Aires, Argentina[10]

Los Pinos is an informal settlement surrounded by gated communities in Escobar, in the metropolitan area of Buenos Aires. It is a low-income area that has grown through informal land occupation, progressively attracting international immigrants (mostly from Peru, the Plurinational State of Bolivia and Paraguay), who today represent 68 per cent of the local population. It has long been overlooked in local planning, and is not connected to local water and sewage networks nor served by public transport. It has no health and education facilities. In addition, the area is prone to recurrent floods.

In recent years, and in collaboration with the NGO known as TECHO, the community has undergone a bottom-up process to promote upgrading and regularization of the settlement. The "compass", a participatory methodology to collect and compare data on access to land, housing, infrastructure, social services as well as food, livelihood and environmental security, was used to guide the decision-making process. The methodology allowed the facilitation of a discussion within the community and with municipal authorities to establish priority actions to improve access to basic services and opportunities for the people in Los Pinos. The identified priorities included: 1) a neighbourhood-level urban plan to prevent encroachment on open spaces critical for sunlight, ventilation, and recreation; 2) infrastructural improvements (street lighting, roads and a drainage system) to enhance accessibility and personal security,

---

10 Based on F. Murillo, Migration and urbanization paths: Emerging challenges of reshaping the human geography of Latin America (2014). Background Paper for the *World Migration Report 2015: Migrants and Cities: New Partnerships to Manage Mobility*, International Organization for Migration, Geneva.

and prevent flooding; 3) better access to affordable sanitation systems and potable water; and 4) improved waste management, by designating a site for dumping waste and negotiating the weekly removal of rubbish with the public waste collection company.

Various forms of self-organization that are typical to the migrants' places of origin in the Andes region were instrumental to improving local standards of living. The neighbourhood association organized fundraising events to pay for streetlights and drainage. Community members contributed labour to infrastructure projects through solidarity mechanisms (so-called *minga*), which are routinely used for private work such as housing construction, especially in favour of those most in need. Rotating savings and credit associations financed local micro-businesses, while mothers organized to establish collective childcare.

The experience in Los Pinos is now being replicated in all of Escobar's slums. It should be noted, however, that the progressive formalization of service provision can potentially reduce their affordability, and result in reduced access for the poorest members of the community. In addition, the successful experience of Los Pinos has led to some discontent in other communities, as people perceive that the assistance received by migrants is unfair to them. In order to reduce the potential for inter-communal conflicts, settlers of formal and informal neighbourhoods are now taking part in "Participlan", a gathering in which municipality-wide strategies to address the issue of informality are being discussed. The success of these community-led efforts is based on strong social ties and trust among members, which are identified and leveraged throughout the bottom up decision-making process.

Migrant involvement in disaster risk management systems

Local-level efforts by multiple actors, in particular, can help address the specific factors of vulnerability faced by migrants in times of disasters. Japanese prefectures and municipalities, for instance, provide multilingual hazard awareness and risk information documentation and training,[11] while the Japanese government agency, the Council of Local Authorities for International Relations, has developed a toolkit for multilingual emergency communications.[12] Such efforts, often complemented by those of non-governmental organizations and academic institutions, have also been essential to providing warnings and information to linguistic minorities before, during and after the 2011 Tohoku triple disaster (Carrol, 2012; Miyao et al., 2007).

Local media can also be key to the circulation of information in disasters. New Orleans' Spanish-language radio station in the US disseminated evacuation alerts and key relief and recovery information in Spanish, despite the lack of translated official communications. In the 2007 fires in San Diego, it was Spanish-speaking TV channels that disseminated evacuation and relief information, including through

---

11 http://mief.or.jp/en/bousai.html
www.hyogo-ip.or.jp (in Japanese only).
12 http://sic-info.org/en/

WORLD MIGRATION
REPORT 2015
Migrants and Cities:
New Partnerships
to Manage Mobility

103

their own live coverage of the event (Benavides, 2013). In Nairobi, the UNHCR has partnered with local radio stations and telecommunication companies to disseminate early warnings and emergency messages to spatially segregated refugee groups (Sturge, 2014).

Involvement of culturally and linguistically diverse communities is a priority for many local authorities governing increasingly diverse communities. City-level risk management institutions in Australia, for instance, have worked with representatives of local migrant communities to set up preparedness, warnings, evacuation and displacement management that are informed by local cultural and linguistic diversity.[13] Better inclusion is also pursued through the set-up of specific liaison structures and through direct involvement of representatives of foreign groups, specifically newcomers and young migrants and refugees, as volunteers or staff members within risk management structures.[14]

Migrants as actors of risk reduction

Such efforts often also recognize the potential for migrants and their networks to contribute to managing risks for the community at large. Migrants are often overrepresented in healthy, productive age groups and provide a set of diversified skills that can support disaster preparedness, response and recovery efforts, particularly in ageing societies. In addition, they might be able to more easily access spatially and socially neighbourhoods and communities.

After the Northridge earthquake in the United States, Hispanic immigrant groups (also including undocumented individuals) collaborated with local NGOs in delivering assistance to affected areas that were not adequately covered by official responders. This led to the creation of the Pico Union Cluster, a community-based, independent preparedness structure, which eventually joined Los Angeles' official NGO disaster preparedness and response coordination body (Wisner, 2002b). Involvement of migrants in emergency assistance, search and rescue, rubble removal and early recovery and reconstruction efforts was also observed in the aftermath of Hurricane Sandy in New York in 2012 by Asian migrant groups,[15] after the 2014 floods in Liguria, Italy,[16] and after the Tohoku disaster in Japan in 2011, when Pakistani, Filipino and Chinese groups managed emergency shelters and food distribution facilities (Duncan, 2013).

The inflow of people to cities after urban disasters, in fact, is often essential to provide the resources needed for recovery (Hugo, 2008), something that was observed in New Orleans after the 2005 Hurricane Katrina in the United States, when newly migrated Latino workers were instrumental for running building, demolition, hauling and sanitation efforts (Vinck et al., 2009; Elliott and Pais, 2006). Migrants' trans-local resources based on the fact that they interact with different locations can also benefit host cities as a whole: following the 2012 earthquake in the Emilia-Romagna region of northern Italy, affected towns received funding and in-kind resources from the migrants' societies and communities of origin in order to help cope with and recovery from the disaster.[17]

---

13 www.maribyrnong.vic.gov.au/Page/Page.aspx?Page_Id=2814
14 www.em.gov.au/Documents/Project%20Red%20-%20Consultation%20Report%20-%20FINAL%20-%20June%202011%20-%20PDF.PDF
15 www.democracynow.org/2012/11/2/residents_of_nycs_chinatown_turn_to
16 www.famigliacristiana.it/articolo/anche-tanti-immigrati-tra-gli-angeli-del-fango.aspx (in Italian only).
17 www.ilmessaggero.it/PRIMOPIANO/CRONACA/terremoto_emilia_la_carica_dei_volontari_tra_loro_tantissimi_stranieri/notizie/197648.shtml (in Italian only).

3.6

CONCLUDING
REMARKS

Cities can drastically expand the migrants' access to essential resources, services and opportunities. For most migrants, moving to a city is a sound well-being and resilience decision. However, migration, in particular when inadequately managed, can actually result into conditions of exclusion and vulnerability for those moving, as well as for their host communities. Migrants often face specific barriers and obstacles that result in specific patterns of marginalization. As a consequence, they often end up over-represented among the weakest, most vulnerable social groups within urban communities – those that are worst affected by natural and man-made hazards.

At the same time, examples from around the world show that good planning and local coordination can help reduce these risks. Inclusive policies are key to making migrants more resilient, and more resilient migrants help reduce risk for both communities of origin and of destination. The exchanges of material and immaterial resources that migration fosters help to build socially and culturally vibrant, economically dynamic and more resourceful human settlements. Proactive and inclusive urban planning at the local level and effective national mobility management policies are therefore essential not only to prevent the potential vulnerabilities linked with movement into cities, but also to leverage the potential of building the resilience and increasing the well-being of migrants.

WORLD MIGRATION
REPORT 2015
Migrants and Cities:
New Partnerships
to Manage Mobility

105

Migrant voices

Rebuilding through hope: A Chadian in Lagos

When Didier moved from N'Djamena, the capital city of Chad where he grew up, to Lagos, he found the city astonishing, "You cannot compare Lagos to N'Djamena, it is very different, and there are so many people in Lagos." Lagos, the vibrant commercial capital of Nigeria, has an estimated 17 million inhabitants compared to around 1.5 million in N'Djamena. The city is the melting pot of the country and one of the fastest growing urban areas in the world. Didier has called Lagos home for three years and describes it thus: "Lagos is a city that welcomes anyone. If you are hard-working, you will always find something to do, you will survive."

His journey from N'Djamena to Lagos was difficult. Having fled Chad by boat to Cameroon, concerns for his safety there forced him to flee again to Nigeria. Through the aid of the Government and some local friends, Didier settled in Borno, north-eastern Nigeria, where he ran a small grocery store for over a year. However, new concerns about his security meant another forced relocation to Abuja, and then to Lagos.

Didier sells second-hand shoes while completing a diploma in mechanical engineering and computer networking. He has had to overcome numerous challenges in his integration process in Lagos. "I initially wanted to find a job," he says, "Everywhere I applied the first question they always asked was where I am from and if I can speak the local language, which I don't. These counted against me." He did not let this discourage him though. "Although I could not find a job, I realized that Lagos was a place that, if you had something to sell, you would at least have small money to eat daily. That is why I started selling shoes." The high cost of accommodation remains an ongoing challenge. After initially squatting for several months, Didier finally got an affordable place through a friend. The room does not have electricity or running water. Intermittent harassment by security officers also presents a daily struggle.

Despite these challenges, Didier is slowly becoming a full-fledged Lagosian. "It was very difficult at first," he reveals, "Everything in Lagos is very fast. Now I can even go toe-to-toe with anyone in Pidgin English," he adds proudly showing off his newly acquired language skills. Didier maintains links to home through numerous telephone calls and talks with his mother and other members of his family still in Chad. He is also a chair of the Chadian association in Lagos. Didier currently does not earn enough money to send any remittances home but remains optimistic about the future. "I am not satisfied with my current situation," he explained, "I would like to not only make more money but also contribute to development in Nigeria and in Chad. I believe I have the knowledge to do much more than I am doing now."

REFERENCES

Adams, V., T. van Hattum and D. English
2009   Chronic disaster syndrome: displacement, disaster capitalism, and
            the eviction of the poor from New Orleans. *American Ethnologist*,
            36(4): 615–636.

Adeola, F.
2009   Katrina Cataclysm: Does Duration of Residency and Prior Experience
            Affect Impacts, Evacuation and Adaptation Behaviour Amongst
            Survivors? *Environment and Behavior*, 41(4): 459–489.

Alami, N.N. et al.
2014   Morbidity and Mortality Weekly Report, *Trends in Tuberculosis –
            United States 2013*. Centres for Disease Control and Prevention (CDC),
            Atlanta. Available from www.cdc.gov/mmwr/pdf/wk/mm6311.pdf

Albuja, S. and M. Ceballos
2010   Urban displacement and migration in Colombia. *Forced Migration
            Review*, 34:10–11. Available from www.fmreview.org/en/urban-
            displacement/FMR34.pdf

Alirol, E. et al.
2010   Urbanisation and infectious diseases in a globalised world. *The
            Lancet, Infectious Diseases*, 11(2): 131–41.

Arlikatti, S., H.A. Taibah and S.A. Andrew
2014   How do you warn them if they speak only Spanish? Challenges for
            organizations in communicating risk to Colonias residents in Texas,
            USA. *Disaster Prevention and Management*, 23(5): 533–550.

Benavides, A.D.
2013   Four major disaster occurrences and the Spanish language media: a
            lack of risk communication. *Disaster Prevention and Management*,
            22(1):29–37.

Bolin, B.
2006   Race, class and disaster vulnerability. *Handbook of Disaster Research*
            (I. Rodriguez, H. Quarantelly and R. Dynes, eds.). Springer, New York,
            pp. 113–130.

Bosiakoh, T.A.
2011   The Role of Migrant Associations in Adjustment, Integration and
            Social Development : The Case of Nigerian Migrant Associations in
            Accra, Ghana. *Ghana Journal of Development Studies*, 8(2): 64–73.

Brookings Institution
2013   *Under the Radar: Internally Displaced Persons in Non-Camp Settings*.
            Brookings Institution, Washington. Available from www.brookings.
            edu/~/media/research/files/reports/2013/10/noncamp-displaced-
            persons/under-the-radaridps-outside-of-camps-oct-2013.pdf

WORLD MIGRATION
REPORT 2015
Migrants and Cities:
New Partnerships
to Manage Mobility

107

Cannon, T.
2008   Vulnerability, "innocent" disasters and the imperative of cultural understanding. *Disaster Prevention and Management*, 17 (3) 350–357.

Carrillo, A.C.
2009   Internal displacement in Colombia: humanitarian, economic and social consequences in urban settings and current challenges. *International Review of the Red Cross*, 91(875): 527–546.

Carrol, T.
2012   *Multilingual or Easy Japanese? Promoting Citizenship via Local Government Websites*. Language and Citizenship in Japan (N. Gottlieb ed.). Routledge, New York.

Crimella, C. and C.S. Dagnan
2012   The 11 March triple disaster in Japan. In: *State of environmental migration 2011* (F. Gemenne, P. Bruecker and D. Ionesco, eds.). Institute for Sustainable Development and International Relations and the International Organization for Migration, Paris and Geneva, pp. 35-46. Available from www.iddri.org/Publications/Collections/Analyses/SEM%202011_web.pdf

Davies, A.A., C. Blake and P. Dhavan.
2011   Social determinants and risk factors for non-communicable diseases in South Asian migrant population in Europe. *Asia Europe Journal*, 8(4): 461–473.

De Haas, H.
2007   Turning the Tide? Why Development Will Not Stop Migration. *Development and Change,* 38(5): 819–841.

de Sherbinin, A. et al.
2012   Migration and risk: net migration in marginal ecosystems and hazardous areas. *Environmental Research Letters*, 7(4): 1–13.

Donner, W. and H. Rodríguez
2008   Population Composition, Migration, and Inequality: The Influence of Demographic Changes on Disaster Risk and Vulnerability. *Social Forces*, 87(2): 1089–1114.

Duncan, H.
2013   Immigrant integration as a factor in disaster preparedness: The case of the 2011 Tōhoku earthquake in Japan. In: *Migration Policy Practice*, 3(2). International Organization for Migration, Geneva. Available from http://publications.iom.int/bookstore/index.php?main_page=product_info&cPath=50&products_id=952

Duong, L.B., T.G. Linh and N.T.P. Thao
2011   *Social protection for rural-urban migrants in Vietnam: Current situation, challenges and opportunities*. CSP Research Report 08. Centre for Social Protection, Institute of Development Studies, Brighton. Available from www.ids.ac.uk/files/dmfile/Research Report08REVISE.pdf

Elliott, J.R. and J. Pais

2006   Race, class, and Hurricane Katrina: Social differences in human responses to disaster. *Social Science Research*, 35 (2), 295–321. Available from http://ac.els-cdn.com/S0049089X06000135/1-s2.0-S0049089X06000135-main.pdf?_tid=51ab4ca0-fb25-11e4-99ec-00000aab0f26&acdnat=1431710023_bb2e10851b367e213f95c716ff2d522e

Enarson, E. and B.H. Morrow

2000   A Gendered Perspective: The Voices of Women. In: *Hurricane Andrew: Ethnicity, Gender, and the Sociology of Disasters* (W.G. Peacock, B.H. Morrow and H. Gladwin, eds.). International Hurricane Center, Laboratory for Social and Behavioral Research, Miami, pp. 116–137.

Esnard, A.M. and A. Sapat

2014   *Displaced by disaster: Recovery and resilience in a globalizing world.* Routledge, New York.

Eswaran, H. et al.

2011   The Anthroscape Approach in Sustainable Land Use. In: *Sustainable Land Management: Learning from the Past for the Future* (S. Kapur, H. Eswaran and W.E.H. Blum, eds.). Springer, Berlin, p.1–50.

European Centre for Disease Prevention and Control (EDC) and World Health Organization (WHO) Regional Office for Europe

2014   *HIV/AIDS surveillance in Europe 2013.* EDC and WHO, Stockholm and Copenhagen. Available from http://ecdc.europa.eu/en/publications/Publications/hiv-aids-surveillance-report-Europe-2013.pdf

European Foundation for the Improvement of Living and Working Conditions (Eurofund)

2007   *Housing and integration of migrants in Europe.* Dublin.

Ferris, E. and S. Ferro-Ribeiro

2012   Protecting people in cities: the disturbing case of Haiti. *Disasters.* 36(s1): S43–S63.

Gaillard, J.C. et al.

2010   Alternatives for Sustained Disaster Risk Reduction. *Human Geography,* 3(1): 66–88. Available from http://scholars.wlu.ca/cgi/viewcontent.cgi?article=1015&context=geog_faculty

Greiner, C. and P. Sakdapolrak

2012   Rural-urban migration, agrarian change, and the environment in Kenya: a critical review of the literature. *Population and Environment,* 34(4): 524–553. DOI: 10.1007/s11111-012-0178-0.

Hardoy J. and G. Pandiella

2009   Urban poverty and vulnerability to climate change in Latin America. *Environment and Urbanization*, 2009 21(1): 203–224. Available from http://eau.sagepub.com/content/21/1/203.full.pdf+html

Hardoy J., G. Pandiella and L.S. Velásquez Barrero

2011   Local disaster risk reduction in Latin American urban areas. *Environment and Urbanization,* 2011 23(2): 401–413. Available from http://eau.sagepub.com/content/23/2/401.full.pdf+html

WORLD MIGRATION
REPORT 2015
Migrants and Cities:
New Partnerships
to Manage Mobility

109

Haysom, S.
2013   *Sanctuary in the city? Urban displacement and vulnerability - Final report*. Overseas Development Institute, London. Available from www.odi.org/sites/odi.org.uk/files/odi-assets/publications-opinion-files/8444.pdf

Hu, X., S. Cook and M. Salazar
2008   Internal migration and health in China. In: *The Lancet,* 372 (9651): 1717–9.

Hugo, G.
2008   Migration, Development and Environment. *Migration Research Series, No. 35*. International Organization for Migration, Geneva. Available from http://publications.iom.int/bookstore/free/MRS_35.pdf

Internal Displacement Monitoring Centre (IDMC)
2014   *Global Estimates 2014: People displaced by disasters*. Internal Displacement Monitoring Centre, Geneva. Available from www.internal-displacement.org/publications/2014/global-estimates-2014-people-displaced-by-disasters

International Federation of Red Cross and Red Crescent Societies (IFRC)
2012   *World Disasters Report 2012 - Focus on forced migration and displacement*. International Federation of Red Cross and Red Crescent Societies, Geneva. Available from www.ifrc.org/en/publications-and-reports/world-disasters-report/world-disasters-report-2012---focus-on-forced-migration-and-displacement/

International Organization for Migration (IOM)
2008   *Migrants and the host society: Partnerships for success*. International Dialogue on Migration No. 11. International Organization for Migration, Geneva. Available from http://publications.iom.int/bookstore/free/IDM_11_EN.pdf
2013   *World Migration Report: Migrant Well-being and Development*. International Organization for Migration, Geneva. Available from http://publications.iom.int/bookstore/free/WMR2013_EN.pdf

International Organization for Migration (IOM), World Health Organization (WHO) and Office of the High Commissioner for Human Rights (OHCHR)
2013   *International Migration, Health and Human Rights*. IOM, WHO and OHCHR, Geneva. Available from http://publications.iom.int/bookstore/free/IOM_UNHCHR_EN_web.pdf

Jacobsen, K. and K. Howe
2008   *Internal displacement to urban areas: the Tufts-IDMC profiling study - Case 3: Santa Marta, Colombia*. Tufts University, Boston, and IDMC, Geneva. Available from www.internal-displacement.org/assets/publications/2008/200809-am-colombia-urban-displacement-santa-marta-country-en.pdf

Jones-DeWeever, A.A. and H. Hartmann
2006   Abandoned Before the Storms: The Glaring Disaster of Gender, Race, and Class Disparities in the Gulf. In: *There is no such Thing as a Natural Disaster: Race, Class and Hurricane Katrina* (C. Hartman and G.D. Squires, eds.). Routledge, New York, pp.85-102.

Juzwiak, T., E. McGregor and M. Siegel

2014   *Migrant and Refugee Integration in Global Cities, the Role of Cities and Businesses*. The Hague Process on Refugees and Migration, The Hague. Available from http://thehagueprocess.org/wordpress/wp-content/uploads/2014/04/MigrantRefugeeIntegrationGlobalCities.pdf

Koike, K.

2011   Forgotten and unattended: refugees in post-earthquake Japan. *Forced Migration Review,* 38: 46–47. Available from www.fmreview.org/en/technology/46-47.pdf

Koser, K.

2014   Protecting non-citizens in situations of conflict, violence, and disaster. In: *Humanitarian crises and migration: causes consequences and responses* (S.F. Martin, S. Weerasinghe and A. Taylor, eds.). Routledge, New York.

Ku, L. and M. Jewers

2013   *Health Care for Immigrants: Current Policies and Issues*. Migration Policy Institute, Washington. Available from www.migrationpolicy.org/research/health-care-immigrant-families-current-policies-and-issues

Kyobutungi, C. et al.

2008   The burden of disease profile of residents of Nairobi's slums: Results from a Demographic Surveillance System. In: *Population Health Metrics,* 6 (1).

Li, W. et al.

2008   Surviving Katrina and its Aftermath: A comparative analysis of community mobilization and access to emergency relief by Vietnamese Americans and African Americans in an Eastern New Orleans Suburb. In: *Journal of Cultural Geography,* 25(3): 263–286.

Lindell, M.K. and R.W. Perry

2004   *Communicating Environmental Risk in Multiethnic Communities*. SAGE Publications, California: http://dx.doi.org/10.4135/9781452229188

Lyons, M. and S. Snoxall

2005   Creating Urban Social Capital: Some Evidence from Informal Traders in Nairobi. In: *Urban Studies,* 42(7): 1077–1097.

Majidi, N.

2011   *Urban returnees and internally displaced persons in Afghanistan*. Middle East Institute, Washington. Available from www.refugeecooperation.org/publications/afghanistan/pdf/01_majidi.pdf

Marlowe, J.

2013   Resettled refugee community perspectives to the Canterbury earthquakes: Implications for organizational response. *Disaster Prevention and Management* 22(5): 434–444.

WORLD MIGRATION
REPORT 2015
Migrants and Cities:
New Partnerships
to Manage Mobility

111

Mberu, B. et al.

Regional Synthesis on Patterns and Determinants of Migrants' Health and Associated Vulnerabilities in Urban Setting of East and Southern Africa. Forthcoming.

MercyCorps
2012   Analysis of Host Community-Refugee Tensions in Mafraq, Jordan.

Metcalfe, V., S. Haysom and E. Martin
2012   Sanctuary in the city? Urban displacement and vulnerability in Kabul. Humanitarian Policy Group Working Paper. Overseas Development Institute, London. Available from www.odi.org/sites/odi.org.uk/files/odi-assets/publications-opinion-files/7722.pdf

Miyao, M. et al.
2007   Mobile Interaction - Multilingual Disaster Information System for Mobiles Phones in Japan. Symposium on Human Interface, HCI International 2007, Beijing. In: *Lecture notes in Computer Science*, Vol. 4558: 592–599.

Mosca, D., B. Rijks and C. Schultz
2013   A role for health in the global migration and development debate? Looking ahead at the UN High-level Dialogue on International Migration and Development (HLD) and other forums. In: *Migration Policy Practice*, IOM, Geneva, (3)2: 19–24. Available from http://publications.iom.int/bookstore/free/MigrationPolicyPracticeJournal10_15May2013.pdf

Murillo, F.
2014   Migration and urbanization paths: Emerging challenges of reshaping the human geography of Latin America. Background Paper for the *World Migration Report 2015: Migrants and Cities: New Partnerships to Manage Mobility*. IOM, Geneva.

Ompad, D. et al.
2007   Social determinants of the health of urban populations: Methodologic considerations. *Journal of Urban Health: Bulletin of the New York Academy of Medicine*, New York, 84 (3 Suppl): i42-53. Available from www.ncbi.nlm.nih.gov/pmc/articles/PMC1891644/

Orozco, M.
2008   Diasporas and development: Issues and impediments. In: *Diasporas and International Development: Exploring the Potential*. (J.M. Brinkerhof, ed.). Lynne Rienner, Boulder. Available from www.worldbank.org/afr/diaspora/200802hlseminar/Diaspora%20and%20Development%20Orozco.pdf

Østergaard-Nielsen, E.
2011   Codevelopment and citizenship: the nexus between policies on local migrant incorporation and migrant transnational practices in Spain. *Ethnic and Racial Studies* 34(1): 20–39.

Owusu, T.
2000   The Role of Ghanaian Immigrant Associations in Toronto, Canada. *International Migration Review,* 34(4): 1155–81.

Perlman, J.E.
2002   Marginality: From Myth to Reality in the Favelas of Rio de Janeiro, 1969–2002. In: *Urban Informality: Transnational Perspectives from the Middle East, Latin America and South Asia* (A. Roy and N. Al Sayyad, eds.). Lexington Books, Oxford, pp. 105–146.

Perry, R.W. and A.H. Mushkatel
2008   *Minority Citizens in Disasters.* University of Georgia Press, Athens.

Phillips, B.D.
1993   Cultural diversity in disasters: sheltering, housing and long-term recovery. *International Journal of Mass Emergencies and Disasters* (IJMED) 11(1): 99–110. Available from www.ijmed.org/articles/368/

Sabates-Wheeler, R.
2009   Social security for migrants: Trends, best practice and ways forward, Working Paper 12. ISSA project "Examining the Existing Knowledge on Social Security". International Social Security Association, Geneva.

Sabates-Wheeler, R. and I. Macauslan
2007   Migration and Social Protection: Exposing problems of access. *Development* 50(4). Society for International Development, Washington.

Sall, B.
2005   Remittances and Economic Initiatives in sub-Saharan Africa. In: *Migration, Remittances and Development.* OECD, Paris, p. 265–278.

Schultz, C.
2014   Migration, Health and Urbanization: Interrelated Challenges. Background Paper for the *World Migration Report 2015: Migrants and Cities: New partnerships to manage mobility.* IOM, Geneva.

Seibert, T.
2014   A city of arrival and its wild growth. In: *World Risk Report 2014.* UN-EHS, United Nations University, Bonn, pp. 24–29. Available from   http://worldriskreport.entwicklung-hilft.de/uploads/media/ WorldRiskReport_2014_online-II_01.pdf

Serageldin, M., F. Vigier and M. Larsen
2014   Urban Migration Trends in the MENA Region and the Challenge of Conflict Induced Displacement. Background Paper for the *World Migration Report 2015: Migrants and Cities: New partnerships to manage mobility.* IOM, Geneva.

Shepherd, J. and K. van Vuuren
2014   The Brisbane Flood: CALD Gatekeepers' risk communication role. *Disaster Prevention and Management,* 23(4): 469–83. DOI:10.1108/ DPM-08-2013-0133.

WORLD MIGRATION
REPORT 2015
Migrants and Cities:
New Partnerships
to Manage Mobility

113

Sherwood A, et al.

2014   *Supporting Durable Solutions to Urban, Post-Disaster Displacement: Challenges and Opportunities in Haiti*. Brookings Institution and International Organization for Migration, Washington and Geneva. Available from http://publications.iom.int/bookstore/free/ Supporting_Durable_SolutionstoDisplacement_Haiti_Feb2014_ Brookings.pdf

Shetty, P.

2011   Health care for urban poor falls through the gap. In: *The Lancet*, 377(9766): 627–628. Available from www.thelancet.com/pdfs/ journals/lancet/PIIS0140-6736(11)60215-8.pdf

Somerville W., J. Durana and A.M. Terrazas

2008   *Hometown Associations: An Untapped Resource for Immigrant Integration?* Migration Policy Institute, Washington. Available from www.migrationpolicy.org/research/hometown-associations- untapped-resource-immigrant-integration

Sturge, G.

2014   *Nairobi, Kenya. A Case Study from Migrant and Refugee Integration in Global Cities: The Role of Cities and Businesses*. The Hague Process on Refugees and Migration. Available from http://thehagueprocess.org/ wordpress/wp-content/uploads/2014/04/NairobiTHP.pdf

Tacoli, C., G. McGranahan and D. Satterthwaite

2014   Urbanization, Rural-urban Migration and Urban Poverty. Background Paper for the *World Migration Report 2015: Migrants and Cities: New Partnerships to Manage Mobility*. IOM, Geneva.

UNAIDS

2014   *The Gap Report*, UNAIDS, Geneva, pp. 84 and 159. Available from www. unaids.org/sites/default/files/en/media/unaids/contentassets/ documents/unaidspublication/2014/UNAIDS_Gap_report_en.pdf

United Nations Development Programme (UNDP)

2009   *Human development Report 2009 - Overcoming barriers: Human mobility and development*. United Nations, New York. Available from http://hdr.undp.org/sites/default/files/reports/269/hdr_2009_en_ complete.pdf

United Nations High Commissioner for Refugees (UNHCR)

2014a   *Jordan Refugee Response - RRP6. Protection Sector Achievements, January to September 2014*. UNHCR, Geneva.

2014b   *UNHCR Lebanon Shelter Update, September 2014*, UNHCR, Geneva.

United Nations Human Settlements Programme (UN-Habitat)

2003   *The Challenge of Slums. Global Report on Human Settlements 2003*. United Nations Settlement Programme. New York. Available from http://unhabitat.org/?wpdmact=process&did=MTQ3OS5ob3RsaW5r

2014a   *City Profile Aleppo, Multi-Sector Assessment*. UN-Habitat, Damascus. Available from http://unhabitat.org/?wpdmact=process&did=MTQ5 Ny5ob3RsaW5r

2014b   *City Profile Lattakia, Multi-Sector Assessment*. UN-Habitat, Damascus. Available from http://unhabitat.org/?wpdmact=process&did=MTQ5 Mi5ob3RsaW5r

Vinck, P. et al.
2009   Inequalities and Prospects: Ethnicity and Legal Status in the Construction Labor Force after Hurricane Katrina, *Organization and Environment*, 22(4): 470–478.

Vu L. et al.
2009   Evacuation and Return of Vietnamese New Orleanians Affected by Hurricane Katrina. *Organization & Environment,* 22(4): 422–436.

Wang, M.Z., M. Amati and F. Thomalla
2011   Understanding the vulnerability of migrants in Shanghai to typhoons. *Natural Hazards.* 60(3):1189–1210.

Wei, X. et al.
2009   Barriers to TB care for rural-to-urban migrant TB patients in Shanghai: a qualitative study. In: *Tropical Medicine and International Health*, 14(7): 754–760. Available from http://onlinelibrary.wiley.com/ doi/10.1111/j.1365-3156.2009.02286.x/epdf

Weiss Fagen, P.
2014   Flight to the cities: urban options and adaptations. In: *Humanitarian crises and migration: causes consequences and responses* (S.F. Martin, S. Weerasinghe and A. Taylor, eds.). Routledge, New York.

World Health Organization (WHO)
2008   *Closing the gap in a generation: Health equity through action on the social determinants of health, Final Report of the Commission on Social Determinants of Health*. WHO, Geneva. Available from http:// whqlibdoc.who.int/publications/2008/9789241563703_eng.pdf

2015   *Factors that contributed to undetected spread of the Ebola virus and impeded rapid containment: One year into the Ebola epidemic*. January 2015. Available from www.who.int/csr/disease/ebola/one- year-report/factors/en/

WHO and IOM
2014   *Tuberculosis Prevention and Care for Migrants*. WHO and IOM, Geneva. Available from www.who.int/tb/publications/WHOIOM_ TBmigration.pdf

WHO and UN-Habitat
2010   *Hidden Cities: Unmasking and overcoming health inequities in urban settings*. WHO and UN-Habitat, Geneva, p. 14. Available from www. who.int/kobe_centre/publications/hiddencities_media/who_un_ habitat_hidden_cities_web.pdf

WORLD MIGRATION
REPORT 2015
Migrants and Cities:
New Partnerships
to Manage Mobility

115

Wisner, B.
2002a   Goma, Congo: City Air Makes Men Free? RADIX online.
2002b   Assessment of capabilities and vulnerabilities. *Mapping Vulnerability:
             Disasters, Development and People* (G. Bankoff , G. Frerks and D.
             Hilhorst, eds.). Wiley.

Wisner, B. et al.
2004   At Risk: Natural hazards, people's vulnerability and disasters.
             Routledge, London and New York. Available from www.preventionweb.
             net/files/670_72351.pdf

Zetter, R. and G. Deikun
2010   Meeting humanitarian challenges in urban areas. *Forced Migration
             Review,* 34: 5–7. Available from www.fmreview.org/en/urban-
             displacement/FMR34.pdf

Urban migration
and economic
development

CHAPTER 4

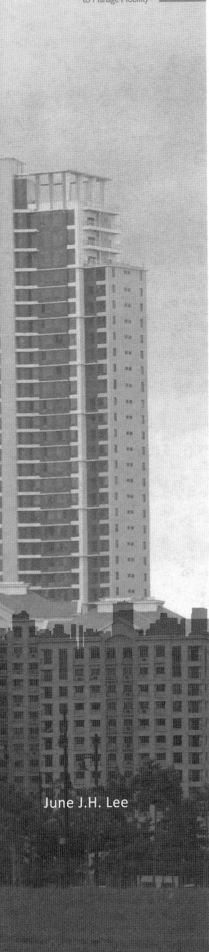

June J.H. Lee

WORLD MIGRATION
REPORT 2015
Migrants and Cities:
New Partnerships
to Manage Mobility

117

HIGHLIGHTS

- There are strong links between urbanization and economic development. The concentration of economic activity in urban areas can facilitate trade and help fuel growth. Data shows that industrialized economies with higher rates of per capita GDP also have higher rates of urbanization. However, these links are not recognized by low- and middle-income countries which see migration as a drain on urban areas and thus tend to pursue policies to discourage it. Instead, policies are needed to harness the economic potential of migration and turn it to the benefit of city destinations.

- Cities can turn urban diversity arising from migration into a social and economic advantage. Migration can help increase productivity if it is strategically managed and linked to the formal economy. Fostering the inclusion of migrants into the labour market can have positive benefits for both the place of origin and of destination as links are maintained between the two. Support to migrant entrepreneurs aids not only their own socioeconomic integration but also local development. Both city governments and the private sector can play an important role in the inclusion of migrants into labour markets through policies and practices aimed at the provision of information and training as well as networking and livelihood opportunities.

- Urban migrants can be agents of international development, supporting and promoting the economic growth of countries of origin. Innovative local development partnerships between host and sending countries which involve city-city relationships, twinning arrangements and diaspora-led initiatives have been shown to yield economic dividends for communities back home.

- The number of practices on the ground aimed at tackling urban integration and fostering participative economic growth among city authorities, urban practitioners, civil society leaders, business development communities, migrant associations and diasporas, mostly in the developed world, are growing fast.

- Coherent policy development requires an understanding of the character of migration flows, new patterns of circular, temporary and commuter mobility as well as an assessment of labour market needs. The lack of systematic data collection establishing the exact links between migration and urbanization is a significant constraint.

This chapter examines how urbanization and new mobility patterns contribute to urban poverty reduction, growth and development and enhance migrant well-being. It also examines how cities can turn urban diversity into a social and economic advantage, through facilitating migrant access to formal labour markets and encouraging migrant-led businesses. Finally, the chapter looks at the emerging innovative partnerships involving cities which have the potential to enhance the development impacts of migration.

WORLD MIGRATION
REPORT 2015
Migrants and Cities:
New Partnerships
to Manage Mobility

119

4.1

INTRODUCTION

Migrants make significant and essential contributions to the economic, social and cultural development of their host cities and their communities back home. Yet these contributions often go unrecognized or, at best, are measured only in terms of the remittances they manage to send back home. The Declaration adopted at the 2013 UN High-level Dialogue on International Migration and Development in New York highlighted the need for migrants to be at the centre of national and global migration and development agendas. Sustained and inclusive economic growth is the goal that most cities strive to achieve. Migration policies and programmes are integral to urban development planning and management for an increasing number of cities.

Cities and towns are places where practical solutions linking migration and sustainable development can be tested. For large emerging economies, like China and India, managing internal migration and urbanization will be critical for their economic and political future. Despite the need for more study on migration issues in low- and middle-income country urban destinations, a growing number of research findings demonstrate that migration can have a transformative power and lead to poverty reduction as people adopt circular mobility patterns and livelihood strategies based on maintaining links to multiple locations.

Rapid city growth can, if unmanaged, undermine this potential as the urban infrastructure, environment and social fabric will be insufficient to support urban migrants in their efforts to improve the situation for themselves, their families and communities. Well-managed urbanization, whereby cities invest in providing adequate services, is essential in order to bring about economic growth and development which can be sustained.

Cities are responding to these challenges by exploring flexible forms of governance for development that draw on urban diversity as a source of innovation. Mayors and city councils of cities like New York have established immigrant affairs functions within their city planning administrations. The European Union (EU) continues to refine the knowledge and toolkits to support cities to turn urban diversity into a social and economic advantage. Cities, such as Lisbon, Rotterdam, Chicago, Buenos Aires, Sao Paulo, Nairobi, Auckland and Kuala Lumpur, are also paying increasing attention to the role of migrants and attempting to create an opportunity structure for natives and newcomers alike through partnerships with migrants, the private sector and civil society.

4.2

MIGRATION AND URBAN POVERTY REDUCTION

4.2.1. Urbanization and economic development

There are strong links between urbanization and economic development as the concentration of economic activity in particular areas fuels growth. Statistics show that countries with higher rates of per capita GDP have higher rates of urbanization. These links are not recognized by low- and middle-income countries which sometimes seek to discourage migration as a perceived drain on urban areas.

The links between urbanization, migration and economic development are complex: economic development and urbanization are linked but the contribution of migration to urbanization is more nuanced. Empirical data and research on the complex links between migration and urbanization remain inadequate. This is because the basic premise for making the links between migration and urbanization are constantly shifting. The traditional dichotomy of rural–urban mobility simply no longer applies in many parts of the world, nor does urbanization necessarily equate with urban development or only occur as an outcome of migration.

The Chinese experience demonstrates that urbanization involves not only the net movement of people towards and into urban areas but also the progressive extension of urban boundaries and creation of new urban centres. A major characteristic of China's urbanization process in the 1980s and 1990s has been the emergence and development of in situ urbanization (Friedmann, 2005; Zhu, 2000; Zhu et al., 2012). In the process of in situ urbanization, rural settlements and their populations transform themselves into urban or quasi-urban settlements without too much geographical relocation of residents (Zhu, 2004). Between the 1982 and 1990 censuses, almost 70 per cent of total urban population growth can be attributed to reclassification of rural areas that were previously defined as rural. Only in the recent period, between the 2000 and 2010 censuses, did rural–urban migration overtake reclassification as the most important source of urban population growth (ibid.).

Urbanization does not always lead to urban development or industrialization. Urbanization in developing countries is often linked with industrialization; across much of Asia and Latin America, population movements meant movement of labour from agriculture into industries that manufacture goods for domestic and international markets (Jedwab, Gollin and Vollrath, 2013). However, countries that are rich in natural resources have urbanized even without industrializing. High incomes due to natural resource endowments create needs for the kinds of urban goods and services that require workers in non-tradable services. This consumption-based, not production-based, urbanization accounts for 30–50 per cent of the experience in Africa and the Middle East (ibid.).

Sometimes urbanization is not accompanied by economic development but by significant international migration. In the Pacific region, due to the slow economic growth and development in most countries, the formal labour market with regular employment opportunities can absorb only a small portion of the rapidly growing working-age populations. Increasing education and growth in urban populations have meant educated islanders look for jobs abroad in the labour markets of Australia, New Zealand and the United States, while their home countries suffer from the shortage of skilled workers in such sectors as health care and education (Bedford and Hugo, 2011). For these small island developing States, strategic planning of cities that retain and attract skilled human resources is critical and will help keep them connected to global markets.

WORLD MIGRATION
REPORT 2015
Migrants and Cities:
New Partnerships
to Manage Mobility

121

Urbanization does not necessarily deprive rural areas of economic development. In fact, urban development cannot be studied without reference to rural development. For instance, internal and international migration and urbanization trends need to be factored into labour market strategies that affect both rural and urban development. The United Nations (UN) reports that cities are drivers for economic growth and poverty reduction in both urban and rural areas and recommend strengthening rural–urban pathways, not delinking them (UN DESA, 2014).

Notwithstanding the exceptions discussed above, it is widely acknowledged by both economists and development practitioners that sustained economic growth does not take place without urbanization (Guranton, 2014). Urbanization and economic development are associated. Urbanization has economic benefits because cities provide for economies of agglomeration, in that businesses benefit from being close together and can generally profit from the mobility of capital, labour, ideas and internal and international connections. By bringing together the various factors of production, cities can offer the possibility of securing new economic advantages and scaling them up (Glaeser and Joshi-Ghani, 2013). It is known that sustained economic growth comes with urbanization (World Bank, 2009). Figure 6 shows that, when examining the urbanization and economic growth for the past three decades, countries with the highest per capita GDP also have the highest levels of urbanization.

Cities in Asia and Africa are expected to account for the major part of global economic growth in the coming decades (UN DESA, 2012) which will inevitably involve increased urbanization but this is not without its challenges. Slums are a regular sight in many of the world's burgeoning cities. Many cities in sub-Saharan Africa are unable to provide for the most basic of human needs, such as clean drinking water. Urban violence is pervasive in many Latin American neighbourhoods. Limited transport options can turn daily commutes in Asia's megacities into arduous journeys.

In order for the cities in the low-income countries to become engines of economic growth, policymakers and local authorities need to put in place institutional support. Migration of people can promote urbanization and hence economic development but for this to work effectively, the infrastructure and services need to be in place to meet the needs of these arrivals. A recent statistical review of regional variations in India's economic growth noted the economic importance of facilitating migration, for example, by providing more adequate transportation infrastructure as well as laws and welfare policies that do not discriminate against migrants (Das, Ghate and Robertson, 2015).

Figure 6

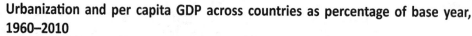

Urbanization and per capita GDP across countries as percentage of base year, 1960–2010

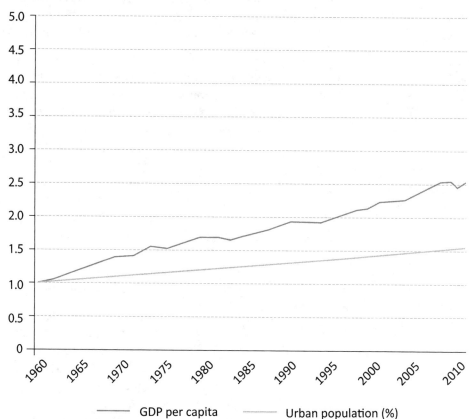

——— GDP per capita   ——— Urban population (%)

Source: State of the World's Cities 2012/2013, Prosperity of Cities, UN-Habitat, 2013.

4.2.2. Rural–urban migration and poverty reduction

There is little evidence to suggest that migration drives up urban poverty (Tacoli, McGranahan and Satterthwaite, 2014). Conversely, studies show that migration has economic advantages for migrants themselves, who may benefit at an individual level through increased livelihood opportunities and also contribute to poverty reduction in their home communities by sending back money and resources.

In spite of the strong correlation between urbanization and economic growth, the majority of governments (80 % of 185 countries reviewed), especially in low- and middle-income nations in Africa and Asia, had policies to lower rural to urban migration (UN DESA, 2013). These policymakers tend to assume that most migrants "transfer" their poverty to urban contexts. However, this does not recognize the complexity of such population movements. Migrants are not a homogeneous group and have differentiated access to resources and institutions, and differing capacities to undertake migration.

There is little evidence to suggest that migration drives up urban poverty. In fact those moving to urban contexts are relatively better off. Permanent migrants from rural areas tend to have sufficient resources to move to a further location

WORLD MIGRATION
REPORT 2015
Migrants and Cities:
New Partnerships
to Manage Mobility

123

for employment or education purposes (Massey, Axinn and Ghimire, 2007). For instance, in the Upper West Region of Ghana, wealthy migrants were found to move more often to the urban centres of the south, including Accra, while the poor and illiterate migrated over shorter distances, usually to the Brong Ahafo region (Van der Geest, 2011). Also, often, those who move to urban centres are not from rural areas but from another urban centre (ibid.).

Those who are poor have more limited choices and, rather than migrating to urban areas, are more likely to seek work in other rural destinations. Rural to rural migration is most prevalent among the poorest who take advantage of the seasonal demand for waged agricultural labour for commercial farming, or family farming for high-value products, such as fresh fruit and vegetables. Using these migrant remittances, their families often hire labourers to compensate for shortages of family labour. Thus out-migration to urban centres stimulates in-migration from other rural areas (Tacoli, 2011; Hoang, Dinh and Nguyen, 2008).

Conversely the economic benefits of migrating from rural to urban areas are well evidenced. A recent study among the poor migrants living and working in two urban informal settlements in Accra (Nima and Old Fadama) indicates that, despite living in a harsh environment with little social protection, an overwhelming majority of the migrants (88%) believed that their overall well-being had been enhanced by migrating to Accra (Awumbila, Owusu and Teye, 2014). Migrants in these informal settlements tend to be optimistic and try to move out of poverty, despite the obvious challenges. In another study in Harare, Zimbabwe, in 2001, prior to hyperinflation, about half of sampled rural–urban migrants estimated that their standard of living had improved in comparison to their rural areas of origin (Potts, 2006).

Migration plays a critical role in establishing linkages between rural origins and urban destinations, and these linkages have multifaceted impacts on individuals, families and communities. In some Asian countries, the younger, better educated members of origin communities tend to migrate to urban areas. The benefits of these linkages between rural and urban areas as part of the migration process partially offset the negative impacts on rural communities and families members left behind. Such connections certainly bring positive effects to migrant families and communities and need to be properly maintained (Zhu et al., 2013). Research on migrants from the poorer parts of western Kenya shows that they fare much better in urban destinations and maintain strong contacts with their origins through remittances. The vast majority of migrants expect to return to their homes eventually to lead better lives than the non-migrants and contribute to their communities' development (Oucho, Oucho and Ochieng, 2014).

In order to make rural–urban migration effective in poverty reduction, institutional arrangements are required such as improvements in access to social services and benefits. This is critical in order, for example, that migrant residents in cities may evolve into a new burgeoning middle-class that drives consumption growth (Chan, 2012). In the Philippines too, internal migration is growing especially to smaller towns with bigger growth potential than urban centres. Guiguinto in Central Luzon has attracted large numbers of internal migrants due to its proximity to Metro Manila, as well as to its dynamic economy and the positive role of local government in supporting infrastructure and services. However, in order to reap the benefits of internal migration, the local governance systems of small towns need to be strengthened (Basa, Villamil and de Guzman, 2009).

Improved communication, increasing movements of people and goods, and changes in land use have reshaped the relationship between urban and rural areas and blurred any clear distinction between them. People travel for much longer distances than before and their economic interactions take place over much wider areas than before. Urban and rural areas enjoy different and often complementary assets, and better integration between them is important for socioeconomic performance. National, regional and local policymakers need to build effective and sustainable rural–urban partnerships, especially those fostered through migration links, for better economic development (OECD, 2013).

4.2.3. International and internal remittances

International remittances are key to alleviating poverty and their potential can be maximized by instituting schemes and programmes that link urbanization, rural migration, expatriate involvement and national growth. Less has been studied about the effects of internal remittances on poverty reduction but given that the number of internal migrants far exceeds the number of international migrants, the potential of internal remittances must not be overlooked.

International remittances, investments and manpower, skills and expertise from diaspora communities abroad can accelerate urban growth in their countries of origin. The aggregate positive effects of international remittances on income and employment in migrant-sending regions have transformed many towns and cities. The Moroccan diaspora, for example, has invested in urban-based real estate and businesses in their home regions, which in turn has attracted more investments and internal migration. In 2013, the Ministry in Charge of Moroccans Living Abroad and Migration Affairs launched the Maghir Bank to further enhance Moroccan expatriate financial connections to their origin country. In Egypt, the foreign exchange earning shortage experienced in the aftermath of the 2011 political crisis was partially offset by an increase in remittances and donations from diasporas to the Egypt Development Fund (Serageldin, Vigier and Larsen, 2014). Migrant investors tend to prefer larger cities than small towns, although investments in hometowns and villages continue as they can confer a greater status on the migrants than in large urban centres (ibid.).

Less has been studied about the effects of internal remittances on poverty reduction. A clear and nuanced understanding is needed about the way that rural–urban linkages are forged in the migration process and the diverse forms they take, especially given that, in many countries, internal migrants outnumber international migrants. The number of internal migrants globally is at least 740 million, nearly four times the number of international migrants (UNDP, 2009). Migration is a livelihood strategy pursued by poor households in order to spread livelihood risks, secure and increase income, and acquire investment capital. Remittances are central elements of such household strategies to overcome local development constraints. For example, in India and Ghana, censuses and recent household surveys show that internal migrants greatly outnumber international migrants and result in a significant amount of internal remittances, in both countries. Furthermore, internal remittances are particularly important to the poorest regions of Ghana and the poorest states of India (Castaldo, Deshingkar and McKay, 2012). Families of internal migrants tend to be poorer than those

WORLD MIGRATION
REPORT 2015
Migrants and Cities:
New Partnerships
to Manage Mobility

125

of international migrants as the amount of remittances tend to be smaller than international remittances.

However, there is clearly the potential to improve standards of living and overall well-being with possible multiplier effects for origin areas (McKay and Deshingkar, 2014). As examined in six countries in Africa and Asia – Nigeria, Rwanda, South Africa, Uganda, Bangladesh and Viet Nam – internal remittances flow to a large number of receiving households, mainly in poor rural areas, improve living standards and overall well-being of those households. In India, circular migration has become the enduring mobility pattern of the poor in agriculturally marginal areas. Migration among chronically poor households is higher and plays an important role in managing risk, improving standards of living and household well-being, and maintaining rural livelihood. As a result of migration, these poor families are able to repay debts faster, eat more regularly, spend on education, health, agriculture and housing, and borrow large sums when needed. There are costs, however, as migration increases the risk of injury and exposure to disease and other hazards, as well as the negative impacts of long separation from families (Deshingkar, 2011; Deshingkar and Farrington, 2009).

Experiences in China illustrate the multiplier effect of international and internal remittances working in tandem to support the dramatic growth of towns and cities. The south-eastern Chinese provinces of Fujian, Jiangsu, Zhejiang and Guangdong greatly benefitted from remittances and investment from overseas Chinese in the 1970s and 1980s during the early stage of town and village enterprise development. Their contributions helped overcome the constraints of the lack of investments, infrastructure and skilled labour in rural development. Later internal migrants from inland areas to those south-eastern provinces started remitting significant funds to help their hometown development. The China Rural Household Survey in Guizhou province in early 2000 found that some 82 per cent of male migrants and 73 per cent of female migrants sent remittances to their hometowns in the year of the survey, contributing as much as 30 per cent of the total income of migrant households. These remittances sent by Chinese internal migrants as a whole may be as high as 160 billion Yuan per year (Zhu, 2014). The impact of these remittances is significant on the socioeconomic development and rural–urban transformation of migrant hometowns as well as on migrant households.

This Chinese experience illustrates that a virtuous circle can be established between urbanization, rural migration, expatriate investment and national growth. Timely regulations and investment by central and local governments was critical in providing the necessary support. An earlier study of five semi-urban communities of origin in Latin America and the Caribbean has shown that fragile local economies and high costs of living can hinder the ability of remittance recipients to save and mobilize those savings. This is especially acute where there is inadequate support by governments, civil society and private sector to recipient families (Orozco, 2008). This attests to the value of remittance-leveraging policies at the local level as shown in text box 18.

Text box 18

Remittance policies in Mexico and Argentina[1]

The Mexico–United States "Tres por Uno" (Three for One) initiative encourages effective use of remittances in order to promote local development. In this initiative, Mexican migrants living abroad, mainly in the United States, agree to contribute a third of the capital needed to carry out improvement work in their regions of origin, with the other two thirds of the required capital provided by the Mexican federal, state and municipal governments.

Argentina shares a similar partnership with a Bolivian migrant cooperative called "Saropalca" for public infrastructure improvement projects in the municipalities of Toropalca, a very poor region in Bolivia. Saropalca has an extensive network of producers who provide a significant proportion of fruits and vegetables for the entire city of Buenos Aires. Most of the members keep and expand their housing facilities in their places of origin and contribute through charitable organizations to help the youth and the elderly in their communities. The cooperative finances the building of a mill and a seed mixer to facilitate micro-business rural activities, thus also adding to the value of their own production chain. Migrants have succeeded in linking up with the national government to work in partnership with a private actor, their own cooperative, for the benefit of seven municipalities in their communities of origin.

4.2.4. Informal urban economies and migrant livelihoods

Migrants make a significant contribution through the informal economy in low-paid insecure jobs but their efforts are not recognized by policymakers nor are they harnessed by policy frameworks aimed at promoting local development.

Unstable, low-paid jobs in the informal sector are common among the urban poor, especially among migrants who lack skills, education and especially the social networks to gain access to better employment. Most migrants in African cities have little education and end up in the informal sector which accounts for 93 per cent of all new jobs and 61 per cent of urban employment in Africa. Among residents of low-income settlements in 11 cities in Southern Africa, about half of both migrant and non-migrant workers do not earn their incomes from regular wage work (Crush, 2012).

Informal activities in many developing cities in Asia and Africa provide employment opportunities for millions of people beyond the formal economy. This can account for more than 60 per cent of urban employment in Africa (Awumbila, 2014), providing a main source of employment and income for a majority of the poor in

---

1   Taken from F. Murillo, Migration and Urbanization Paths: Emerging challenges of reshaping the human geography of Latin America, 2014. Background Paper for the *World Migration Report 2015: Migrants and Cities: New Partnerships to Manage Mobility*. International Organization for Migration (IOM), Geneva.

WORLD MIGRATION
REPORT 2015
Migrants and Cities:
New Partnerships
to Manage Mobility

127

urban centres and poor urban women in particular. The informal economy is an arena of considerable heterogeneity, a space where the poor, the not-so-poor and middle-income earners make a living (see text box 19).

Text box 19

E-waste business in African slums[2]

The e-waste business, which involves salvaging materials from discarded electronic and electrical equipment for sale to industries, appears to be one of the most profitable jobs in the slums studied. This economic activity is mainly undertaken by male migrants from northern Ghana, Niger and Nigeria. A chain of e-waste-related activities, namely collection, recycling, repair and refurbishment, and trading of metals are in existence. This hierarchical e-waste business is highly lucrative, despite its risky nature, with earnings of between USD 7.50 daily for scrap collectors to as high as between USD 20 and USD 100 per day for e-waste refurbishers, who are higher in the hierarchy of labour relations. These amounts are higher than the salary of lower and middle level officers in Ghana's public service and certainly several times higher than what they were earning in their home regions. Some of the scrap dealers can earn as much as USD 500 on a very good business day. When one compares these earnings with what they could have obtained from their rural areas, it is clear that migration has improved their earning capacity.

In India, urban slums are an integral part of the process of urbanization and a clear manifestation of rural to urban migration. Slums (Sassen, 2011) exist in many global cities including Mumbai where half the population lives in slums. According to the 2011 census, one in five persons living in urban areas in India was living in a slum (Bhagat, 2014). Slums provide an array of services and products to the advanced sectors and their employees, and a range of working connections also exists with local and global markets. Dharavi, Mumbai, has over 5,000 small-scale industries and 1,500 single room factories generating a turnover of half a billion USD each year. The leather industry alone employs about 200,000 workers in Dharavi. Daily commuting to Dharavi is greater than those who leave it for work in the city. It has a large number of recycling industries, handling plastic, paper and scraps, and manufacturing industries producing plastic tags, suitcase wheels, paper files and leather products sold in the international market. Even high-tech products, such as surgical threads, are produced from the intestines of goats in some areas of Dharavi. Various processed food, catering and printing services are provided and there are shops with a reservoir of highly qualified craftsmen like tailors, carpenters and potters (ibid.).

However, this type of contribution to the urban economy and social life is seldom recognized by policymakers and planners and policy frameworks do not adequately harness the power of migration for local development. In India, the circumstances and integration of migrants can vary significantly depending on whether they are classified as notified or non-notified slums according to a government system. The older slums (notified) tend to have better infrastructure and basic services such as electricity and drinking water and are occupied by a few

2   Taken from A. Awumbila, Linkages between Urbanization, Rural-Urban Migration and Poverty Outcomes in Acfrica, 2014. Background Paper for the *World Migration Report 2015, Migrants and Cities: New Partnerships to Manage Mobility*, IOM, Geneva.

generations of the settled lower-middle class with education and homeownership interests. Newer slums have almost non-existent infrastructure, no basic services or outside support, and tend to be occupied by recent migrants who retain strong ties with families in rural areas and for whom debt repayment is the priority (Tacoli, McGranahan and Satterthwaite, 2014).

Text box 20

Opportunities for women in urban areas

Urbanization can present women with increased economic and social opportunities, better access to services, greater independence and fewer economic and cultural constraints. Women who migrate from rural to urban areas have better opportunities of owning property, gaining exposure to urban life, and are able to remit back home with little economic activity, particularly in dry seasons (Awumbila and Ardayfio-Schandorf, 2008). Migrating to the city can be a way for women to escape traditional gender roles, gender-specific discrimination or gender-based violence, all push factors identified as having a specific dimension in rural areas. In parts of Africa and Asia, many rural women who otherwise have little opportunity or access to international migration relocate to cities to gain training and connections before migrating abroad (Jolly and Reevew, 2005). Women, especially widows, are often denied the right to secure property titles in rural areas, which acts a push factor to migrate to cities where property acquisition may be easier. However, gender gaps in employment and wages, tenure rights, access to and accumulation of assets, personal security and safety, and political representation persist and women are often the last to benefit from the prosperity of cities (Tacoli, 2013).

Informal street trading alone occupies about two-thirds of women, accounting for about 10 to 20 per cent of total employment in cities in Ghana, Zimbabwe and South Africa and providing an important source of livelihood with low barriers to entry. In Ghana, slums are booming with various forms of entrepreneurial businesses, mainly in the informal sector which tends to be gendered (Awumbila, Owusu and Teye, 2014). Migrant women work mainly as petty traders, food vendors, catering assistants, head porters, shop assistants and hairdressers. Young girls from rural areas, particularly the northern regions, move to markets in the urban centres of Accra and Kumasi to serve as *kayayei* (female porters), who carry goods on their heads for a negotiated fee (Awumbila and Ardayfio-Schandorf, 2008). Migrant men work as artisans, construction workers, *okada* (motor bike) operators and in other trades such as e-waste business. The challenges and opportunities facing migrant women in urban areas are discussed in text box 20.

Informal traders generally work under hostile conditions (African Centre for Cities, 2014). Street traders and other informal workers tend to operate in areas with heavy human and vehicular traffic, creating tension with authorities over the use of public space. In Zimbabwe, local authorities often harass migrants working in the informal sector and demand unofficial payments before they can do any business (Awumbila, 2014). Cross-border trade in Africa is often dominated by women, especially in the 11 countries in Southern Africa, where the busiest border points are Lebombo in South Africa and Beitbridge in Zimbabwe. Most

WORLD MIGRATION
REPORT 2015
Migrants and Cities:
New Partnerships
to Manage Mobility

129

traders cross borders frequently for short visits to trade various food produce. Female traders face significant challenges at border crossings including high and fluctuating duties, unwarranted confiscation of goods, long queues and physical harassment (ibid.).

Alone in the big city of Accra: Building a future one load at a time

The main market place in Accra, popularly known as Makola, is bursting with life day and night. If one looks closely while walking in the streets, you will see women carrying large pans or flat wooden boards, some piled high with fresh fruits and vegetables, cartons of canned foods, soaps and other market goods, hurrying along to deliver their order or in search of a load to carry for a fee. They are called *Kayayei* in the local language, meaning female head porters. Most of these *Kayayei* have migrated to Accra from northern Ghana, the most poverty stricken part of the country that is affected by droughts and floods. Many survive only on subsistence farming.

Adamu, 27 years of age, grew up in a small farming village called Walewale in Ghana. Determined to succeed, she travelled to Accra to work, baking, selling bread and doing housework before becoming a *Kayayo*. Working as a *Kayayo* is a challenging trade with little trust and respect from customers, "Life in Accra is not easy".

Finding food and shelter is a constant problem for *Kayayei* in general and Adamu currently shares one small wooden structured room with 11 other girls. Others sleep in open spaces in front of shops after they close. Those staying in shared rooms or open spaces are far from the comforts of home and are often forced to lay cardboard on the floor and sleep on it. The space is so small that turning while sleeping is almost impossible. They have access to water, toilets and electricity but these facilities are public ones, often at a distance from their room, and are at an additional prohibitive cost. None of them feel safe as robbery and rape are a common occurrence in their neighbourhood. The open sleeping places also expose *Kayayei* to predators looking for easy sex, leading to many teenage pregnancies.

Among the *Kayayei*, there are people from other parts of Ghana and Burkina Faso, according to Adamu. She realized that with no assistance from NGOs or other groups, there was a need to organize the *Kayayei* together to improve their living situation. Earlier this year, she started a group called "Together We Stand". They held meetings for three months but, due to the nature of their work schedule, it was difficult to encourage others to join and the group disbanded.

Despite these daily challenges, Adamu remains hopeful. "Because of the work I do here, I can financially help my mum and siblings at home," she explains, "I am the firstborn so I am the one taking care of them." Adamu returns home every two to three months to see her loved ones and enjoy her community. In five years' time, "I plan to have a trade, and continue to work in Accra", says Adamu. She has a great interest in bead work and is currently saving money to enrol in a three-month bead course to better her future.

Adamu is one of the estimated tens of thousands of *Kayayei* who live and work in Accra in search of opportunities and to support their extended families. The majority of *Kayayei* begin as adolescent girls, with some as young as seven years old, and they labour for an estimated GHS 3 or just over USD 0.93 per day. Over the last thirty years, the proportion of the Ghanaian population (24 million) living in urban areas has grown from 30 per cent to over 50 per cent. This includes the sustained migration of women from rural northern areas to urban centres. Although many travel with the support and connections of families and friends, an increasing number are migrating without any support network, increasing their vulnerability to abuse and exploitation.

4.3

URBAN DIVERSITY AND ECONOMIC ADVANTAGE

4.3.1. Economic potential of migration

Diversity arising from the presence of migrants is shown to increase productivity and be of benefit to urban areas, if strategically managed.

As in informal settlements, immigrants play a vital role in creating economically vibrant, competitive cities as they contribute to a dynamic labour force and spur economic growth. Immigrants are more likely to start businesses and create jobs in their cities. Immigrants are also critical to helping cities counteract population decline and make cities more attractive by raising housing values (Vigdor, 2013). Higher levels of education among immigrants contribute to a talented workforce (AS/COA, 2014).

Immigrants have added USD 3.7 trillion to the housing wealth in the United States, created manufacturing jobs in cities such as Baltimore and St. Louis, and helped stabilize communities across the country. New migrants have helped reverse population decline. For example, in Chicago the 600,000 or so immigrants arriving in the city and surrounding Cook County since the 1970s has helped offset the loss of over 900,000 local residents. In Utica, the old industrial centre of New York, the arrival of Bosnians, Burmese, Somalis, Vietnamese, Iraqis and others has almost halted the serious decline in the population.

European cities are in search of policies and governance arrangements that can engage emerging hyper-diversity successfully in order to foster social mobility, social cohesion and economic performance. Recent research findings contradict prevailing views on migration from Eastern Europe draining local resources. Migrants are young and working-age EU mobile citizens who fill gaps in the labour market, especially for low-skilled occupations, become entrepreneurs and support the development or sustainment of core sectors of the local economy. The research found that migration is not placing a major burden on public services but that migrants have limited access to housing, education and the labour market, and interact little with local citizens (Ernst & Young Global Limited, 2014).

Migration-induced diversity is positively correlated with productivity, as it may increase the variety of goods, services and skills available for consumption, production and innovation (Kemeny, 2013). Therefore, diversity is increasingly considered as an instrument for strengthening the competitive advantage of cities. In the United States, racial heterogeneity and a social mix bring about a variety in abilities, experiences and cultures, which may be productive and lead to innovation and creativity. Researchers have argued that some areas with high levels of social mix in the city provide an easier environment for migrants,

WORLD MIGRATION
REPORT 2015
Migrants and Cities:
New Partnerships
to Manage Mobility

131

especially newcomers, wishing to start small businesses, due to the easy access to information through the well-developed networks (Saunders, 2010). It is also said that diversity contributes to the attraction of knowledge workers and increases the creative capital of cities (Florida, 2002). Such arguments tend to focus on the contributions of highly skilled migrants as well as on the transnational economic and business connections immigrants establish with their places of origin.

An immigrant influx alone does not yield competitive cities. In fact, immigrant-driven diversity challenges social cohesion and, in the past, has contributed to heightened racial and ethnic polarization in diverse cities like Los Angeles in the United States. Therefore, cities need to strategically develop inclusive policies to build a stable community and to take advantage of diversity dividend.

In the United States, immigrant integration efforts have long been at work in big cities across the nation. The loss, however, of manufacturing jobs, slow population growth and a crippled local economy has propelled city officials and civic leaders of the relatively homogenous Midwest to consider the potential contribution of immigrants to economic competitiveness, social diversity and community renewal. Many of these welcoming policies are motivated by self-interest as city leaders recognize the value of both skilled and unskilled labour from diverse backgrounds.

The range of initiatives and programmes adopted throughout the Midwest[3] is wide, from entrepreneur training, small business incubators and multilingual business services to programmes focusing on education, social integration or civic participation (Kerr, McDaniel and Guinan, 2014). Across the region, local governments are allocating resources, funding and staffing to ensure that a government body is equipped for structuring, monitoring and implementing immigrant-integration initiatives, often leveraging resources through collaborations with a variety of community-based organizations and broader networks, such as Welcoming America and the Global Great Lakes Network.

4.3.2. Migrant inclusion in local labour markets

The inclusion of migrants in labour markets needs to be managed if it is to be effective rather than be left to occur haphazardly. City governments can facilitate this inclusion as policymakers, mediators, employers and customers. The private sector has a role in assessing the labour market and in providing tailored vocational training programmes.

The knowledge economy is growing in importance and the search for talent is becoming as competitive as it is global. Skilled migrants can offer a compelling comparative advantage to the local labour markets while the demand for unskilled workers is also on the rise. The latter is particularly true as the high cost of living is making lower-paying jobs unattractive to local youth while at the same time populations are ageing fast. This means local economies cannot rely solely on local labour markets for their labour needs (OECD, 2006).

These days, urban job markets are characterized by growing occupational polarization along with a move away from manufacturing to financial and business

---

3   The Midwest is defined in this report as the 12-state Midwest, which includes Illinois, Indiana, Iowa, Kansas, Michigan, Minnesota, Missouri, Nebraska, North Dakota, Ohio, South Dakota, and Wisconsin. Pittsburgh, Pennsylvania, and Louisville, Kentucky, have also been referenced in this report given their geographic proximity to the region and participation in regional collaborations.

administration jobs. Job growth is occurring at both the top and bottom end of the labour sector while "dropping off" at the centre. Most of the low-paid work is to service the growing professional and managerial segment of the city economies and a significant proportion of these low-paying jobs in the global city are being filled by foreign-born workers. Against this backdrop, cities such as London have experienced a dramatic increase of a foreign-born population (May et al., 2007).

Yet migration may or may not match the demands of the local labour markets. Migration has a relatively uneven geography with most migrants moving to cities, especially to certain gateway cities. This leads to local variations in both the size and structure of the immigrant population. Demand for immigrants' skills and labour can vary considerably across regions and localities depending on the existence of regional industry clusters, the availability of local skills and regional demographical trends. A fast aging rural population may need health professionals and agricultural workers for their commercial farmland, not engineers and technicians who are better suited to high tech industries in cities (Sumption, 2014). Text box 21 sets out the challenges faced by migrants in entering local labour markets.

Text box 21

Challenges migrants face entering local labour markets[4]

- **Unemployment**

- **Underemployment** - employment that does not correspond to the migrants' skills and qualifications, leading to deskilling.

- **Concentration of migrant workers in particular sectors** and industries, especially unskilled services, construction, healthcare, domestic work.

- **Qualifications not recognized**

- **Lack of language skills**

- **Lack of business and social networks**

- **Discrimination**

- **Loss of motivation:** The transition from a native to a foreign labour market can be a lengthy one. During this process of trial and error, motivation can deteriorate while skills depreciate.

- **Additional obstacles:** As recent arrivals in a local area, immigrants are more susceptible to the indirect factors which can prevent people from accessing work, such as exclusion from important social networks, geographical isolation in cheaper housing areas and other issues which derive from relative social exclusion. Financial pressures may encourage migrants to take the most immediately available and accessible jobs to ensure a living, even if these jobs are not at a level commensurate with their skills and experience.

- **Exploitation in the informal economy**, including lack of insurance, forced labour, low wages, poor working conditions, virtual absence of social protection, denial of freedom, and of association and union rights.

---

4   Organisation for Economic Co-operation and Development (OECD), *Immigration to Integration: Local Solutions to a Global Challenge* (Paris, 2006).

WORLD MIGRATION
REPORT 2015
Migrants and Cities:
New Partnerships
to Manage Mobility

133

Role of city governments

City governments have multiple roles and can facilitate migrants' labour market inclusion in more than one way:

As policymaker, cities can include low-skilled migrant workers into the political discourse of "competitive"/"creative" cities, highlighting their contribution to the economic base of globally oriented cities (May et al., 2007). Cities can facilitate the recognition of foreign degrees and qualifications and provide migrants with information about the local labour market.

As mediators, cities can create partnerships between various local stakeholders involved in migrants' labour market insertion and overcome policy fragmentation at the local level. In fact, the wide variety of different stakeholders involved at the local level in supporting the integration of immigrants into the labour market to some extent reflects the diversity of barriers which immigrants face.

Key stakeholders for labour market insertion that cities should liaise with include:

- **Public employment service**

- **Civil society actors, including non-governmental organizations,** which are often the main providers of supportive environments and individualized one-stop shop approaches

- **Colleges and vocational schools**

- **Employers**

- **Local chambers of commerce** which can play the part of "not-for-profit" brokers between employers and employees

- **Not-for-profit private sector**, including social enterprises, local development companies and community foundations

- **Trade unions**

- **Immigrant associations**.

City-led employment initiatives are found in all areas of policy concerns such as social inclusion, community development, entrepreneurship assistance, education and training. These services are often relatively small scale, linked to a limited target group and delivered in a single location. However, training institutions and non-governmental organizations often operate without up-to-date information about labour market needs, hence providing relatively generic labour market advice. There is a lot of duplication in services among organizations who lack expertise in the local labour market and links with employment services. This can lead to a limited focus on the migrants' perceived lack of personal confidence and job search skills rather than on helping migrants to understand and respond to local demands (OECD, 2006). Given the fast speed of change of the local labour market, organizations need to be aware of the latest labour market demands in order to accurately guide migrants towards realistic employment routes.

As employers, cities can diversify the public workforce and improve the intercultural skills of municipal staff. Public administrations offer essential services for migrants but are often also among the biggest employers in cities. Successful strategies combine a mixture of change in organizational structures, including appointing a representative for integration or finding new cooperation partners, new ways of recruiting employees taking into consideration cultural diversity, and staff intercultural training (Weber, 2012).

As customers of many local businesses, cities can promote diversity in procurement, for example, by subcontracting migrant-led companies or companies with a highly diverse workforce.

See text box 22 for an example of integration measures by the Canton of Vaud, Switzerland.

Text box 22

Cantonal Integration Programme of Vaud, Switzerland: Public policy challenges and objectives

The Canton of Vaud has the third highest proportion of foreign residents (32%), after the Cantons of Geneva and Basel City which have 35 per cent each. Among the 240,741 foreign nationals living in Vaud, 73 per cent are from the European Union. Portuguese and French nationals make up 23 per cent and 17 per cent respectively.[5] Migrant workers and students from all over the world are drawn to the canton for its labour opportunities and universities as well as its favourable fiscal policies and proximity of the international airport of Geneva.

PIC (Programme d'intégration cantonal): A public policy on integration with communes and migrants' associations as partners

Currently all Swiss cantons are implementing the four-year (2014–2017) cantonal integration programmes (PICs) that have been designed to strengthen social cohesion, encourage respect and tolerance among migrants and Swiss residents, and ensure migrant participation in public life. These programmes were developed based on the Federal Act on Foreign Nationals, effective since 1 January 2008, which clearly defines the cooperation between the Confederation and the cantons on migrant integration.[6]

The Cantonal Office for the Integration of Foreigners and Prevention of Racism (Bureau cantonal pour l'intégration des étrangers et la prévention du racisme [BCI]) is responsible for the PIC.[7] It has a strong implementation partnership with the communes including Lausanne, Nyon, Renens, Vevey and Yverdon-les-Bains which have appointed an integration officer who manages the communal integration programme, a "Mini-PIC". The Mini-PICs include measures to provide initial information and advice, language training, coaching for job-seekers, and programmes targeting migrant children, elderly migrants and unemployed migrant women. As

5   Statistique Vaud. See www.scris.vd.ch/
6   Art. 53, paras. 4 and 5, Federal Act on Foreign Nationals (LEtr), 2005. See www.admin.ch/opc/en/classified-compilation/20020232/index.html (Unofficial translation for information purposes only).
     Arts. 2 and 18, Ordonnance sur l'intégration des étrangers, OIE, 2007 (Foreign Nationals Integration Order). See www.admin.ch/opc/fr/classified-compilation/20070995/
7   Programme d'intégration cantonal (PIC) 2014–2017 (Cantonal Integration Programme 2014–2017 of Vaud) is available from the BCI website www.vd.ch/themes/vie-privee/population-etrangere/integration-et-prevention-du-racisme/programme-dintegration-cantonal/

WORLD MIGRATION
REPORT 2015
Migrants and Cities:
New Partnerships
to Manage Mobility

135

information providers with linguistic and cultural skills and migration experience, migrants' associations are increasingly being called upon by government bodies to provide their expertise and representation potential as part of public policies (Matthey and Steiner, 2008).

Integration into the labour market: A cantonal policy priority

In the Canton of Vaud, foreign nationals make up 35 per cent of the working population but represent 52 per cent of job-seekers, possibly due to the mismatch between their education and the requirements of the labour market.[8] The PIC strives to develop measures to assist and support people in their search for employment, by providing them with appropriate training, by promoting ongoing training in companies, by encouraging the recognition of prior learning and by offering guidance in making career choices. The priority target groups for these measures are young people (15 to 18 years old), isolated and/or vulnerable women and refugees.

Efforts are made to enhance cooperation among relevant governmental and private stakeholders. The Canton encourages private sector organizations particularly to develop in-house projects for migrant labour market integration and to engage with other companies and migrant associations.

Contributed by Amina Benkais-Benbrahim, Déléguée à l'intégration et cheffe du BCI, Bureau cantonal pour l'intégration des étrangers et la prévention du racisme, Vaud.

---

8   Statistique Vaud. See www.scris.vd.ch/

Migrant voices

Making new plans for the future: A Syrian refugee in Vienna

The streets were empty and quiet. It was early in the morning when Sipan arrived in Austria. He had fled from the Syrian Arab Republic and decided to go to Austria because his brother had already been living there for three years. In his home country, Sipan lived in a city with about 100,000 inhabitants. Living in Vienna for him means being part of a city which Sipan associates with museums, the Danube and St. Stephen's Cathedral. He feels comfortable in the area he lives in although he does not really like his apartment because it is old and run-down.

Many of Sipan's friends are also from his home country, even his neighbours. He likes to spend his free time in the park close to his apartment and participates in activities of the Syrian community. However, it is not too important to him whether he spends time with Syrians or with other nationalities, as long as it is fun.

Sipan passed his A-levels (British qualification taken at the age of 17–18 years of age) in the Syrian Arab Republic and would like to have them recognized in Austria. "I don't think this would work", he fears, although he thinks that passing an A-level is much harder in his homeland than in Austria. He thinks Austrian education is not as tough as it is in his home country. "In Syria, you have to know entire books by heart", he explains. In Austria, Sipan is attending a school for basic qualifications. He likes going to school and finds the subjects easy. It is the language that is difficult. Sipan is also thinking about starting an apprenticeship though he is not quite sure yet which profession he would like to pursue. Back home, he would be studying at university by now, if it wasn't for the war and the subsequent obligatory military service for young men. He thus had no choice. "Either you run or you die", he sums up.

"Politics give me a headache", Sipan answers when asked if he participates in political activities in Vienna. He stresses he just wants to have a normal life. In Austria, he feels safe and he believes that living a normal life is possible. However, "the police make me nervous", he explains, "I do not trust everyone who works for the authorities." He has been living in Vienna for ten months now. "It would be great to have more opportunities to learn about the Austrian culture and to get to know the people", he wishes. The nineteen-year-old is happy that he can stay in touch with his parents who are still in the Syrian Arab Republic. "I hope they will come to Austria soon", Sipan says. It is time for him to make new plans for the future. What he knows for sure is that he wants to stay in Austria until the situation in the Syrian Arab Republic improves. Maybe he will return to his country someday, but as he is now used to the modern standard of living, he thinks that returning may be difficult.

WORLD MIGRATION
REPORT 2015
Migrants and Cities:
New Partnerships
to Manage Mobility

137

Role of the private sector

Both businesses and governments face similar employment-related challenges in terms of skills shortages and talent mobility and share concerns about economic growth and competitiveness (THP, 2014). The private sector, as a potential employer, can also make a major contribution to migrant inclusion in cities by informing cities about labour market needs and assisting with the design of tailored vocational trainings (OECD, 2006).

Both the private sector and local government can help migrants acquire the vital skills needed for finding work or starting a business, for instance through language teaching, explaining the administration and structures, and guidance for developing contacts and support networks. Other initiatives comprise developing financial instruments to reuse old buildings, including social housing in new private housing development, and negotiating lower mortgages for migrants. Partnerships with information communications technology companies can help cities manage the effects of human mobility and engage in inclusive urban planning through knowledge-sharing and collaborative policymaking. Employers of migrant workers can provide a critical link to the broader community via access to community-based financial or educational resources, such as access to language and financial literacy classes, or information on home ownership and citizenship – all of which can play a pivotal role in successful integration (Koser, 2014).

Cities in developed countries have fostered public–private partnerships in sectors such as health care, education, energy, transport and welfare but these have not, to date, specifically targeted migrants. Given the multiple benefits that can be shared among migrants, cities and businesses, initiatives similar to the efforts of Rotterdam to connect migrants and their potential private sector employers (see text box 23) are multiplying in cities such as Auckland, Copenhagen, Halifax, London and Wuppertal in Germany (Cities of Migration, 2012).

Text box 23

Business–city partnerships in Rotterdam, the Netherlands

- **Businesses** are increasingly struggling to fill skills gaps from within their local labour market. The Organisation for Economic Co-operation and Development (OECD) 2012 survey found that one in four employers are unable to find the right people to fill positions in their company. Tapping into the migrant labour force more effectively could help alleviate this problem.

- **Cities** are faced with the challenge of effectively integrating migrants, including easing access to the labour market. Capitalizing on the skills migrants have to offer reduces the level of unemployment in the city whilst allowing migrants to contribute to its economic and development.

- **Migrants** need employment, thus contributing to the local economy and actively participating in their new community whilst also earning an income.

The Hague Process on Refugees and Migration (THP), a non-profit foundation, has designed a project in the city of Rotterdam to help create a formal partnership between the city and the private sector in order to improve labour market outcomes in the city and increase migrant community participation in the labour market. The business community in the Rotterdam region is to participate in addressing labour shortages and skills gaps through the migrant community. Based on recommendations and outcomes of direct discussions with the business community, models and measures are drawn up whereby labour and skills shortages can be addressed in part by making migrants in the labour pool more employable. Specifically, the THP creates a knowledge-base of labour and skill shortages and a human resources pool based on direct consultations with business leaders, migrants and their associations. Through the partnership, the most viable solutions can be found and put in place.

The THP business-city partnership project helps upskill migrants to enter the labour market, leading to further economic growth in the city. Businesses in the city are assisted in filling skills and labour gaps and, at the same time, expanding their employee pool to include skills offered by migrants. This leads to greater efficiency and increased productivity in the company. In this way, the city benefits from increased integration and access to jobs by migrants. This reduces the potential cost to the welfare system that migrants could incur. Similarly, migrants themselves become more active participants in their host communities and contribute to the city.

Based on the contribution by Nava Hinrichs, Managing Director, The Hague Process on Refugees and Migration

4.3.3. Migrant entrepreneurship[9]

Migrant entrepreneurs in urban areas contribute to their own socioeconomic integration as well as to the development of the local economy. Policies aimed at providing information, networks, training and recruitment can support this process.

Impact of migrant entrepreneurship

Generally immigrant entrepreneurship tends to be concentrated in urban areas, especially ethnic enclaves (European Commission, 2008). Immigrant entrepreneurship can be an efficient means of socioeconomic integration of the migrants themselves, while at the same time contributing to the local economy. The evidence is mixed, however, in terms of the impacts of entrepreneurship on migrant integration. In the United States and the Netherlands, entrepreneurship has been shown to contribute to the socioeconomic integration of immigrants (Irastorza, 2010; Teder and Golik, 2006) especially among those who take up entrepreneurship out of necessity as an alternative to unemployment or bad working conditions. In Germany, there is also evidence that immigrant entrepreneurs have higher incomes than employed immigrants (Constant, Shachmurove and Zimmermann, 2007). In Sweden, the opposite is the case

---

9   The information in this section, 4.3.3., including table 3 and text box 24, is based on K. Marchand and M. Siegel, Immigrant Entrepreneurship in Cities, 2014. Background Paper for the *World Migration Report 2015: Migrants and Cities: New Partnerships to Manage Mobility*, IOM, Geneva.

WORLD MIGRATION
REPORT 2015
Migrants and Cities:
New Partnerships
to Manage Mobility

139

(Hammarstedt, 2001; Hjerm, 2004). It may be that the welfare state in Sweden has an impact on who becomes an entrepreneur as does the level of discrimination towards immigrants in the labour market and the bureaucracy involved in opening a business (Irastorza, 2010). The correlation between entrepreneurship and economic growth is quite strong (Audretsch and Thurik, 2004; Naudé, 2010) but only for opportunity entrepreneurs, as opposed to the necessity entrepreneurs who have no other alternative to unemployment.

The question of whether migrants are more entrepreneurial has been an area of study (Kloosterman, van der Leun and Rath, 1998). Research from the United States on the significant role played by migrants in high-tech entrepreneurships note that positive diversity effects will be most likely observed in "knowledge-intensive" activities and industries (Fujita and Weber, 2003). Close to a quarter of patent applications in the United States are made by migrants, a proportion that is roughly twice their share of the population (Hunt and Gauthier-Loiselle, 2009). This success is put down to positive self-selection in terms of skills and entrepreneurial abilities (Borjas, 1986) and translocal networks. Heterogeneity in backgrounds, skills and culture can also lead to the increased generation of ideas through the complementarities of individuals coming together (Berliant and Fujita, 2009). In comparison with the native population, the share of people holding a degree in science or engineering is also much higher among the immigrant population.

On a more global level, the 2012 Global Entrepreneurship Monitor survey attempted to measure the innovation of enterprises by the number of new products or services they introduced across sixty-nine countries and whether the enterprises in question were owned by a migrant or non-migrant. Analyses of the survey results could not find significant differences between the innovativeness of migrant and non-migrant entrepreneurs (Vorderwülbecke, 2012). Preliminary research in South Africa shows that immigrant entrepreneurship creates opportunities that have important implications for the country's economy. By contributing to job creation and innovation, immigrant entrepreneurs can play a role in the reduction of inequality and poverty and be a positive factor for the economic growth of South Africa (Kalitanyi and Visser, 2010; Tengeh et al., 2012).

Urban policies for immigrant entrepreneurship

Effective policies can help attract potential entrepreneurs from abroad, provide an attractive environment for new start-up companies and provide practical support programmes for potential entrepreneurs in general and specifically for migrants. As immigrant entrepreneurs are far from being a homogeneous group, a wide variety of policies and support programmes need to be developed to address the different strengths, weaknesses and needs.

Given the growing interest in migrant entrepreneurship and economic growth, an increasing number of countries are introducing specific policy measures for this group (see table 3). However, these types of policies focus on migrants with start-up capital and who are willing to invest in the country of destination. A large proportion of immigrant entrepreneurs do not qualify for this type of visa, most likely due to a lack of capital and experience, and so they usually enter the country through another channel. However, a significant number of migrant entrepreneurs are also pushed into self-employment by a lack of other options.

Table 3 **Admission criteria of immigration policies for self-employment and entrepreneurship in OECD countries**

Admission Criteria	Countries using Criteria	
	Self-employment	Business Investment
Experience	Australia, Austria, Belgium, Canada, Denmark, Finland, Germany, Greece, Ireland, Italy, Japan, the Netherlands, New Zealand, Norway, Portugal, Spain, Sweden, Switzerland	Australia, Canada, New Zealand (unless investment is over a threshold where no experience is required)
Minimum Investment	Czech Republic, New Zealand, United Kingdom (It is generally required to submit proof of financial resources for living expenses and set-up of the business)	Australia, Canada, France, Greece, Ireland, Republic of Korea, the Netherlands, New Zealand, Portugal, Spain, United Kingdom, United States
Business Plan	Austria, Belgium, Denmark, Finland, France, Germany, Ireland, the Netherlands, New Zealand, Norway, Poland, Spain, Sweden, Switzerland	Greece, Ireland, the Netherlands
Restriction of Field of Activity	Australia, Canada, Czech Republic, Denmark, Japan	Australia, Republic of Korea
Show Relevance to Local Economy	Austria, Belgium, Denmark, Finland, Germany, Greece, Ireland, the Netherlands, Poland, Switzerland	Greece, Ireland, Portugal, United States

Successful migrant entrepreneur support programmes

For immigrants already in the country of destination, there may be more practically oriented policies and programmes at the local level. These initiatives may be planned nationally but implemented at the city level and involve support programmes available in various cities to address the different needs of potential entrepreneurs, especially for new business start-ups. In addition, some cities offer specific programmes for migrants in terms of language learning, access to credit and country- and city-specific human capital. However, in general, immigrants are much less likely than natives to take advantage of such programmes. They rather turn to informal support and rely on their social, often ethnic, networks when opening a business.

Immigrant entrepreneurs often face many obstacles that include administrative challenges, complex procedures and criteria to be fulfilled in order to set up a business. These might include financial obligations, tax-related requirements, labour regulations, social security regulations, safety and health requirements as well as environmental factors. They often face language barriers and are disadvantaged in terms of country-specific knowledge (Desiderio, 2014).

WORLD MIGRATION
REPORT 2015
Migrants and Cities:
New Partnerships
to Manage Mobility

141

Migrant entrepreneurs can benefit from general programmes and those intended especially for migrants. An example of a multi-faceted programme for migrants is given in text box 24. Such programmes may comprise one or more of the elements of information provision, networking, mentoring and counselling, training, investment and partnership.

Information Provision: Migrants may well lack knowledge of local business opportunities and procedures, which in turn might hinder investments. In order to encourage new start-ups, many cities offer information provided by administrative units, chambers of commerce, business associations, labour unions and private organizations. Information is also made available through events, websites, telephone hotlines and information sheets catering for specific trades, which are especially common start-ups.

Networking: Networking organizations provide an opportunity for potential and new immigrant entrepreneurs to meet other entrepreneurs, either immigrant or native, make local contacts with suppliers and potential customers, discuss potential partnerships and find relevant business partners. These networking meetings can be in person or through online services.

Mentoring and Counselling: The new entrepreneur is matched up with a mentor from possibly the same business sector, ethnic background or language abilities for a limited period of time. During this period, frequent interaction takes place on a variety of relevant issues. This type of programme is common, targeting immigrant entrepreneurs or entrepreneurs in disadvantaged urban areas.

Training: Entrepreneurship training programmes help aspiring entrepreneurs to gain the relevant knowledge and skills necessary for starting up a successful business; these include market research, business plan development, administrative support and business management. The provision of information on financing opportunities is critical.

Investment: As access to credit is one of the major challenges faced by migrant entrepreneurs, this type of programme is crucial for many new businesses. A business plan is scrutinized by a team of experts with regard to multiple factors that are determined by each organization individually. Only the most promising proposals can be offered financing for a limited time frame.

Partnerships: A partner organization can take the form of a business incubator or a business angel. A business angel invests capital in projects for financial return. They can be involved in developing the business project and managing it, especially in the early stages. There are business "incubators", who provide sponsored networking opportunities with local employers, as well as support with administrative procedures. In Chicago, for example, public and private-sector groups have established several services aimed at supporting migrant entrepreneurs. Both these types of support arrangements help maximize the contributions immigrant entrepreneurs can make to the city's economy.

Ethnic Entrepreneurship Programme in Glasgow, Scotland, United Kingdom

Glasgow has the highest ethnic minority population in Scotland and the number of ethnic minorities living in the city has increased from 31,510 in 2001 to 68,684 in 2012. The contribution of immigrant businesses to the Scottish economy overall, and especially to Glasgow, is significant. In addition, many of the immigrants had previously run businesses in their home country and wished to do the same in Glasgow. Based on this, the Ethnic Entrepreneurship Programme was established in 2005 by the Business Gateway. The Glasgow Business Gateway employs a specialist ethnic adviser to investigate and tackle barriers to self-employment and to help promote strategies for integration into wider Scottish society through business creation. The target group of the programme are recognized refugees, Scots from ethnic minorities, EU immigrants as well as individuals on a post-study visa who all face common challenges in entering the labour market and for whom self-employment is a viable option. The Ethnic Entrepreneurship Programme offers a wide variety of services all aimed at the support and training of potential new immigrant entrepreneurs. It is a low-tech approach where personal relationships and trust are built up over an extended period of time.

4.4
MIGRANTS AS AGENTS OF INTERNATIONAL DEVELOPMENT

Migrants can support development back home through partnerships with countries of origin. Decentralized development approaches, for instance, cooperation between cities of the host and sending countries or programmes which draw on diaspora support can help harness the potential of migrants as agents for development.

Decentralized development approaches

Migrants can help promote development back home with their ideas, skills, labour, remittances and investments, as temporary foreign workers, permanent settlers as well as remitters and investors in the diaspora. Diaspora communities abroad also help create boomtowns in their countries of origin through remittances, investments and physical returns.

Decentralized cooperation through, for example, city twinning, is an approach to development cooperation that puts local governments at the centre of development efforts by utilizing local-to-local transnational ties and by involving public, private and civil society actors as well as migrants. Policies which allow the devolution of budgetary responsibility to municipal or city authorities foster such twinning as cities are able to negotiate their own arrangements across borders and/or with migrant and diaspora groups.

In Europe, cities and municipalities of different sizes and some border region municipalities have forged city twinning mainly with Morocco, Turkey and Suriname as migrant-sending countries. The most common form is based on an agreement between two local governments aiming to work together and encourage

WORLD MIGRATION
REPORT 2015
Migrants and Cities:
New Partnerships
to Manage Mobility

143

exchange of information and activities between their staff members (Van Ewijk, 2008). The main objectives include contributing to the local development and capacity-building of both local government bodies. These twinning arrangements seek to promote mutual understanding between migrant and host societies, social cohesion, and integration of migrants through contacts and the exchange of information. Activities can range from cultural exchange programmes to support programmes on waste management, water and sanitation, housing and public administration. The objectives may vary, for instance, the main concern may be migrant integration efforts in the destination countries rather than the intention of bringing measurable economic or trade benefits. Alternatively, the goal may be learning and benefits for the country of origin, especially if the twinning has an "aid" element.

The literature on city-to-city partnerships considers mutuality as one of the aims but the notion is not generally made explicit. As such an evaluative framework to gauge the success or failure of such partnerships is not established and "benefits" for municipalities in the destination countries remain unclear in practice (Van Ewijk, 2013). Many local governments in the Netherlands are pulling out due in part to budget cuts. Another challenge that municipalities in both origin and destination countries face is that they are at different stages of the decentralization process and have different budgets and opportunities for action at their disposal (ibid.).

Broadly, there are numerous and growing translocal or intercity cooperation examples that are not framed by city twinning arrangements but focus on harnessing migration's benefits for local development. For example, in response to the call for new, broader partnerships, including migrants and their associations, as reflected in the discussions on the post-2015 development agenda, the European Commission established the Joint Migration and Development Initiative (JMDI) which the UN and the International Organization for Migration (IOM) support. Its aim is to facilitate local development by building translocal links of migrants and empowering local authorities in partnership with civil society and other small scale actors in European Union Member States and their counterparts in lower income countries of migrant origin (JMDI, 2013).

Joint Migration and Development Initiative[10]

The view of migration as a local development tool is gaining more support than ever before as it can sustain local development and enhance the dynamism of origin and destination communities of migrants. Migrants are allies of cities and local communities as agents of positive change as they contribute to the social and economic development through the various resources they possess. Furthermore, migrants and diasporas are building development links between cities as they assert a transnational presence which changes the local environment of the population in territories of origin and destination.

The experience of the JMDI has shown that the most successful and sustainable interventions to link migration and development are those that have been developed by diaspora groups having a strong relationship with local governments in countries of origin and destination. Where migrants and diaspora interventions

10 This section is based on the contribution provided by Cécile Riallant, Programme Manager, Joint Migration and Development Initiative (JMDI), an EC and Swiss-funded global programme led by UNDP and implemented in close partnership with IOM, ILO, UNHRC, UN Women, UNITAR and UNFPA.

are not aligned with local needs and capacities, the mid-term to long-term impact on development is uncertain. The JMDI has, since 2013, engaged in the scaling-up of 16 promising initiatives of local authorities in eight countries around the world. The JMDI strives to take into account the migration continuum and how this has an impact on policies and practices which should be put in place both in sending and receiving communities. Some of the preliminary lessons learnt from this global programme are described below.

Migration needs good local governance to achieve development impact:

Migrant contributions to local development depend, to a large extent, on the relationship they establish with local actors and their ability to cope with the potential shortcomings of their local institutional environment. More often than not, migrant activities are limited to marginal associative fields and rely on autonomous and direct personal relationships, with few interactions with local stakeholders. For the local development impact of migration to flourish, it is essential to acknowledge and integrate migrants' contributions into local development by creating a conducive and inclusive environment. Essentially, this is about applying the principles of good local governance to migration.

Increasingly cities are compelled to reflect on the needs, rights and resources that are made available to newcomers in the host society. In the case of returning migrants, cities are looking into facilitating their reintegration into the local labour market and building on the potential skills and networks acquired during their migratory experience.

Cities are best placed to act as the focal point that brings together the voices, needs and expertise of all local actors. This includes providing migrants with a space for their opinions to be heard, establishing transparent frameworks that enhance trust between local stakeholders and migrant associations, and increasing the capacity of migrants to develop projects (be they profit driven or philanthropic) with new partners in communities of origin and destination. Successful examples of such practices exist in many cities around the world.

Articulated strategies to harness the benefits of migration for local development need also to strongly look into upholding the political, economic, social and cultural rights of migrants. Cities' initiatives to promote integration or reintegration (in the case of returning migrants) are therefore highly linked to preserving and enhancing the capacities of migrants as development actors.

Migration needs to be integrated into local development planning:

Enhancing the contribution of migration to local development requires more than marginal support or subsidies from cities. It demands that cities understand the specificities of migrant resources and how they take shape at the local level. Cities can then develop a strategy to reach out to the relevant stakeholders and articulate migrant activities with local development actions to maximize the positive impacts that migration can provide in terms of social cohesion, cultural diversity and economic development and so minimize the negative consequences.

WORLD MIGRATION
REPORT 2015
Migrants and Cities:
New Partnerships
to Manage Mobility

145

Taking this one step further, it is in the interest of cities concerned by high migration flows to firmly engage in improving policy coherence in city planning by mainstreaming migration across the board, given that many sectoral policies can affect or can be affected by migration. This process is essential to move from punctual or isolated interventions towards sustained and coherent city planning, considering all the dimensions of the impact of migration on local development. Figures 7 and 8 summarize how the local development cycle can be articulated with the migration continuum and provides snapshots of possible policy interventions.

For increased positive impact, vertical policy coherence (between local, national and international levels) should also be ensured since, to date, this seems to be one of the most important obstacles to the implementation of effective interventions to connect migration and development.

Figure 7   **Local development cycle**

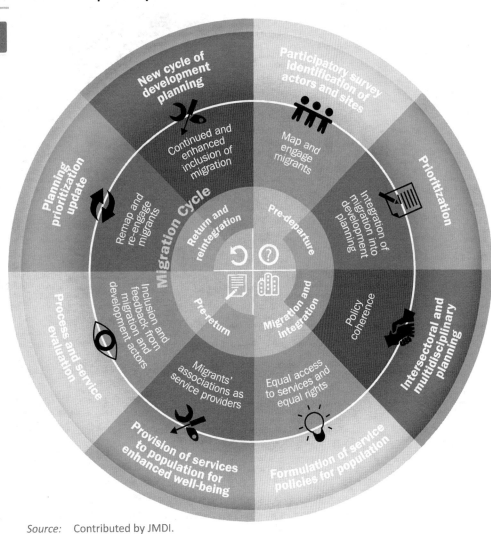

Source: Contributed by JMDI.

Figure 8   **Migrants as a bridge between cities**

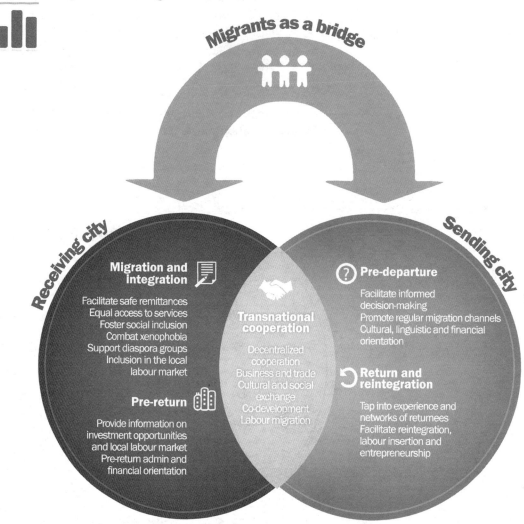

Source: Contributed by JMDI.

Cities need to be connected internationally along migratory corridors:

City-to-city links are often created or maintained due to the presence of large migrant populations connecting them. If they can share a common vision and establish peer-to-peer cooperation, this represents a formidable development opportunity. Whilst local authorities are at the heart of decentralized partnerships for development, migrant and diasporas communities can play an important role in supporting these partnerships and in facilitating or undertaking some of the related activities. Specifically, migrants and their associations can connect and provide expertise and information on the communities of origin, and in this way facilitate economic relations between cities.

In Senegal, for example, a local government is helping to build a transnational cooperation process between the cities of Dakar and Venice by partnering with the Senegalese Confederation for the Promotion of Small and Medium Enterprises and Entrepreneurship among Migrants which provides support for Senegalese

WORLD MIGRATION
REPORT 2015
Migrants and Cities:
New Partnerships
to Manage Mobility

147

diaspora businessmen and women with business investment opportunities in Dakar.[11]

Cities with strong and long lasting migratory connections also have an interest in cooperating and possibly in coordinating their actions along the migration continuum. A city of origin can provide information on labour market conditions and needs at the destination end which can greatly facilitate the integration of migrants and bring economic benefits for the host community. Very few cities, however, are reaping the benefits of these connections through migration. Dialogue among mayors, such as the Mayoral Forum on Mobility, Migration and Development held in Barcelona in 2014, has the potential for facilitating the connections and transnational actions of cities building on the development potential of migration.

Cities of origin of migrants could also be an active participant in mainstreaming migration into local development planning. They can proactively plan their work in order to first address the various concerns of their residents whose family members are migrants working overseas. These efforts will also increase the cities' understanding of the specific resources of their migrants. Cities can then develop a partnership with migrants and their families and formulate jointly concrete action plans to maximize the positive impacts that migration can provide in terms of social cohesion, cultural diversity and economic development and minimize the negative consequences. Naga, a city of 200,000 inhabitants in central Philippines, is such an example. Its local government pioneers the mainstreaming of migration and development into its local planning process through various project activities in conjunction with local research partners and international agencies including IOM (see text box 25).

Text box 25

Mainstreaming migration into local development planning in Naga City, the Philippines

Capacity-building through participatory planning

A multi-sectoral technical working group was organized in early 2011 to build up local capacity in migration and development mainstreaming. The working group comprised members of the City Council, officials and representatives from the national government, academia, the local church, the federation of civil society organizations (the Naga City People's Council) as well as the banking sector and the chamber of commerce.

The regional unit of the Overseas Workers Welfare Administration provided information on the number of Filipino contractual workers (Overseas Filipino Workers or OFWs) from the city, and the Bangko Sentral ng Pilipinas (the Central Bank of the Philippines) submitted an estimate of the remittances that are sent. These were cross-referenced with local sources such as the Community-Based Monitoring System, a citywide survey which the city government was also implementing for the first time.

---

11 This transnational migration and development cooperation process is supported by the Joint Migration Development Initiative project, "Linking migrants, local authorities, investors and economic actors for local development".

These secondary data were supplemented with a series of workshops where concerns facing the Overseas Filipino sector were discussed with OFWs' families, their children and school counsellors, the business sector, the urban poor and local banks. (The "Overseas Filipino sector" is an encompassing term that, in addition to the OFWs, includes Nagueños, who have become citizens or permanent residents abroad, as well as the undocumented migrants.)

A series of citywide consultations were then held to discuss the research and workshop results with the participants of the Overseas Filipino sectoral workshops. A prioritization exercise enabled the participants to identify which programmes, projects and activities should be pursued by the city government.

Finally, an initial draft of the local Comprehensive Development Plan (CDP) was presented for review at a National Stakeholders Consultation in Manila in September 2011. The CDP included the vision statement that highlighted the developmental impacts of migration, the city migration profile, the Overseas Filipinos subsector plan and the local development investment programme. Based on the suggestions made, a final version of the CDP was drawn up and endorsed by the City Development Council in June 2012 before being adopted by the Sangguniang Panlungsod (the legislative body of the City Council) in November 2012.

Institution building

Realizing the immense value of the work done by the technical working group, Mayor John G. Bongat decided to create an institutional home for the mainstreaming programme. Through Executive Order No. 2012-006, the City Advisory Committee on Overseas Filipinos was born, tasked, among others, to provide expert advice and strategic guidance to the city government in the continuing effort to mainstream migration into local planning and policymaking, programme development and project implementation in Naga City.

Next steps

The city's pioneering effort did not escape the attention of both national and international migration agencies. In 2013, the City Planning and Development Office was approached by the Commission on Filipinos Overseas to help the Province of Pangasinan in scaling up the Naga City experience at the provincial level. The successful partnership led to another collaboration, which will position the city to become the first Philippine local government to offer online and mobile payment systems and services in 2015 in a bid to capture Filipino diaspora philanthropy and investments. Since April 2014, it has been helping 15 provinces, cities and towns in the Bicol Region develop their own capacity on migration and developing planning, institution building and service development.

Contributed by Wilfredo B. Prilles Jr., Coordinator, City Planning and Development Office, Naga City, the Philippines

WORLD MIGRATION
REPORT 2015
Migrants and Cities:
New Partnerships
to Manage Mobility

149

Working towards a multicultural Seoul: A Vietnamese marriage migrant

"I didn't know a small advertisement would change my life forever," said Pham Thi Quynh Hoa, aged 34, a marriage migrant who moved from Hanoi, Viet Nam to Seoul, Republic of Korea. Quynh Hoa works as a manager in the Multiculturalism Division of Seoul City Hall, "I feel lucky to have a job that I can perform better than the locals".

A wife and mother of two, Quynh Hoa moved to Seoul from Hanoi ten years ago to be with her Korean husband. Quynh Hoa started her masters' degree at Seoul National University with a Korean Government scholarship the year she moved to Seoul. Luckily, the university allowed the couple to live in one of the family residences at the university. "It was a huge financial relief for us, because private housing in Seoul is extremely expensive."

After living in student accommodation for eight years, the family moved to an apartment near the university in 2012. This is when Quynh Hoa experienced discrimination after her landlord found out that his tenants were a so-called multicultural family, "I can put up with occasional discrimination, because there are many Koreans who have been nice to me". Quynh Hoa thinks her background as a migrant has been useful in performing her current job, "I feel lucky to have a job. Maybe this way I can repay what I have received from all the kind people in Korea who have helped me."

At work, Quynh Hoa organizes a classroom-based educational programme to boost understanding of multiculturalism among youth in Seoul. The programme has 35 instructors from 29 countries with different migrant backgrounds, such as migrants by marriage and foreign students, who all regularly visit schools in Seoul, providing classes on multiculturalism, "I am glad to see the efforts of the city of Seoul. They come up with policies and practices in favour of migrants and multicultural families every year".

Even though Quynh Hoa is satisfied with life in Seoul, her heart is still in Hanoi. After her children grow up, she is planning to settle in Hanoi with her husband. "With the degree and work experience I have acquired in Korea, I can have a very good job in Viet Nam. I am most interested in teaching Korean Studies at one of the universities in Hanoi". She beams while saying this, looking hopeful and resolved.

4.5

CONCLUDING REMARKS

There is a clear need to develop effective urban policies to create "opportunity structures" for sustained and inclusive economic growth that empower both migrants and local residents. The number of practices on the ground to tackle urban integration issues and foster participative economic growth among city authorities, urban practitioners, civil society leaders, business development communities, migrant associations and diasporas, mostly in the developed world, are growing fast. There is little evidence as yet, however, that these practices are being systematically captured and translated into higher level policy.

The lack of empirical data is a constraint. There is no common method for analysing the interplay among mobility patterns, demographic transition and urban growth. Empirical data and research remains inadequate to establish the exact nature of the links between migration and urbanization; the traditional dichotomy of rural–urban mobility no longer applies in many parts of the world with the diversification of mobility patterns including circular, temporary, urban–urban migration and international migration. Furthermore, urbanization does not necessarily lead to urban development, nor does it necessarily only occur due to migration.

The term "urban transition" reflects the transformative nature of mobility as a key driver of urban migration. The concept can also encompass the concurrence of urban and rural development as they are closely linked through increasing mobility. Therefore, at a policy level, internal and international migration and urbanization trends need to be factored into labour market strategies as they affect both rural and urban development.

This chapter has examined a growing body of evidence showing the potential and real benefits of well-managed migration for urban growth. Local strategies for migrant inclusion can strengthen the negotiating position of cities seeking to do business with the world. Cities can gain dividends through policies aimed at migrant inclusion which involve attracting skilled migrants, innovators, investors and students, and ensuring the flow of remittances.

WORLD MIGRATION
REPORT 2015
Migrants and Cities:
New Partnerships
to Manage Mobility

151

Migrant voices

A business built on mutual trust and kindness: A migrant entrepreneur in Moscow

Good day! My name is Usman. Currently, I live and work in Moscow. I was born in Uzbekistan and moved with my family to Russia about three years ago. I came to Moscow because I wanted to have more opportunities for personal development. Here, there are many more possibilities than back home, so here I am.

All my life I wanted to start a business which would make people happier. In Moscow, I managed to do exactly that and opened a small zoo for kids. In the beginning, it was not easy. When I was trying to get my business off the ground, I had to deal with fraudsters who tried to cheat me. At the same time, I met a lot of good people, who sincerely tried to help.

One of them was a Russian lady. She helped me with opening and registering my current business. By bringing somebody else into the business, I knew that I was taking some risks. However, I saw that this person also sincerely wanted to create a place where families with kids could come and spend time having fun and interacting with animals. Quite soon, she became my real business partner. I trusted my heart and took some risks. Now, I know that it was the right decision and helped make my dream come true.

Moscow is a very big city. There are a lot of newcomers, migrants from other countries and people from other parts of Russia as well. There are a lot of languages spoken in Moscow, and Russian and English seem to be the most popular. I feel very comfortable and safe in Moscow and I freely communicate with the people who live here. When my kids grow up, they will go to school here in Moscow and have the opportunity to get a good education. As for myself, in the future, I see myself as a happy and successful person.

I have met a lot of people of different nationalities in my life. I believe there are no bad nationalities, but just bad people. It is not fair to judge a whole nation by the actions of one person. Therefore, when anyone says that migrants from Uzbekistan, Kyrgyzstan and Tajikistan are bad, this is simply a prejudice. It may be a result of cultural misunderstanding.

We need to try to get to know more about each other, to better understand each other. We all should try to trust each other and not be afraid of people whose nationality or culture is different from our own. My personal life experience tells me that the world is built on mutual trust and kindness, no matter where you live and no matter the nationalities of the people around you.

REFERENCES

African Centre for Cities

2014   *Urban Informality and Migrant Entrepreneurship in Southern African Cities*. Conference Report, 10–11 February 2014. African Centre for Cities, University of Cape Town. Available from http://imrc.ca/wp-content/uploads/2013/11/Cape-Town-Informality-Conference-Report.pdf

Americas Society / Council of the Americas (AS/COA)

2014   *Immigrants & Competitive Cities,* Get the Facts Series. AS/COA, New York. Available from www.as-coa.org/sites/default/files/ImmigrantsandCompetitiveCities.pdf

Audretsch, D. and R. Thurik

2004   A model of the entrepreneurial economy. *International Journal of Entrepreneurship Education*, 2(2): 143–166.

Awumbila, M.

2014   Linkages between Urbanization, Rural-Urban Migration and Poverty Outcomes in Africa. Background Paper for the *World Migration Report 2015, Migrants and Cities: New Partnerships to Manage Mobility.* IOM, Geneva.

Awumbila, M. and E. Ardayfio-Schandorf

2008   Gendered poverty, migration and livelihood strategies of female porters in Accra, Ghana. *Norwegian Journal of Geography*, 62(3): 171–179.

Awumbila, M., G. Owusu and J. K. Teye

2014   Can Rural-Urban Migration into Slums Reduce Poverty? Evidence from Ghana. Working Paper 13. Migrating out of Poverty Research Programme Consortium, University of Sussex, Brighton. Available from http://r4d.dfid.gov.uk/Output/196216/

Basa, C., L. Villamil and V. de Guzman

2009   Migration, local development and governance in small towns: two examples from the Philippines. Working Paper No. 17. Working Paper Series on Rural-Urban Interactions and Livelihood Strategies, International Institute for Environment and Development (IIED), London. Available from http://pubs.iied.org/pdfs/10576IIED.pdf

Bedford, R.D. and G. Hugo

2011   Migration, urbanisation and new diaspora: reflections on future migration in the Pacific. Presentation at the Pathways, Circuits and Crossroads Conference, Immigration in the Second Decade of the 21st Century, Wellington, 12–13 December 2011.

Berliant, M. and M. Fujita

2009   The dynamics of knowledge diversity and economic growth. Conference Paper, 56th Annual North American Meeting, Regional Science Association International, San Francisco, 18–19 November 2009.

WORLD MIGRATION
REPORT 2015
Migrants and Cities:
New Partnerships
to Manage Mobility

153

Bhagat, R.B.
2014   Urban Migration Trends, Challenges and Opportunities in India.
            Background Paper for the *World Migration Report 2015: Migrants
            and Cities: New Partnerships to Manage Mobility*. IOM, Geneva.

Borjas, G.J.
1986   The Self-employment Experience of Immigrants. *The Journal of
            Human Resources*, 21(4): 485–506.

Castaldo, A., P. Deshingkar and A. McKay
2012   Internal migration, remittances and poverty: Evidence from Ghana
            and India. Working Paper No 7. Migrating out of Poverty Research Pro-
            gramme Consortium, University of Sussex, Brighton. Available from
            http://migratingoutofpoverty.dfid.gov.uk/files/file.php?name=wp7-
            internal-migration-remittances-and-poverty.pdf&site=354

Chan, K.W.
2012   Crossing the 50 Percent Population Rubicon: Can China Urbanize to
            Prosperity? *Eurasian Geography and Economics*, 53(1): 63–86.

Cities of Migration
2012   *Good Ideas from Successful Cities*: Municipal Leadership on Immigrant
            Integration. Maytree Foundation, Toronto. Available from http://
            citiesofmigration.ca/wp-content/uploads/2012/03/Municipal_
            Report_Main_Report2.pdf

Constant, A., Y. Shachmurove and K. F. Zimmermann
2007   What Makes an Entrepreneur and Does it Pay? Native Men, Turks and
            Other Migrants in Germany. *International Migration*, 45(4): 71–100.

Crush, J.
2012   *Migration, Development and Urban Food Security*. Urban Food
            Security Series No. 9, Queen's University and the African Food
            Security Urban Network, Kingston, Ontario, and Cape Town. Available
            from www.afsun.org/wp-content/uploads/2013/09/AFSUN_9.pdf

Das, S., C. Ghate and P.E. Robertson
2015   Remoteness, Urbanization, and India's Unbalanced Growth. *World
            Development*, 66: 572–587.

Deshingkar, P.
2011   Migration, remote rural areas and chronic poverty in India. ODI Working
            Paper 323 and CPRC Working Paper 163. Overseas Development
            Institute, London, and Chronic Poverty Research Centre, University of
            Manchester, Manchester. Available from www.odi.org/sites/odi.org.
            uk/files/odi-assets/publications-opinion-files/5510.pdf

Deshingkar, P. and J. Farrington (eds.)
2009   *Circular Migration and Multilocational Livelihood Strategies in Rural
            India*. Oxford University Press, New Delhi.

Desiderio, M.V.
2014   *Policies to Support Immigrant Entrepreneurship*. Migration Policy
            Institute, Washington, D.C. Available from www.migrationpolicy.org/
            research/policies-support-immigrant-entrepreneurship.

Ernst & Young Global Limited

2014   *Evaluation of the impact of the free movement of EU citizens at local level. Final Report*. European Commission, DG Justice, Brussels. Available from http://ec.europa.eu/justice/citizen/files/dg_just_eva_free_mov_final_report_27.01.14.pdf

European Commission

2008   *Supporting Entrepreneurial Diversity in Europe - Ethnic Minority Entrepreneurship / Migrant Entrepreneurship*. Conclusions and Recommendations of the European Commission's Network "Ethnic Minority Businesses". European Commission, Brussels.

Florida, R.

2002   *The Rise of the Creative Class: And How It's Transforming Work, Leisure, and Everyday Life*. Basic Books, New York.

Friedmann, J.

2005   *China's Urban Transition*. University of Minnesota Press, Minneapolis and London.

Fujita, M. and S. Weber

2003   Strategic Immigration Policies and Welfare in Heterogeneous Countries. Institute of Economic Research Working Papers, Kyoto University, Kyoto. Available from http://alfresco.uclouvain.be/alfresco/download/attach/workspace/SpacesStore/1c3438bc-6679-4f4f-844c-96f335a95c64/coredp_2003_95.pdf

Glaeser, E. and A. Joshi-Ghani

2013   Rethinking Cities: Toward Shared Prosperity. Economic Premise No. 126. World Bank, Washington, D.C. Available from http://siteresources.worldbank.org/EXTPREMNET/Resources/EP126.pdf

Guranton, G.

2014   Growing through Cities in Developing Countries. Policy Research Working Paper Series, No. 6818. World Bank, Washington D.C. Available from http://elibrary.worldbank.org/doi/pdf/10.1596/1813-9450-6818

Hammarstedt, M.

2001   Immigrant self-employment in Sweden - its variations and some possible determinants. *Entrepreneurship & Regional Development*, 13(2): 147–161.

Hjerm, M.

2004   Immigrant entrepreneurship in the Swedish welfare state. *Sociology*, 38(4): 739–756.

Hoang, X., T. Dinh and T. Nguyen

2008   Urbanization and rural development in Viet Nam's Mekong Delta: Livelihood transformations in three fruit-growing settlements. Working Paper 14, Working Paper Series on Rural-Urban Interactions and Livelihood Strategies. International Institute for Environment and Development (IEED), London. Available from http://pubs.iied.org/pdfs/10555IIED.pdf

WORLD MIGRATION
REPORT 2015
Migrants and Cities:
New Partnerships
to Manage Mobility

155

Hunt, J. and M. Gauthier-Loiselle
2009   How much does immigration boost innovation? IZA Discussion Paper
          No 3921. Institute for the Study of Labour (IZA), Bonn. Available from
          www.econstor.eu/bitstream/10419/35709/1/589802992.pdf

Irastorza, N.
2010   *Born Entrepreneurs? Immigrant Self-Employment in Spain.*
          International Migration, Integration and Social Cohesion in Europe
          (IMISCOE) Dissertations. Amsterdam University Press, Amsterdam.

Jedwab, R., D. Gollin and D. Vollrath,
2013   Urbanization with and without Industrialization. Working Paper Series
          IIEP-WP 2014–1, Institute for International Economic Policy (IIEP),
          The George Washington University, Washington, D.C. Available from
          www.gwu.edu/~iiep/assets/docs/papers/Jedwab_IIEPWP_2014-1.
          pdf

Joint Migration Development Initiative (JMDI)
2013   *Mapping Local Authorities' Practices in the Area of Migration and
          Development.* JMDI, Brussels. Available from www.migration4devel-
          opment.org/content/mapping-local-authorities%E2%80%99-practic-
          es-area-migration-and-development-new-jmdi-report

Jolly, S. and H. Reevew
2005   *Gender and Migration: Overview Report.* Institute of Development
          Studies, Brighton. Available from www.bridge.ids.ac.uk/reports/CEP-
          Mig-OR.pdf.

Kalitanyi, V. and K. Visser
2010   African Immigrants in South Africa: Job takers or job creators. *South
          African Journal of Economic and Management Sciences*, 13(4): 376–
          390.

Kemeny, T.
2013   Immigrant Diversity and Economic Development in Cities: A Critical
          Review. SERC Discussion Paper 149. Spatial Economics Research
          Centre, London School of Economics and Political Science, London.
          Available   from   www.spatialeconomics.ac.uk/textonly/SERC/
          publications/download/sercdp0149.pdf

Kerr, J., P. McDaniel and M. Guinan
2014   *Reimagining the Midwest: Immigration Initiatives and the Capacity
          of Local Leadership.* The Chicago Council on Global Affairs and the
          American Immigration Council, Chicago and Washington, D.C.
          Available from www.thechicagocouncil.org/publication/reimagining-
          midwest-immigration-initiatives-and-capacity-local-leadership

Kloosterman, R.C., J. van de Leun and J. Rath
1998   Across the border: immigrants' economic opportunities, social capital
          and informal business activities. *Journal of Ethnic and Migration
          Studies*, 24(2): 249–268.

Koser, K.
2013   The business case for migration: Engaging with the private sector
            to encourage more proactive migration policies in the interest of
            economic growth and prosperity. *Migration Policy Practice*, III (5):
            14–17. Available from http://publications.iom.int/bookstore/free/Mi
            grationPolicyPracticeJournal13_3Dec.pdf

Massey, D., W. Axinn and D. Ghimire
2007   Environmental Change and Out-migration: Evidence from Nepal.
            Research Report 07–615, Population Studies Center, Institute for
            Social Research, University of Michigan, Ann Arbor. Available from
            www.psc.isr.umich.edu/pubs/pdf/rr07-615.pdf

Matthey, L. and B. Steiner
2008   *Nous, moi – les autres. Les associations de migrants et la formation
            de l'identité : Une approche internaliste.* Commission fédérale pour
            les questions de migration, Berne. Available from www.ekm.admin.
            ch/dam/data/ekm/dokumentation/materialien/mat_nous_f.pdf

May, J. et al.
2007   Keeping London working: global cities, the British state and London's
            new migrant division of labour. *Transactions of the Institute of British
            Geographers*, 32(2): 151–167.

McKay, A. and P. Deshingkar
2014   Internal remittances and poverty: Further evidence from Africa and
            Asia. Working Paper 12. Migrating out of Poverty Research Programme
            Consortium, University of Sussex, Brighton. Available from http://
            migratingoutofpoverty.dfid.gov.uk/files/file.php?name=wp-
            12---mckay-and-deshingkar-internal-remittances-and-poverty.
            pdf&site=354

Naudé, W.
2010   *Entrepreneurship and Economic Development.* Palgrave Macmillan,
            Basingstoke.

Organisation for Economic Co-operation and Development (OECD)
2006   *Immigration to Integration: Local Solutions to a Global Challenge.*
            OECD, Paris.
2013   *Rural-Urban Partnerships: An Integrated Approach to Economic
            Development.* OECD, Paris.

Orozco, M.
2008   Remittances in Latin America and the Caribbean: Their impact
            on local economies and the response of local governments. In:
            Decentralization and the Challenges to Democratic Governance
            (Organization of American States, ed.) OAS, Washington D.C., pp. 25–
            44. Available from www.oas.org/sap/publications/2008/English%20
            Decentraliztion.pdf

WORLD MIGRATION
REPORT 2015
Migrants and Cities:
New Partnerships
to Manage Mobility

157

Oucho, J., L. Oucho and V. Ochieng
2014   Is migration the solution to poverty alleviation in Kenya? Rural-
            urban migration experiences of migrants from Western Kenya to
            Kisumu and Nairobi. Working Paper 21. Migrating out of Poverty
            Research Programme Consortium, University of Sussex, Brighton.
            Available from http://migratingoutofpoverty.dfid.gov.uk/files/file.
            php?name=wp21-oucho-oucho-ochieng-2014-is-migration-the-so-
            lution-to-poverty-in-kenya.pdf&site=354

Potts, D.
2006   'Restoring Order'? Operation Murambatsvina and the Urban Crisis in
            Zimbabwe. *Journal of Southern African Studies,* 32(2): 273–291.

Sassen, S.
2011   The Global City and the Global Slum. *Forbes,* 22 March. Available
            from www.forbes.com/sites/megacities/2011/03/22/the-global-city-
            and-the-global-slum

Saunders, D.
2010   *Arrival City: How the Largest Migration in History is Reshaping Our
            World.* Random House, New York.

Serageldin, M., F. Vigier and M. Larsen
2014   Urban Migration Trends in the MENA Region and the Challenge of
            Conflict Induced Displacement. Background Paper for the *World
            Migration Report 2015: Migrants and Cities: New Partnerships to
            Manage Mobility.* IOM, Geneva.

Sumption, M.
2014   *Giving Cities and Regions a Voice in Immigration Policy: Can National
            Policies Meet Local Demand?* Migration Policy Institute, Washington,
            D.C. Available from www.migrationpolicy.org/research/giving-cities-
            and-regions-voice-immigration-policy-can-national-policies-meet-
            local-demand

Tacoli, C.
2011   Not only climate change: mobility, vulnerability and socio-economic
            transformations in environmentally fragile areas in Bolivia, Senegal
            and Tanzania. Human Settlements Working Paper Series: Rural-Urban
            Interactions and Livelihood Strategies – 28. International Institute for
            Environment and Development (IIED), London. Available from http://
            pubs.iied.org/pdfs/10590IIED.pdf
2013   The benefits and constraints of urbanization for gender equality.
            Environment and Urbanization Brief-27. International Institute for
            Environment and Development, London. Available from http://pubs.
            iied.org/10629IIED.html

Tacoli, C., G. McGranahan and D. Satterthwaite
2014   Urbanization, Rural-urban Migration and Urban Poverty. Background
            Paper for the *World Migration Report 2015: Migrants and Cities:
            New Partnerships to Manage Mobility.* International Organization for
            Migration, Geneva.

Teder, J. and M. Golik

2006   Ethnic minorities and entrepreneurship in Estonia. Paper presented at the 14th Nordic Conference on Small Business Research, Stockholm. Available from www.researchgate.net/publication/237684036_ ETHNIC_MINORITIES_AND_ENTREPRENEURSHIP_IN_ESTONIA

Tengeh, R. et al.

2012   Do immigrant-owned businesses grow financially? An empirical study of African immigrant-owned businesses in Cape Town Metropolitan Area of South Africa. *African Journal of Business Management,* 6(19): 6070–6081.

The Hague Process on Refugees and Migration (THP)

2014   *Engagement with the Private Sector on International Migration: Mapping Study.* The Hague Process on Refugees and Migration, The Hague. Available from http://thehagueprocess.org/engagement-with-the-private-sector-on-international-migration/

United Nations Department of Economic and Social Affairs (UN DESA)

2012   *World Urbanization Prospects: The 2011 Revision.* United Nations, New York. Available from www.un.org/en/development/desa/ population/publications/pdf/urbanization/WUP2011_Report.pdf

2013   *World Population Policies 2013.* United Nations, New York. Available from www.un.org/en/development/desa/population/publications/ pdf/policy/WPP2013/wpp2013.pdf

2014   *World Urbanization Prospects, The 2014 Revision - Highlights.* United Nations, New York. http://esa.un.org/unpd/wup/Highlights/ WUP2014-Highlights.pdf

United Nations Development Programme (UNDP)

2009   *Human Development Report 2009, Overcoming barriers: Human mobility and development.* United Nations, New York. Available from http://hdr.undp.org/en/content/human-development-report-2009

Van der Geest, K.

2011   *The Dagara farmer at home and away: Migration, environment and development in Ghana.* African Studies Centre, Leiden. Available from https://openaccess.leidenuniv.nl/handle/1887/17766

Van Ewijk, E.

2008   *Decentralized cooperation between Dutch municipalities and municipalities in migrant countries: Main developments and main theoretical debates illustrated by several case studies. Report for NCDO.* Amsterdam Institute for Metropolitan and International Development Studies, Amsterdam. Available from http://hdl.handle. net/11245/2.66647

2013   *Between local governments and communities: Knowledge exchange and mutual learning in Dutch-Moroccan and Dutch-Turkish municipal partnerships.* PhD Dissertation, University of Amsterdam, Amsterdam. Available from http://dare.uva.nl/document/2/129540

WORLD MIGRATION
REPORT 2015
Migrants and Cities:
New Partnerships
to Manage Mobility

159

Vigdor, J.L.

2013   *Immigration and the Revival of American Cities: From Preserving Manufacturing Jobs to Strengthening the Housing Market.* Americas Society / Council of the Americas (AS/COA), New York. Available from www.as-coa.org/sites/default/files/ImmigrationUSRevivalReport.pdf

Vorderwülbecke, A.

2012   Entrepreneurship and Migration. In: *Global Entrepreneurship Monitor 2012 Global Report* (S.R. Xavier et al., eds.), Global Entrepreneurship Research Association, London, pp. 42-50. Available from www.gemconsortium.org/report

Weber, D.

2012   Dealing with cultural diversity from a labour market perspective: Intercultural competencies for stakeholders. In: *Migration Policy Practice*, II (4): 23–26. Available from http://publications.iom.int/bookstore/free/MigrationPolicyPracticeJournal_11Sept2012.pdf

World Bank

2009   *World Development Report 2009: Reshaping Economic Geography.* The World Bank, Washington D.C. Available from https://openknowledge.worldbank.org/handle/10986/5991

Zhu, Y.

2000   *In Situ* Urbanization in Rural China: Case Studies from Fujian Province. *Development and Change*, 31(2): 413–434.

2004   Changing Urbanization Processes and In Situ Rural–Urban Transformation: Reflections on China's Settlement Definitions. In: *New Forms of Urbanization: Beyond the Urban–Rural Dichotomy* (A.J. Champion and G. J. Hugo, eds.). Ashgate Publishing, Aldershot, pp. 207–228.

2014   In situ urbanization in China: Processes, Contributing Factors, and Policy Implications. Background Paper for the *World Migration Report 2015: Migrants and Cities: New Partnerships to Manage Mobility.* IOM, Geneva.

Zhu, Y. et al.

2012   *Zhongguo De Jiudi Chengzhenhua: Lilun Yu Shizheng* (China's in Situ urbanisation: Theories and empirical evidence). Science Press, Beijing. (In Chinese only)

2013   Rural-urban linkages and the impact of internal migration in Asian developing countries. An introduction. In: *Asian Population Studies*, 9 (2): 119–123.

WELCOME
Bienvenue
Chào Mừng
добро пожаловать
ДВРО РАЖАВАТ
어서오세요
مرحبا
Bienvenido
歡迎
خوش آمدید
स्वागत
LIBRARY INFORMATION
VOLUNTEERS

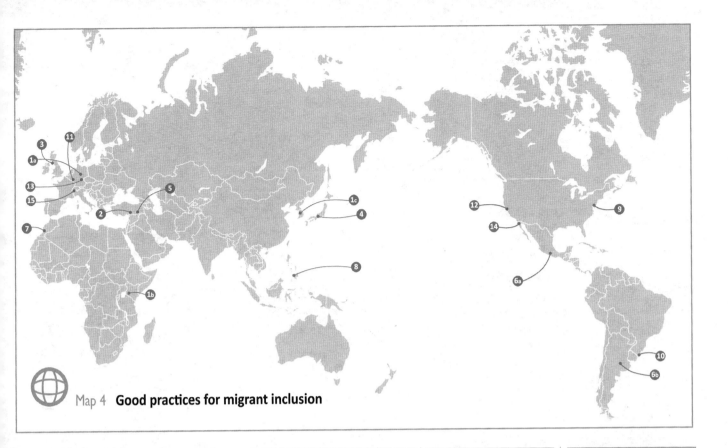

Map 4 **Good practices for migrant inclusion**

---

(1) **(a) Berlin and other German cities (b) Nairobi, Kenya (c) Seoul, Republic of Korea**

Text box 13: Examples of effective partnerships in health care

Networks of voluntary doctors are providing health services in German cities.
A community health centre brings health care closer to people in Nairobi.
Access to health care for undocumented migrants is facilitated in Seoul.

---

(2) **Gaziantep, Turkey**

Text box 15: Gaziantep: A story of inclusion

With the support of the local communities, the city has adopted a comprehensive programme for the Syrians displaced by conflict, providing adequate assistance and integration support, without undermining the well-being of host communities.

---

(3) **Glasgow, Scotland, United Kingdom**

Text box 24: Ethnic Entrepreneurship Programme in Glasgow, United Kingdom

Established in 2005, the Glasgow Business Gateway has employed a specialist ethnic adviser to investigate and tackle barriers to self-employment, and to help promote strategies for integration into wider Scottish society through business creation.

---

(4) **Hamamatsu and other Japanese cities**

Text box 6: Migration and localities in Japan: The Committee for Localities with a Concentrated Foreign Population

Established in 2001, the Committee promotes migrant integration through employment and language support for migrants, facilitation of migrant children's education and promotion of cultural understanding for host communities.

---

(5) **Mardin, Turkey**

Text box 31: Mardin, Turkey: Migrants asagents for city-making

Migrants from Mardin living in various European cities help their origin city achieve a global profile by promoting its historical, cultural, religious and socioeconomic facets, with support from the city leaders.

---

(6) **(a) Mexico (b) Argentina**

Text box 18: Remittance policies in Mexico and Argentina

Mexican migrants in Texas contribute resources for improvement work in their regions of origin, with the financial support of the Mexican Government.
The Argentinian Government supports a Bolivian cooperative for public infrastructure improvement projects in Toropalca, Bolivia.

---

(7) **Moroccan transit cities**

Text box 29: Need for improved national and local governance on migration management in Morocco

The Government of Morocco established an immigration policy to better attend to the basic rights of migrants and for the provision of services in support of cities hosting increasing numbers of transit migrants.

---

(8) **Naga City, the Philippines**

Text box 25: Mainstreaming migration into local development planning in Naga City, the Philippines

Naga City pioneers the mainstreaming of migration and development in its local planning process through various projects with local research partners and international agencies, including IOM.

---

(9) **New York City, United States of America**

Text box 1: How the American Community Survey is used in New York, United States of America

The annual American Community Survey provides information on New York's 3.1 million immigrants, representing 37 per cent of the city's 8.4 million residents, and is widely used by the city and its communities.

---

(10) **Porto Alegre, Brazil**

Text box 30: Participatory budgeting and migrant inclusion in Porto Alegre, Brazil

Porto Alegre, in the southern part of Brazil, seeks social inclusion through participation of various groups, including internal migrants, in building the city infrastructures and institutions. Today, 15,000 locals take part in the participatory budgeting each year.

---

(11) **Rotterdam, the Netherlands**

Text box 23: Business–city partnership in Rotterdam, the Netherlands

Rotterdam implemented a formal partnership between the city and the private sector in order to improve labour market outcomes in the city and increase migrant community participation in the labour market.

---

(12) **San Francisco and other US gateway cities**

Text box 27: A legacy of sanctuary in gateway cities in the United States

Some US cities are not enquiring into an individual's immigration status, representing a more inclusionary attitude towards newcomers. Most of the gateway cities have either formal or de facto sanctuary policies.

---

(13) **Stuttgart, Germany**

Text box 28: Stuttgart, Germany: intercultural city – arrive, stay and shape

Stuttgart is a cultural and economic hub in Europe, with migrants from over 180 countries representing 40 per cent of its population. Migrants actively participate in integration programmes as collaborators or city employees.

---

(14) **Tijuana, Mexico**

Text box 5: A city where returning migrants and migrants in transit are offered assistance: Tijuana, Mexico

Established in 2013, the State Council for the Attention of Migrants provides support in Tijuana for returning migrants from the United States and migrants in transit.

---

(15) **Vaud, Switzerland**

Text box 22: Cantonal integration Programme of Vaud, Switzerland: Public policy challenges and objectives

The Canton of Vaud, which has the third highest proportion of foreign residents (32%) in Switzerland, established a public policy on integration and works closely in partnership with migrant associations.

Urban partnerships to manage mobility

CHAPTER 5

WORLD MIGRATION
REPORT 2015
Migrants and Cities:
New Partnerships
to Manage Mobility

163

HIGHLIGHTS

- New and innovative policies are needed to meet the biggest challenges facing urban governance today of ensuring adequate infrastructure and service delivery to diverse and growing populations. Migration and how it is governed is thus at the frontline of urban planning and sustainable development.

- Fragmentation of policy between the national and local level is a key challenge when it comes to managing migration in cities. Central government is responsible for setting overall migration policy but this often does not factor in the impacts of migration at the local level in terms of pressures on housing, jobs and services, the domain of city level administrations. Any major disjuncture between central migration policies and local urban development plans and capacities exists mainly in the area of finance.

- Some cities in high-income countries are proactively developing their own plans for integration to the extent that they have the autonomy to do so. Good examples of efforts to build institutional structures to promote social cohesion can be found in numerous cities around the world. Partnerships with migrants and migrant associations are key. Notably, city administrations in low- and middle-income countries do not have the resources to institute similar measures.

- Migrants can play a role as city-makers, helping their adopted cities achieve a global profile by promoting the historical, cultural, religious and socioeconomic facets, providing the right opportunities exist to enable this to happen.

June J.H. Lee

This chapter examines some of the urban governance conditions needed to enable local governments to take an inclusive and participatory approach to migrants. It looks at how national and local government relations work together to share financial, budgetary and administrative authority in order to shape opportunities that help link migrant inclusion to economic growth and global competitiveness.

WORLD MIGRATION
REPORT 2015
Migrants and Cities:
New Partnerships
to Manage Mobility

165

5.1 INTRODUCTION

The world is urbanizing and its impacts are wide-ranging far beyond the boundaries of cities, metropolises, megacities and metropolitan regions. Those boundaries are seriously blurred not only between the urban and rural but also on an urban, regional, national and global scale through the ever increasing connections among them. Cities are characterized not only by their population density, economic agglomeration or infrastructure concentration but also as a dynamic site and by the outcome of broader social transformation processes. Urban governance therefore assumes the challenges of coordinating such complex interconnections, while the growth of the city remains essential to the politics of cities.

Human mobility is a major contributor to this urbanization, both as a narrow demographic change as well as a broad societal transformation, and migrants contribute to the cities' complex interconnections through their sustained global communication, institutional linkages and exchange of resources among migrants, homelands and wider diasporas. Migrants can be key players in city development, growth, resilience and sustainability. They are often found among the architects and constructors of growing cities, the service providers, the entrepreneurs, employers, innovators and as part of a global diaspora, "bridge builders", traders, business links and humanitarian support between countries. As migration flows diversify, different opportunities become available to migrants in their specific localities. A mobile and diverse world requires flexible migration governance that can account for change and transition.

As cities are nested in a hierarchy of regional, state, federal or even supranational entities, migrant inclusion is intimately intertwined with the relationship among different levels of governance. Effective immigration management by the national government can be a considerable boost for local economies as migrants could help create jobs and fuel growth. Yet cities in general do not actively participate in the policymaking processes that influence such migrant movements. Urban citizenship is a pragmatic policy tool to further enable migrants' inclusion and an important element of such opportunity structures.

5.2 MIGRANT INCLUSION AND URBAN GOVERNANCE

The biggest challenge for urban governance is the need to ensure adequate infrastructure and service delivery to diverse and growing populations. This requires new and innovative policy approaches that recognize urban diversity as a positive aspect and take an inclusive approach to all segments of society. Human mobility contributes to this global urban transition and the way in which cities and countries manage this transition is critical to their future. Migration and how it is governed is thus at the frontline of urban planning and sustainable development.

The participation and inclusion of migrants in their host cities is an indispensable part of building stable, open and vibrant communities that assure the socioeconomic future of a country. Ensuring adequate infrastructure and service delivery to diverse and growing populations poses the biggest challenge for urban governance. Recent research has found a strong correlation between the effective provision of services and urban development in all of the major emerging economies (EPF and CIRD, 2013). In pursuing more inclusive urban governance, cities today can link local urban social cohesion to economic growth and global competitiveness (Metropolis, 2011).

An important implication of increasing urban diversity is the need for new and innovative policy instruments and governance arrangements that recognize urban diversity as a positive aspect and that increase interaction and communication between the diversity of groups in urban society and improve participation to satisfy the needs of the communities. In this new policy approach, equal rights, access and opportunities for all urban inhabitants are assured while addressing some specific social and material needs of vulnerable groups, women, and children, the elderly and migrants with an irregular status (UCLG, 2013).

Cities are thus at the centre of a shift in the debate on multiculturalism and migrant integration to a more inclusive approach to community building and public participation in municipal tasks that involves, but does not single out, immigrants. Local initiatives, such as Berlin's "socially integrative urban development" projects, are offering new integrated models of urban citizenship for the whole community. Under these projects, monitoring of various social conditions such as employment and housing for all residents is implemented throughout the city as part of neighbourhood management.[1]

A holistic approach for community development is necessary, yet it is equally important to look beyond the conventional actors in migrant inclusion. Broadening the scope is especially relevant for cities of countries where some of the major local governance actors are either absent, less relevant or unwilling to contribute to migrant inclusion at the local level (OECD, 2011). The shift to urban "governance" and its broad-based partnership has led to some of the most innovative responses to decision-making in cities of less-developed countries, for example, participatory budgeting in Brazil (see text box 30, Participatory Budgeting and Migrant Inclusion (Kingsley, 2012)) and South Africa's integrated development plans. Integrated Development Planning involves the entire municipality and its citizens in finding the best solutions to achieve good long-term development and is an attempt to overcome the racial division in areas of work, residence and services, a legacy of Apartheid.[2] However, significant groups of people continue to be excluded from urban policymaking and planning (Stren, 2012).

In cities everywhere, urban governance should be both inward- and outward-looking in order to manage migration for optimal development outcomes. Affordable local solutions to housing, health, clean air, water and transportation are key markers not only for migrant inclusion and community vitality but also for global economic development. Local strategies of inclusion and cohesion can strengthen cities and help successfully negotiate connections to global markets, for example as production hubs, knowledge centres and tourist destinations or through remittances. These cities are likely to attract skilled migrants, innovators, investors, students, returnees and diaspora groups who are essential for the city to reap the dividends of investing in migrant inclusion.

The lives of urban migrants are dominated by transnational practices including sustained communication, institutional linkages and resource exchanges with home communities and diasporas. Thus migrants can be part of the solution to manage rapid urban transition,[3] as they help make the links function between smart migration policy and urban planning. Local migrant communities can

---

1   See also www.stadtentwicklung.berlin.de/wohnen/quartiersmanagement/index_en.shtml
2   See www.etu.org.za/toolbox/docs/localgov/webidp.html
3   See the IOM website on the 7th World Urban Forum in Colombia in 2014: www.iom.int/news/iom-actively-participates-7th-world-urban-forum-held-medellin-colombia

WORLD MIGRATION
REPORT 2015
Migrants and Cities:
New Partnerships
to Manage Mobility

167

participate in the broad consultative process and act as the front players in integrative community development and co-development between cities of origin and destinations. A host of partners, including international community actors, can assist effectively in building the knowledge base, capacities and commitments towards change and good policymaking and practice across countries.

By 2050, the UN estimates some 66 per cent of the global population, or around 6.3 billion people, will be living in urban areas. The pattern of this urban population growth will vary but almost 90 per cent is expected to occur in Africa and Asia. Human mobility contributes to this global urban transition and the way in which cities and countries manage this transition is critical to their future. Migration and how it is governed is thus at the frontline of urban planning and sustainable development.

5.3

MULTILEVEL GOVERNANCE FOR MIGRANT INCLUSION

There is often incoherence between national and local policies when it comes to managing migration to cities. National policy and admission can regulate entry of migration to particular countries but integration in specific cities or locations is not planned for but is left to cities. This fragmentation results in a mismatch between migrant numbers and characteristics and the needs and capacities in cities in which they arrive. Some cities in high-income countries are proactively developing their own plans for integration to the extent that they have the autonomy to do so. Notably, city administrations in low- and middle-income countries do not have the resources to institute similar measures.

A lack of coordination and consistency between national migration policies and local urban needs and capacities is at the heart of challenges in managing migrant integration in urban areas. Overall immigration and residence policies are usually the jurisdiction of central governments, but the impacts of migrant settlement are experienced at ground level in varying ways in different locations. For instance, the United Kingdom policy on migration is set by the national government but, as the majority of migrants settle in London, the additional demands on public services such as education, housing and social services are managed by the local London boroughs. Budget allocations from national government to local authorities do not necessarily take into account the demands arising from population mobility (Travers et al., 2007).

Moreover, national policies may not meet the demands of different sectors or localities in terms of migration. For example, admissions policies that favour family reunion may not necessarily bring the skills needed to meet local labour demands (Sumption, 2014), as seen in the current debate in the United States about whether current visa programmes are delivering the global talents needed for the United States economy. Furthermore, skilled migrants, business investors and foreign students tend to be attracted to vibrant metropolises, financial hubs or high-tech clusters, while other regions may struggle to attract and retain native and foreign workers alike. In some countries like Australia and Canada, the federal and state governments jointly select and adjust the flow of migrant workers to the needs of the communities, under state-nominated or provincial visa programmes. Text box 26 shows how migration governance is managed at multiple levels of the political system of the United States.

Multilevel migration governance of the United States[4]

In the United States, policies for migrant integration emanate from different levels of government.

Federal level – sets high-level immigration policy, for instance, in terms of the provision of a permanent solution for undocumented immigrant status or an adjustment to visa quotas. There are also national laws that directly and indirectly influence the integration of immigrant newcomers into the United States such as birthright citizenship that is given to a newborn child, even of undocumented migrants, and the Civil Rights Act of 1964 that outlaws discrimination due to race, colour, religion or country of origin.

State level – enjoys considerable independence in creating a variety of policies and laws. State-based legislation is a major factor in the opportunity structures for immigrants, such as the Development, Relief and Education for Alien Minors Act (DREAM) that helps social mobility among migrants. State governments control the appropriation of funds for migrant services, health and education, and set residency requirements for educational institutions. Whether they accept foreign credentials, recognize professional licences, issue driver's licences to undocumented immigrants, permit in-state tuition or choose to enforce federal laws, these issues are driven primarily by state rather than federal legislation.

City level – In order to promote immigration as a component of social and economic development, mayors of large, medium-sized and small cities are formalizing offices dedicated to improving services and engaging immigrant communities through enhanced collaboration with community organizations, academic institutions and the private sector. In the absence of a formal entity to address immigrant affairs, due to a lack of political support, funding and other resources, civic programmes play a critical role and reflect the specific needs of a metropolitan area, such as economic development and business growth by the immigrant population. Global Detroit coordinates numerous immigrant integration and economic development efforts in the region in an effort to revitalize southeast Michigan's economy.

Policy fragmentation at the national and local level is a major challenge to migration governance (OECD, 2006). While national policymakers pursue coherence and control over migrants' access to services, cities have specific challenges in ensuring inclusivity and integration of immigrants. The sanctuary city movement in the United States (see text box 27) is an effort by local jurisdictions and activists to reform federal immigration policies and to challenge federal immigration laws that are perceived to be unfair or unjust.

---

4   Based on J. Kerr, P. McDaniel and M. Guinan, *Reimagining the Midwest: Immigration Initiatives and the Capacity of Local Leadership*. The Chicago Council on Global Affairs, 2014; and M. Price, Cities Welcoming Immigrants: Local Strategies to Attract and Retain Immigrants in US Metropolitan Areas, 2014. Background Paper for the *World Migration Report 2015: Migrants and Cities: New Partnerships to Manage Mobility*, IOM, Geneva.

WORLD MIGRATION
REPORT 2015
Migrants and Cities:
New Partnerships
to Manage Mobility

169

Text box 27

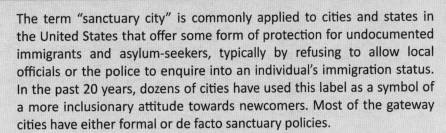

A legacy of sanctuary in gateway cities of the United States[5]

The term "sanctuary city" is commonly applied to cities and states in the United States that offer some form of protection for undocumented immigrants and asylum-seekers, typically by refusing to allow local officials or the police to enquire into an individual's immigration status. In the past 20 years, dozens of cities have used this label as a symbol of a more inclusionary attitude towards newcomers. Most of the gateway cities have either formal or de facto sanctuary policies.

San Francisco was one of the first "gateway" cities to formally pass a municipal sanctuary policy in the 1980s. At that time, the city was experiencing an influx of refugees from El Salvador and Guatemala fleeing civil war. In trying to serve this needy group who were not recognized as refugees, the Board of Supervisors passed San Francisco's City of Refuge Ordinance in 1985. Initially it was to recognize just the people from El Salvador and Guatemala, yet it evolved into protection of all immigrant rights in the city (Ridgley, 2008).

Today most people associate sanctuary cities with efforts in the late 1990s to counter restrictions on migrant access to services with the passing of the Illegal Immigration Reform and Immigrant Responsibility Act of 1996. More cities adopted sanctuary policies in the 2000s as a counter measure to the Department of Homeland Security's 287(g) Agreements that engage local police in immigration control. But now with California's 2014 TRUST Act, the entire state has become a sanctuary.

Some European cities face particular policy challenges to respond to the public service needs of those migrants whose migration status grants only limited entitlements to services but who may present significant welfare needs. The result may be formal or informal exclusion from welfare benefits which is most evident in informal settlements such as La Cañada Real, on the outskirts of Madrid, the largest shanty town in Europe whose residents are mostly migrants, and Oranienplatz in Berlin, a protest camp of asylum-seekers and migrants from Africa with Italian humanitarian status and therefore lacking entitlements to stay in Germany. While state laws, policies and judiciary processes shape migrants' entitlements, migrants' access to services are closely linked to the relationship between the national and local government. Migrants often have to negotiate the complex rules and restrictions with the assistance of informal social networks (Price and Spence, 2014).

Policy fragmentation is particularly the case when it comes to migrant entry into the labour market as jobs tend to be insecure and underpaid with the work often not matching the migrants' professional qualifications. A multi-stakeholder approach is critical in order to develop effective vocational training which

5   Based on M. Price, *Cities Welcoming Immigrants: Local Strategies to Attract and Retain Immigrants in US Metropolitan Areas*, 2014. Background Paper for the *World Migration Report 2015: Migrants and Cities: New Partnerships to Manage Mobility*, IOM, Geneva.

responds to the needs of local labour markets and to engage employers, local chambers of commerce, colleagues and vocational schools in addition to non-profit actors such as social enterprises (see text box 23, Business-city partnerships in Rotterdam, the Netherlands).

Successful migrant inclusion initiatives tend to be those programmes that are tailored to the needs of particular communities. Inclusion happens at multiple levels and is often the outcome of international cooperation, state laws and local policies. In Germany, a highly federalized state where local governments enjoy constitutionally guaranteed autonomy, almost all cities today have their own integration plans, which conform to the binding and verifiable targets for integration set by the national Immigration Law on Integration and the National Integration Plan (Bendel, 2014). Text box 28 sets out the example of Stuttgart.

Text box 28

Stuttgart, Germany: The intercultural city – arrive, stay and shape

Major German cities started implementing a policy of integration and diversity as per the National Integration Plan endorsed in 2007 and based on the new 2005 Immigration Law. All governmental levels (national, federal states and communal), civil society and migrant organizations have agreed on the National Integration Plan with its measures for education, labour, housing, cultural activities, sports and elderly care. Financial responsibilities are shared. National resources support integration courses, counselling for new immigrants and labour market inclusion measures while federal states finance schooling. However, cities and communes have to rely increasingly on external funding from private foundations or the European Union (EU) to maintain successful programmes and initiatives.

Cities have an important role to play in the National Integration Plan, as most integration efforts take place at the local level in everyday interactions. With their expertise based on long experience of integrating increasingly heterogeneous populations, cities can develop successful strategies for social participation of immigrants and ethnic minorities in their respective host community. Cities also have to face the consequences of failed integration processes.

Stuttgart ("the city"), the state capital of Baden-Württemberg, is a cultural and economic hub in the heart of Europe, with migrants from over 180 countries representing 40 per cent of the city's population. Migrants actively participate in integration programmes as collaborators or city employees. The *Forum of Cultures*, an umbrella association of all migrant organizations in Stuttgart, significantly supports this intercultural approach.

The city learns from other cities and civil society institutions through national and international networks and tries to contribute to the development of a common integration framework. For example, the city coordinates the communal working group composed of integration commissioners of some 30 cities and municipalities, representatives of the Federal Office for Migration and Refugees, the Association of German

WORLD MIGRATION
REPORT 2015
Migrants and Cities:
New Partnerships
to Manage Mobility

171

Cities, academic institutions and foundations. The working group issues reference materials on current integration matters that serve as best practices.

On the European level, the city supports the exchange of 35 European cities on local integration policy as part of the European Network of Cities for Local Integration Policies and in cooperation with the European Foundation for the Improvement of Living and Working Conditions, the Council of Europe, the Council of European Municipalities and Regions, and the Committee of the Regions. Through various case studies, effective good practice examples were developed for different government levels for the further development of European integration policy.

The city also partners with the *Cities of Migration* network of the Maytree Foundation, the *Transatlantic Cities Network* of the German Marshall Fund of the United States, the Robert Bosch Foundation, and the Bertelsmann Foundation in order to foster innovative ideas on integration practices.

Contributed by Fritz Kuhn, Mayor of Stuttgart

As a budget tightening effort, many European governments have mainstreamed integration priorities across general policy areas, including education and employment. Yet it is not clear whether or not such mainstreaming will lead to better coordination among agencies at the national and local government levels (Collet and Petrovic, 2014). At the supranational level, the EU has developed a European Fund for the Integration of Third-Country Nationals.[6] However other lower-income regions in the world are not likely to attain this level of convergence. There is a dearth of research on how different state structures and political systems shape migration policies and their impacts on urban development and planning, especially in lower-income regions (Caponio and Borkert, 2010). While cities everywhere try to pursue inclusive and sustainable development, not all cities are equally resourced and motivated to achieve the goal. The degree to which the good practices of high-income countries in diversity management are relevant or useful to low- and middle-income countries facing rapid urban transition is very much a question.

Migration policies of both origin and destination countries can affect cities in positive and negative ways. Restrictive, inadequate or unclear policies on labour mobility in Africa, Asia and Europe have contributed to large irregular migration and the growth of informal urban settlements. Strict border control policies can lead to urban "transit hubs" where migrants become stranded on their way to intended destinations. Text box 29 describes the repercussions on Morocco caught between sub-Saharan migrants trying to reach Europe and the restrictive policies of European countries in seeking to deny them access. On the positive side, overseas worker programmes in origin countries have brought huge remittances that, together with other returns, have helped towns, cities and the economy back home to develop.

---

6   See the European website on integration at http://ec.europa.eu/ewsi/en/policy/legal.cfm

Need for improved national and local governance on migration management in Morocco[7]

With the evolution of Morocco from a country of emigration to a country that is increasingly hosting sub-Saharan Africans, different human rights groups, including the National Human Rights Council and various migrant associations, have called for a re-evaluation and reform of Moroccan migration policy. In September 2013, King Mohammed VI announced that the Government would begin working on a new, more liberal immigration policy that is attentive to the basic rights of migrants and the provision of basic services to them.

One of the key features of the policy, adopted in September 2013, includes the special regularization of certain categories of undocumented migrants. Eligible candidates for special regularization include those with work contracts effective for at least two years, non-nationals who have lived in Morocco for five years or more, non-national spouses of Moroccans who have lived together for at least two years, non-national spouses of regularized non-nationals who have lived together at least four years, children of couples in one of these types of relationships, and those with severe medical conditions who arrived before the end of 2013. As of October 2014, the number of regularization requests had reached nearly 20,000, representing 103 countries. Nearly half of these requests have been approved (IOM, 2014).

Intertwined with this policy shift is the signing of a mobility partnership with the EU, which contains a readmission agreement that places increased pressure and responsibility on Moroccan central and local authorities to effectively and humanely manage returned non-nationals once they are readmitted into Morocco.

A combination of Moroccan foreign policy and cooperation, European security policies and economic situation, and the push and pull factors at work in sub-Saharan Africa is therefore currently transforming Morocco's migrant landscape. Until policy decisions among sending, transit and receiving countries can curb this migratory trend through local development in the migrants' countries of origin, rather than focus on containing it in destination countries, Maghrebi central and local authorities will require more and more resources to govern, integrate and serve this growing population (EMHRN, 2014).

---

7   M. Serageldin, F. Vigier and M. Larsen, Urban Migration Trends in the MENA Region and the Challenge of Conflict Induced Displacement, 2014. Background Paper for the *World Migration Report 2015: Migrants and Cities: New Partnerships to Manage Mobility*, IOM, Geneva.

WORLD MIGRATION
REPORT 2015
Migrants and Cities:
New Partnerships
to Manage Mobility

173

5.3.1. Shared financing of migrant inclusion

Migrant access to services is closely linked to national and local government relations. Except for the citizenship issue, migrant inclusion – language acquisition, education, civic awareness, health service access and public safety measures – is facilitated locally at the cost of the public purse. There is often a major disjuncture between central migration policies and local urban development plans and capacities, mostly in the area of finance.

National and local government relations work well where the federal-local structures permit certain devolution of financial, budgetary and administrative authority and flexibility. Such partnerships can work in terms of infrastructure and basic service delivery when central government responsibility is devolved to local authorities working in partnerships with civil society actors, particularly community-based organizations, migrant associations, the private sector and other interested stakeholders (UN-Habitat, 2007).

- In Italy, along with municipal autonomy, budgetary authority has been devolved to local government for small-scale development projects. In this context, translocal projects involving diasporas and private entrepreneurs are thriving in partnership with communities in the origin countries. The Ghanacoop project, for example, involves Ghanaian migrants in the Italian province of Modena as partners with local government and business in small scale agrarian cooperatives in Ghana. The resulting benefits are community development in Italy and socioeconomic development in Ghana.[8]

- In Catalonia, Spain, co-development funds made available by the State and local authorities support local transnational co-development projects with Moroccan, Senegalese, Colombian and other migrant associations and civil society groups. In this way, the local inclusion of migrants is strengthened while, at the same time, creating small trade links with their countries of origin (Acebillo-Baqué and Østergaard-Nielsen, 2011).

- In China, the economic transformation of cities like Fuqing in Fujian province is largely due to the devolution of the approval of foreign investment projects to local government, combined with the investments of Fuqing expatriates abroad, and flexibility by local government towards foreign investors. The growth in Fuqing and elsewhere has boosted education and created jobs, including for the many internal migrants from rural areas. It has also helped mitigate the rural exodus to over-crowded megacities.

In China, despite successful urbanization in terms of the creation of new centres of growth or the decentralization of services and production to peri-urban areas or smaller cities, there are huge social and administrative challenges facing local governments in the delivery of services to growing numbers of urban residents. Local governments reportedly receive half the country's fiscal revenue but are responsible for eighty per cent of national spending (The Economist, 2014).

In different parts of Africa, urban governments and service providers have encountered tremendous challenges in coping with housing and service deficiencies alongside rapid population growth (Stren, 2014). Sub-Saharan African cities have been obliged to operate increasingly through a decentralized,

---

8   For further details about Ghanacoop, see www.iom.int/jahia/webdav/site/myjahiasite/shared/shared/
    mainsite/microsites/IDM/sessions/92nd/oware_ppt.pdf

more democratically structured local-government system at the encouragement of the World Bank, the main agency involved in urban assistance (ibid). The new constitution of Kenya, for example, gives more power to municipal authorities to manage affairs at the local level, but large urban populations of displaced and irregular migrants are testing capacities on the ground (Haysom, 2013). African cities are seeking solutions cooperatively with civil society actors and others. For example, in South Africa, the privatization of many public services has resulted in disadvantaged migrants being excluded from these services (EPF and CIRD, 2013). Civil society groups and small business networks, however, deliver services through informal systems albeit more precariously than the formal public services (Clunan and Trinkunas, 2010).

In the context of financial austerity after the world economic crisis in 2008, many local governments, even in high-income countries, have had to cut down on municipal budgets, including those for migrant inclusion. This has led to, not only the devolution of inclusion responsibilities to migrants, neighbourhood-based communities and civil society groups, but also the privatization of social services as well as increased support for public-private partnerships for social welfare. More research is needed on the models of central–local cooperation that work best for both migration and urban governance, in particular shared financial and budgetary management across different political and fiscal systems.

One innovative approach to financing municipal inclusion policies is participatory budgeting. It is widely practiced by over 1,700 local governments in more than 40 countries, especially among low-income countries where municipal budgets remain low despite decentralization. See text box 30 for an example from Brazil (Cabannes, 2014). Participatory budgeting usually has access to only a small proportion of municipal budgets, and often less than ten per cent. However, it can be used for optimizing scarce municipal resources to provide basic services that correspond to urban dwellers' expectations and priorities. Its cost-efficiency is also due to lower maintenance costs arising from community oversight. Besides improving basic services, engaging urban dwellers in participatory budgeting can help create new spaces of dialogue between local authorities and urban dwellers, thus establishing a joint decision-making process (ibid.). However, there are limitations to participatory approaches. Migrants, particularly irregular migrants, are among the most vulnerable and are often outside participatory discussions. Temporary or circular migrants might also not stay long enough in one place to learn about or get engaged in participatory forums (Blaser and Landau, 2014).

WORLD MIGRATION
REPORT 2015
Migrants and Cities:
New Partnerships
to Manage Mobility

175

Text box 30

Participatory budgeting and migrant inclusion in Porto Alegre, Brazil[9]

Porto Alegre, in the southern part of Brazil, is a good example of a city seeking social inclusion through participation of various groups, including internal migrants. By participating in local elections and other fora, they are able to express their needs and defend their basic rights and also participate in building city institutions. Within seven years of the establishment of the city's municipal assembly in 1990, the percentage of locals with access to sewers doubled from 46 per cent to 95 per cent. The rate of road building, particularly in the *favelas* (slums), rose five-fold. Tax evasion fell, as people saw what their money was being spent on. Moreover, the process gave a voice to the urban poor. Citizens from the poorest 12 per cent accounted – in 1995 – for a third of the citywide assembly participants. Today, 15,000 locals take part in the *"orçamento participativo"* (participatory budgeting) each year – and one in ten citizens have taken part at some point or other.

5.3.2. Pragmatic initiatives on urban citizenship

Positive efforts are being made among city policymakers to promote social cohesion. There are good examples of institutional structures being formed with the commitment of federal and local level authorities in a number of cities in Europe (for instance, Berlin, Athens, Bilbao and Dublin) and in Asia (Fuzhou in the Fujian Province of China, Singapore and a network of cities in Japan). Cities like Berlin, Dublin and Lille are also forging partnerships with migrant associations to promote citizenship and political participation among migrant groups.

Local governments adopt remarkably similar practices to reduce tensions and increase cohesion among diverse resident groups (Fincher et al., 2014). Urban inclusion policies are often more pragmatic than migration governance at the national level. Instead of considering multi-ethnic societies as a threat, urban policymakers tend to promote the positive aspects of difference for competitiveness and social cohesion.

Many cities today are using their own initiative on migration and urban governance in order, for example, to fill gaps in central governance and policies on migration. In Argentina, the province of Buenos Aires approved a series of laws guaranteeing every child the right to schooling and all people access to public services, regardless of their legal status. This law was passed years ahead of the national Immigration Law of 2004 but needed the national law to facilitate implementation.[10]

One way of institutionalizing inclusive urban citizenship is to encourage the political participation of migrants at the local level. Cities may thus forge partnerships with

---

9   Based on P. Kingsley, Participatory democracy in Porto Alegre. *The Guardian*, 10 September 2012. Available from www.theguardian.com/world/2012/sep/10/participatory-democracy-in-porto-alegre [Accessed on 16 December 2014].

10   In 2004, Argentina's Law 25.871 (Ley de Migraciones de Argentina) uniquely recognized the right to migrate as a human right, favoured the integration of immigrants into society and gave them equal access to social services, public goods, health, justice, education, justice, work and social security across the whole country.

migrant associations and bring migrant representatives into city councils. In several European cities, the active participation of migrants is generally fostered through the creation of participatory bodies such as the "Socially Integrative City" (Soziale Stadt) in Berlin, "Neighbourhood Councils" (Conseils de quartier) in Lille, and the "Dublin City Community Forum" in Dublin, or through specific projects such as "Europe for citizens 2007-2013" from which Turin was able to benefit (Ernst & Young Global Limited, 2014). Neighbourhood and community councils are part of the new systems of participation to enable local authorities to consolidate civil engagement, along with e-democracy and participatory budgeting.

In addition, migrants should be encouraged to exercise their right to vote in municipal elections. Within the European Union, EU-mobile citizens could vote in local elections. However, this right is rarely exercised, mainly due to lack of information (ibid.). In Europe, the Italian municipality of Reggio Emilia has taken the lead on promoting full citizenship and voting rights for immigrants. The municipality has also been recognized by the Council of Europe (CoE) for its Programme 2012–2014[11] on intercultural dialogue and implementation of CoE recommendations.

One pragmatic approach to facilitating active urban citizenship is to grant the rights of urban citizenship to undocumented and unauthorized migrants. As the latter lack legal documentation, providing municipal identification to all inhabitants of a city regardless of migration status allows them to access public services in the city. In the United States, New York City issues municipal identification cards to undocumented immigrants to enable them to open bank accounts, sign apartment leases, receive library cards and gain access to other services. Dublin permits all residents, including non-citizens, to vote in local elections (Cities of Migration, 2012).

Today, there are good reasons for reconnecting "citizenship" with "cities", especially when taking a bottom-up approach to citizenship. The demographic complexity of cities and their attractiveness to migrants establishes the conditions and the need for citizenship as the process of political engagement between diverse groups and individuals. Cities today are more diverse than ever which highlights the need for forms of citizenship that are sensitive to difference while promoting engagement (Painter, 2005).

There are growing expectations that migrants should actively contribute to their own socioeconomic inclusion in cities in high-income countries. Recent findings from the *Divercities* project on hyper-diversified European cities, including Antwerp, Athens, Budapest, Leipzig, Tallinn, Warsaw and Zurich, found that many cities increasingly emphasize the social mobility of citizens, and develop policies to guarantee the equal opportunities, but not outcomes, for individuals. These policies, however, have a bias towards more "creative" and "entrepreneurial" citizens and would need fine tuning so as not to adversely impact disadvantaged groups (Van Kempen, 2014).

From the migrants' perspective, there is evidence that migrants readily identify with host cities. In a recent study, immigrants and members of minorities in France, Germany, the United Kingdom and the United States were found to identify more

11 See the Reggio Emilia Programme 2012–2014 for intercultural dialogue and implementation of the Council of Europe recommendations, available at www.coe.int/t/dg4/cultureheritage/culture/cities/Reggio%20 intercultural%20strategy.pdf

WORLD MIGRATION
REPORT 2015
Migrants and Cities:
New Partnerships
to Manage Mobility

177

readily with the city where they live than with the country of which it is part. As a consequence, towns and cities have a unique role to play in creating a sense of shared community and common purpose (Ash, Mortimer and Öktem, 2013). A bottom-up approach to strengthening migrant identification with their host cities is through migrant volunteering. The Grassroots Integration through Volunteering Experiences (GIVE) project (2012–2014) was an EU-funded IOM initiative piloted in four locations – Dublin, The Hague, Vienna and Ipswich. The overall objective of the GIVE Project was to enhance migrant participation in various aspects of life, in their new communities and to support the creation of inclusive neighbourhoods. The project also contributed to enhancing public perception of migration and diversity through a public awareness campaign.[12]

Finally, many cities have recognized that city-specific identities should be highlighted and celebrated. On various occasions, cities celebrate the cultural diversity of their inhabitants and their inclusion in the local community through events, fora and workshops. Among the main examples are the "Social Inclusion Week" and "One City One People" in Dublin, Berlin's "Carnival of Cultures" (Karneval der Kulturen) and the forum "Starting a Business by Foreigners in Italy" (Fare Impresa per gli Stranieri in Italia) in Turin (Ernst & Young Global Limited, 2014).

Most good practices have only been possible through political commitment at federal and local levels and through urban policies that embrace diversity, such as Vienna's Integration Oriented Diversity Policy, coupled with institutional frameworks which facilitate implementation. Key examples from around the world include:

- New York City's former Mayor, Michael Bloomberg, established an Office of Immigrant Affairs which serves as a model and a resource on immigrant affairs and integration for other cities around the world.[13]

- Berlin's Commissioner and the Senate Representative for Integration and Migration advise the Berlin Senate on integration policy and help break down barriers to migrant inclusion in the city-state.[14]

- Athens set up an Integration Council where 23 migrant associations are active participants and which addresses racism issues based on anti-discrimination principles.[15]

- Bilbao has set up a Local Council of Immigration as part of its internationalization of the city and has proactively improved foreigner-participation in city life.[16]

- Dublin City Council has established its own Office for Integration and a ten-point Charter of Commitment to its multilateral strategy known as, 'Towards Integration: A City Framework' strategy'.[17]

---

12 For further information, see http://www.give-project.eu/en
13 Details are available from www.nyc.gov/html/imm/html/home/home.shtml
14 See the website of the Berlin Government at www.berlin.de/lb/intmig/aufgaben/index.en.html
15 Presentation by Mayor Gjorgos Kaminis, at the Mayoral Forum on Migration, Mobility and Development, 19–20 June 2014, Barcelona.
16 Presentation by O. A. Martinez, Councillor for Equality, Cooperation and Citizenship, at the Mayoral Forum on Migration, Mobility and Development, 19–20 June 2014, Barcelona.
17 www.dublin.ie/uploadedFiles/Culture/Towards Integration Final.pdf

- In Italy, the city of Reggio Emilia has invested in a non-profit social agency, the Mondinsieme Intercultural Centre, to assist with immigrant inclusion.[18]

- Fujian province in China has established a Provincial Office of Opening to the Outside World, which helps local governments to be more flexible towards foreign investors, many of whom are Chinese expatriates (Zhu, 1999).

- Singapore, with a rapidly growing immigrant population, set up a National Integration Council which in turn launched the Community Integration Fund in 2009 to promote interaction and harmony between immigrants and the local community (Yeoh and Lin, 2013).

- In Japan, the Committee for Localities with a Concentrated Foreign Population is a mayors' gathering to devise practical solutions for the challenges of increasing migration-led diversity in their cities (see text box 6).

5.4
MIGRANTS AS CITY-MAKERS

Migrants can play a role as city-makers, helping their adopted cities achieve a global profile by promoting the historical, cultural, religious and socioeconomic facets, provided that the right opportunities exist to enable this to happen.

Cities are nested in a hierarchy of relationships that extends up to state, federal and supranational entities and down to communities, neighbourhood and immigrants. Overcoming, for example, a divergence between national migration policies and local needs and capacities is one of the most challenging aspects of the urban governance of migration.

Supranational level regulations, such as those of the World Trade Organization, binding agreements of regional economic communities, such as the European Commission, and various national and local jurisdictions all affect migrants' economic insertion, employment prospects, wages and entrepreneurial opportunities. Furthermore, cities have a specific institutional structure of governance, culture and history which all contribute to form a "territorialized opportunity structure" (Glick Schiller and Çağlar, 2009).

Cities and migrants can mutually benefit each other. Therefore it is important to understand the relationship between the economic, political and cultural positioning of cities within the global system and the ability of migrants to forge a place for themselves within a specific locality (Glick Schiller and Çağlar, 2013). The city of Mardin is a story of city leaders' efforts to rebuild and reposition their city and emigrants' efforts to re-establish relationships to the city at a particular conjuncture of opportunity structures. It illustrates how specific forms of diversity involving migrant groups became an asset for urban development and also part of the city's bid for an improved position in the world. It shows migrants becoming part of city-making processes as bearers of historical, cultural and religious diversity, as well as agents of economic development (text box 31).

---

18 www.annalindhfoundation.org/members/fondazione-mondinsieme-del-comune-di-reggio-emilia-0

WORLD MIGRATION
REPORT 2015
Migrants and Cities:
New Partnerships
to Manage Mobility

179

Text box 31

Mardin, Turkey: Migrants as agents for city-making[19]

Mardin is a border city in Turkey with historical commercial, cultural and religious ties to neighbouring Syrian Arab Republic, Iraq and the Middle East in general. It has been home to a diverse ethnic and religious population for centuries but several decades have seen the out-migration of Armenians, Christian-Syriacs and Kurds, particularly during the years of armed conflict in the 1980s and the 1990s. Mardin's local economy was decimated; the city depopulated and disempowered in terms of access to national and political power, capital investments, adequate global talent and its positioning within the regional and the global economy. Syriac emigrants abroad have maintained translocal ties spanning several places in Europe and worldwide but not with their hometown of Mardin.

Several efforts by local and national authorities during the 1990s to regenerate Mardin's economy and development failed. This situation changed dramatically in the 2000s with the establishment of a Mutual Aid Association *Karfo* by emigrant Syriacs. The Christian Syriac emigrant population of Mardin in different parts of Europe started reaching back to the city, partially resettling there, and increasingly becoming part of several development projects.

Turkey's EU candidacy and EU's regime of supervision opened up opportunities where the Syriac migrants and the Syriacs in Mardin became valuable assets in this city's efforts. Ironically, the strengthening of hometown ties of migrants from Mardin, for example in Vienna, Zurich and Stockholm, simultaneously incorporated them further into the institutions in Europe and in their places of settlement. They increasingly became active in Christian organizations in Europe.

Mardin's case shows how the migrants from Mardin became the agents in reshaping their locality. As a religious minority, they became part of the efforts to recast the parameters of Mardin's global, regional and national connectedness. The Syriacs in Mardin and the emigrants connecting back to the city became an asset of cultural and religious diversity of particular importance due to Turkey's candidacy for EU membership. The Syriac population's presence, well-being and above all religious freedom in Turkey became critical to the Turkish State's claim of tolerance of religious and cultural differences.

The Syriac emigrants, once displaced populations, became active agents of urban regeneration, revitalization of tourism and city branding. Tourism, especially religious and heritage tourism, has become one of the main areas of economic growth in Mardin.[20] The Syriac emigrants in Europe and their presence in the city, together with the its legacies of

---

19 Based on A. Çağlar, Urban Migration Trends, Challenges and Opportunities, 2014. Background Paper for the *World Migration Report 2015: Migrants and Cities: New Partnerships to Manage Mobility*, IOM, Geneva.
20 This analysis of the location of Syriac emigrants in Mardin does not take into account the recent developments of war in the region.

historical, cultural and religious diversity, acquired importance in Mardin's desires and efforts to attract supranational actors like UNESCO and EU for the empowerment and repositioning of the city. These supranational institutions, in turn, facilitated and shaped the emplacement of Syriac emigrants in the narratives of the city's past and future and in its urban renewal/rehabilitation projects.

Migrants can help cities position themselves on the global stage. Local strategies of migrant inclusion, whether in origin or destination cities, can strengthen the negotiating position of cities seeking to do business with the world. Attracting and retaining highly skilled professionals, innovators, investors and students, essential for the city, can reap the dividends of investing in migrant inclusion. Migrants can also be part of the solution of managing urban transition,[21] as they make the links between smart migration policy and urban planning, and with the rest of the world. Cities that have successfully negotiated connections to global markets, for example as production hubs, knowledge centres and tourist destinations, as in the case of Mardin, or through remittances, are likely to attract skilled migrants for longer term benefits. In a world where people increasingly live between countries and cities, flexible national policies, allowing nationals to hold dual or multiple citizenship or foreign students, entrepreneurs and innovators to adjust their status to permanent residence, can complement efforts by cities to grow their communities while making them more globally competitive.

5.5
CONCLUDING REMARKS

Migrant inclusion occurs at local levels; yet immigration and residence policies are usually the jurisdiction of central governments and not location-specific. Migrant access to services is thus closely related to central–local government relations. There is often a major disconnection between central migration policies and local urban development plans and capacities. Migrant-inclusive cities require financial, budgetary and administrative authority and flexibility.

Cities acknowledge the need for citizenship as a process of political engagement among diverse groups and individuals. As migrants readily identify with their host city, cities can play a unique role in creating a sense of shared community and common purpose through a pragmatic approach to "urban citizenship". Migrants can be city-makers too and support cities to strengthen their place in the global economic and political hierarchy.

---

21 See the IOM website on the 7th World Urban Forum in Colombia in 2014 www.iom.int/news/iom-actively-participates-7th-world-urban-forum-held-medellin-colombia

WORLD MIGRATION
REPORT 2015
Migrants and Cities:
New Partnerships
to Manage Mobility

181

Building a family link across the ocean:
A Brazilian working mother in Lisbon

Lidia came to Lisbon ten years ago to pursue a master's degree. Lidia's initial idea was only to stay in Portugal for her studies and then go back to Brazil, her home country, to find a job and build her life. Lidia was already a university lecturer in her home city, Fortaleza. Ten years have since passed and Lidia still lives in Lisbon. After obtaining a doctoral degree in communication sciences, Lidia now teaches at the Autonomous University of Lisbon and also works as a researcher, enjoying the life in the "beautiful, attractive, culturally rich and, most of all, safe" city. Although Lidia thinks she is well integrated and feels at home in Lisbon, it has not always been easy as she had to face many challenges and some discrimination. Lidia is still sometimes reminded that she is a migrant. "I always think I have to face more difficulties than those who are from here", she says with some sadness in her voice.

Nevertheless, Lidia has managed to overcome difficulties and create strong bonds in Portugal, as she has built her own family life. Together with her partner, she adopted a lovely seven-year-old Portuguese girl two years ago. Very proud of being a mother, Lidia claims everything went just fine with the adoption process, "There was never any problem because I am from Brazil and I was very well received", she points out. Lidia now lives with her family in their newly bought apartment in a very calm neighbourhood near the city centre.

Lidia appreciates living in Lisbon with its proximity to Brazil. "I try to go to Brazil at least once a year. It is important to go there and be with my family and friends. Flights are expensive but direct from Lisbon!" she explains. Lidia also participates actively in the city's cultural and political activities: she votes, keeps herself informed of public campaigns, is a member of a migrant association and attends many cultural programmes. Right now Lidia is trying to create a campaign to encourage her friends to vote for a city project that aims at building parking spots for bicycles, "My daughter wants a bike. We don't know where to park one. I am thinking of creating a campaign on Facebook to gather the most votes possible so this project will become a reality and my daughter can have her bike!"

Asked where she sees herself in five years, Lidia replies without hesitation: "Right here! I see myself in Lisbon, in the same apartment together with my partner and my daughter. Now that I have a Portuguese daughter I want to see her grow here. Only with a more stable working contract", she concludes with a smile.

REFERENCES

Acebillo-Baqué, M. and E. Østergaard-Nielsen
2011   Local dynamics of codevelopment and migrant incorporation in three Catalan cities. Paper presented at the International RC21 conference, 17 June 2011. Available from www.rc21.org/conferences/amsterdam2011/edocs2/Session%203/3-1-Acebillo.pdf

Ash, T.G., E. Mortimer and K. Öktem
2013   *Freedom in Diversity: Ten Lessons for Public Policy from Britain, Canada, France, Germany and the United States*. Dahrendorf Programme for the Study of Freedom, St Antony's College, University of Oxford, Oxford. Available from www-old.sant.ox.ac.uk/esc/FreedomRev10.pdf

Bendel, P.
2014   *Coordinating Immigrant Integration in Germany: Mainstreaming at the Federal and Local Levels*. Migration Policy Institute, Europe, Brussels. Available from www.migrationpolicy.org/research/coordinating-immigrant-integration-germany-mainstreaming-federal-and-local-levels

Blaser, C. and L. Landau
2014   Managing migration in Southern Africa: Tools for evaluating local government responsiveness. Migrating out of Poverty Working Paper 20. University of Sussex, Brighton. Available from http://r4d.dfid.gov.uk/pdf/outputs/MigratingOutOfPov/WP19_Blaser-Landau.pdf

Cabannes, Y.
2014   Contribution of Participatory Budgeting to provision and management of basic services: Municipal practices and evidence from the field. Human Settlements Working Paper. International Institute for Environment and Development, London. Available from http://pubs.iied.org/pdfs/10713IIED.pdf

Caponio, T. and M. Borkert (eds.)
2010   *The Local Dimension of Migration Policymaking*. International Migration, Integration and Social Cohesion in Europe (IMISCOE) Reports. Amsterdam University Press, Amsterdam. Available from www.google.ch/url?sa=t&rct=j&q=&esrc=s&source=web&cd=1&ved=0CCMQFjAA&url=http%3A%2F%2Fwww.oapen.org%2Fdownload%3Ftype%3Ddocument%26docid%3D350732&ei=sYFtVZ7_MoaigwSTt4DICQ&usg=AFQjCNHyVkGUJTVKw1JpbaGqEZQQU5DGLA

Cities of Migration
2012   *Good Ideas from Successful Cities: Municipal Leadership on Immigrant Integration*. Maytree Foundation, Toronto. Available from http://citiesofmigration.ca/wp-content/uploads/2012/03/Municipal_Report_Main_Report2.pdf

Clunan, A.L. and H.A. Trinkunas (eds.)
2010   *Ungoverned Spaces: Alternatives to State Authority in an Era of Softened Sovereignty*. Stanford University Press, Stanford.

WORLD MIGRATION
REPORT 2015
Migrants and Cities:
New Partnerships
to Manage Mobility

183

Collett, E. and M. Petrovic
2014   *The Future of Immigrant Integration in Europe: Mainstreaming
            Approaches for Inclusion.* Migration Policy Institute Europe, Brussels.
            Available from www.migrationpolicy.org/research/future-immigrant-
            integration-europe-mainstreaming-approaches-inclusion

Economic Policy Forum (EPF) and China Institute for Reform and Development
(CIRD)
2013   *Report on 2013 EPF Roundtable Meeting on Urbanization and
            Migration: Creating Equitable Access to Basic Service.* 3 November
            2013, Haikou, Hainan Province, PR CHINA. Available from www.
            economic-policy-forum.org/wp-content/uploads/2014/02/Hainan_
            Documentation1.pdf

Ernst & Young Global Limited
2014   *Evaluation of the Impact of the Free Movement of EU citizens at Local
            Level.* European Commission, DG Justice, Brussels. Available from
            http://ec.europa.eu/justice/citizen/files/dg_just_eva_free_mov_
            final_report_27.01.14.pdf

Euro-Mediterranean Human Rights Network (EMHRN)
2014   *Analysis of the Mobility Partnership signed between the Kingdom
            of Morocco, the European Union and nine Member States on 7 June
            2013.* EMHRN, Copenhagen. Available from http://euromedrights.
            org/wp-content/uploads/2015/03/PM-Morocco_Final-Version-EN.
            pdf

Fincher, R. et al.
2014   Planning in the multicultural city: Celebrating diversity or reinforcing
            difference? *Progress in Planning*, 92: 1–55.

Glick Schiller, N. and A. Çağlar
2009   Towards a comparative theory of locality in migration studies: Migrant
            incorporation and city scale. *Journal of Ethnic and Migration Studies*,
            35(2): 177–202.
2013   Locating migrant pathways of economic emplacement: Thinking
            beyond the ethnic lens. *Ethnicities*, 13(4): 494–514.

Haysom, S.
2013   *Sanctuary in the City? Urban Displacement and Vulnerability.* Overseas
            Development Institute, London. Available from www.odi.org/sites/
            odi.org.uk/files/odi-assets/publications-opinion-files/8444.pdf

International Organization for Migration (IOM)
2014   La mise en œuvre de la nouvelle approche migratoire au Royaume
            du Maroc. *Lettre d'information* no. 24 Maroc. Août-Octobre. IOM,
            Geneva. Available from www.iom.int/files/live/sites/iom/files/
            Country/docs/rabat-newsletter-FR-October-2014.pdf

Kingsley, P.
2012   Participatory democracy in Porto Alegre. *The Guardian*, 10
            September. Available from www.theguardian.com/world/2012/
            sep/10/participatory-democracy-in-porto-alegre

Metropolis
2011   *Integrated Urban Governance: The Way Forward.* Metropolis, World
            Association of the Major Metropolises, Barcelona. Available from
            www.metropolis.org/sites/default/files/media_root/documents/c3-
            metropolis-urban-governance-eng.pdf

Organisation for Economic Co-operation and Development (OECD)
2006   *From Immigration to Integration: Local Solutions to a Global
            Challenge.* OECD, Paris.
2011   *Tackling the Policy Challenges of Migration: Regulation, Integration,
            Development.* Development Centre Studies, OECD, Paris. Available
            from www.oecd-ilibrary.org/social-issues-migration-health/tackling-
            the-policy-challenges-of-migration_9789264126398-en

Painter, J.
2005   Urban citizenship and rights to the city. Background Paper for the
            Office of the Deputy Prime Minister, Centre for the Study of Cities and
            Regions, Durham University, Stockton-on-Tees. Available from www.
            dur.ac.uk/resources/cscr/odpm/Urban_Citizenship.pdf

Price, J. and S. Spence
2014   *City-Level Responses to Migrant Families with Restricted Access to
            Welfare Benefits.* Centre on Migration, Policy, and Society, Oxford
            University, Oxford. Available from www.compas.ox.ac.uk/fileadmin/
            files/Publications/Reports/Report_City_level_responses.pdf

Ridgley, J.
2008   Cities of refuge: immigration enforcement, police, and the insurgent
            genealogies of citizenship in U.S. sanctuary cities. *Urban Geography*
            29(1): 53–77.

Stren, R.
2012   Cities and politics in the developing world: Why decentralization
            matters. In: *The Oxford Handbook of Urban Politics* (P. Mossberger
            and S. E. Clarke, eds.). Oxford University Press, Oxford, pp. 567–589.
2014   Urban service delivery in Africa and the role of international
            assistance, *Development Policy Review* 32(S1): s19–s37.

Sumption, M.
2014   *Giving Cities and Regions a Voice in Immigration Policy: Can National
            Policies Meet Local Demand?* Migration Policy Institute, Washington,
            D.C. Available from www.migrationpolicy.org/research/giving-cities-
            and-regions-voice-immigration-policy-can-national-policies-meet-
            local-demand

The Economist
2014   Special Report on China: Building the Dream. *The Economist,* 19 April.
            Available from www.economist.com/news/special-report/21600797-
            2030-chinese-cities-will-be-home-about-1-billion-people-getting-
            urban-china-work

Travers, T. et al.
2007   *Population Mobility and Service Provision: A Report for London
            Councils.* London School of Economics, London. Available from
            www.lse.ac.uk/geographyAndEnvironment/research/London/pdf/
            populationmobilityandserviceprovision.pdf

WORLD MIGRATION
REPORT 2015
Migrants and Cities:
New Partnerships
to Manage Mobility

185

Van Kempen, R.

2014   Governing Diversity. DIVERCITIES Policy Brief Number 2, European Commission, Brussels. Available from www.urbandivercities.eu/wp-content/uploads/2013/05/DIVERCITIES_Policy_Brief_2.pdf

United Cities and Local Governments (UCLG)

2013   *For a World of Inclusive Cities.* Committee on Social Inclusion, Participatory Democracy and Human Rights of the UCLG, Barcelona. Available from www.uclg-cisdp.org/en/observatory/reports/world-inclusive-cities

United Nations Human Settlements Programme (UN-Habitat)

2007   *International Guidelines on Decentralization and Strengthening of Local Authorities.* United Nations, Nairobi. Available from www.cities-localgovernments.org/committees/dal/Upload/news/ladsguidelines.pdf

Yeoh, B.S.A. and W. Lin

2013   Chinese Migration to Singapore: Discourses and Discontents in a Globalizing Nation-State. *Asia and Pacific Migration Journal* 22(1): 31–54.

Zhu, Y.

1999   *New Paths to Urbanization in China: Seeking More Balanced Patterns.* Nova Science Publishers, New York, p. 131.

Conclusions

CHAPTER 6

WORLD MIGRATION
REPORT 2015
Migrants and Cities:
New Partnerships
to Manage Mobility

187

June J.H. Lee

Migration to cities is on the rise

For the first time in history, the majority of people in the world now live in cities. WMR 2015 has drawn attention to the fact that an increasing proportion of people living in cities are migrants. Migration is currently at an all-time high and has largely become an urban phenomenon with the exodus of people from rural areas to urban settlements. For cities everywhere, diversity is a reality of urban life and has to be factored into governance and development policies as internal and international migration continues to rise. A growing number of cities in the developed world are seeking to embrace the challenges presented by having diverse populations live side by side to build institutional capacity and strengthen partnerships and turn diversity into an asset. In the less developed world, the lack of resources may mean that city authorities are unable to deal with such challenges, resulting in tension among migrant and host communities and the emergence of migrant ghettos of extreme poverty.

Migration to cities brings both challenges and opportunities

Migration to cities may often involve using informal and irregular channels in the absence of regular migration routes. Once in cities, migrants often face difficulties in accessing housing, employment opportunities and other basic services such as health care. Migration is likely to be an important factor in the growth of many informal settlements in the peri-urban areas of less developed countries. In such places, migrants end up working in low-paying jobs and potentially exploitive conditions in the informal economies of these cities.

Migrants move to cities in search of livelihood opportunities and to escape socioeconomic and other pressures in their communities of origin. Yet, migration may increase vulnerability to hazards and reduce resilience to such threats. The urban environments that migrants find themselves in may be prone to disaster and the lack of access to adequate housing, employment and social services renders them less able to cope. Hazards in urban areas disproportionately affect migrants as a subset of the urban poor. Language, knowledge, administrative and legal barriers can serve to aggravate the situation. Mass displacement to urban areas is another phenomenon which brings particular risks and challenges in the delivery of humanitarian assistance.

Nevertheless, in informal settlements, migrants may also find protection and income opportunities despite the lack of basic services and infrastructure. In response to the precarious existence in urban environments, migrant households may engage in circular and temporary migration as well as commuting as a preferred mobility/livelihood strategy. This practice is found in many urban parts of fast-urbanizing Asian and African countries, especially China and India as well as Ghana and Kenya. This migration pattern plays a critical role in establishing linkages between rural origins and urban destinations. These linkages have multifaceted positive impacts on individuals, families and communities. The potential for the co-development of urban and rural communities exists but requires partnerships between the migrants and the local authorities of both communities as well as support from national governments.

Taking the migration enquiry to the city level helps increase the understanding of the local political economies of migration, and the close connection between migration and urban development. It assists to shift the focus away from why people move to how they work, live and shape their habitats. Cities across the development spectrum have growing mobile and diverse populations to manage. In developed countries, one of the main sources of population diversity is international migration while, in less-developed countries, it is most likely internal migration[1] and, to a lesser extent, growing international South–South migration.

While acknowledging the vast differences between international and internal migration scenarios, and also between the ability of rich, emerging countries and poor countries to deal with these, this report has highlighted the growing evidence of the potential benefits of all forms of migration and mobility for city growth and development. In order to maximize the developmental benefits of these new mobility patterns in terms of improving migrant well-being, it is imperative for cities to put inclusive urban policies in place for basic services and socioeconomic inclusion.

Migrants are resourceful partners in urban governance

Migrants can be key players in city development, growth, resilience and sustainability. They can be architects and construction workers of growing cities, service providers, entrepreneurs, employers and innovators. As part of the global diaspora, they can facilitate business and humanitarian support between cities and countries. They can contribute to the growing interconnections between cities through sustained global communications, institutional linkages and the exchange of resources among migrants, homelands and wider diasporas.

Migrants as builders of resilience: Migrants also play an important role in building the resilience of home and host communities through the exchange of resources and support. Migrants and their networks can contribute to managing risk for the community at large. They are often overrepresented in healthy, productive age groups and provide a set of diversified skills that can support disaster preparedness, response and recovery efforts, particularly in ageing societies.

Migrants as agents of local development: Migrants play a central role in forging the links between cities of origin and destination and in mainstreaming migration into local development planning. City-to-city links are often created or maintained due to the presence of large migrant populations. Migrant and diaspora communities can play an important role in supporting local decentralized development partnerships between cities and in facilitating or undertaking some of the related activities such as the provision of expertise and information on the communities of origin.

Migrants as city-makers: Migrants can help strengthen the place of cities in the global economic and political hierarchy. They can do so by promoting historical, cultural, religious and socioeconomic assets of a city if given the opportunity.

Cities and migrants can mutually benefit each other. Cities that seek to strengthen their economic, political and cultural positioning within the global system should draw on the potential opportunities presented by migrant populations living in their communities.

---

1 There is a serious lack of consistent, current and comparable data on foreign-born urban populations in most countries of the Global South.

WORLD MIGRATION
REPORT 2015
Migrants and Cities:
New Partnerships
to Manage Mobility

189

Migrant-inclusive urban governance is needed

Taking the migration enquiry to the city level entails a close examination of migration governance. It is at the city, municipality and community level, at the interface of migration, diversity and urban management, where the care and administration of people takes place. Effective urban governance that provides realistic, affordable and local solutions, in terms of housing, health, clean air, water and green spaces, is key to migrant inclusion and community vitality and also to global economic development. Delivery of services is critical to migrant inclusion as well as for community growth. Affordable housing is necessary for the social integration of immigrants and for local development (Collier and Venables, 2013). Accessible transport systems help migrants to access work which in turn sparks off economic development. Investing in social inclusion strategies is necessary if migration is to pay dividends in terms of economic benefits for cities (Çağlar, 2014).

At a practical level, the most compelling evidence comes from the links between well-governed migration and well-managed development which shows that restrictive policies on migration and urbanization can be damaging for growth and development in a globalized context. With the renewed enthusiasm among international communities and scholars to rethink cities, city mayors and urban policymakers are starting to see immigration reform in major destination countries like the United States as an urgent economic imperative for cities. Urban citizenship becomes an administrative tool of growth and development. Openness to international populations has thus become an indicator of a city's ability to do business with the rest of the world along with such indicators of economic, investment and trade links to the global markets.[2] The capacity of a city to attract international populations and enable them to contribute to its future success[3] is considered a key benchmark for sustainable cities of the future. Such cities will guarantee migrants the right to cities through inclusive urban public policies and empowered civil society and migrant associations.[4] Specifically, the following suggestions can be made:

Cities to develop policies for migrant inclusion: Cities need to know and understand migrant communities. Cities not only provide services to migrants but also employ them and facilitate their access to formal labour markets, and encourage the entry of ethnic and migrant-led businesses into supply chains. Most importantly, cities have governance responsibilities and can develop policy frameworks for migrant inclusion in the cities of both origin and destination.

Urban growth can be sustained when cities invest in their people: Rapid city growth can be difficult to sustain in terms of the impacts on urban infrastructure, environment and social fabric. Cities that are managing these challenges effectively make substantive investments in infrastructure especially in the latest digital technologies. They can empower migrants and provide opportunities that

---

2   The "Global Cities Initiative" launched by the Brookings Institution and JP Morgan Chase to strengthen the economic position, investment and trade links of US cities to the global network of metropolitan areas and which features immigration as one of its indicators of globality. See: www.brookings.edu/about/projects/global-cities/about
www.jpmorganchase.com/content/dam/jpmorganchase/en/legacy/corporate/Corporate-Responsibility/globalcities.htm

3   For more details see: www.opencities.eu/web/index.php?indicators_en

4   For further information, see: Migrants' Inclusion in Cities: Innovative Urban Policies and Practices, http://mirror.unhabitat.org/content.asp?typeid=19&catid=508&cid=10545

facilitate entrepreneurship. Cities are able to coordinate infrastructure, public services and other operations collaboratively with citizens and the private sector. Engagement often best occurs at the community level where projects can be most efficiently managed and financed.

Partnerships with migrants and their inclusion are an essential part of urban governance: Urban governance is a collaborative political and policymaking process where individuals and institutions, both public and private, plan and manage the city together. Through the governance process, diverse interests may be accommodated and cooperative action taken. These kinds of partnerships are relevant to migrant inclusion and involve formal institutions as well as informal arrangements which tap into the knowledge, connections and resources of migrants. As such, urban partnership is a critical tool in tackling one of the major urban challenges of our time – the inclusion of large populations of incoming migrants.

Engaging in partnerships increases social cohesion: Today's migrant flows are very mixed and cities have to manage growing diversity and cater to internal and international migrants, refugees, labour and irregular migrants alike. Engaging migrants in local partnerships builds trust among the migrants themselves, the city and the host community, and increases migrants' visibility in the social fabric of the city. While the contribution of migrants to development in their communities of origin has long been recognized, empowering migrants as actors in their cities of destination could also enhance their human and social potential for co-development.

Engaging in partnerships increases the competitiveness of cities: Cities have become principal actors in global networks of capital and labour. Attracting migrants with appropriate skill levels helps the local economies to be competitive and to meet existing labour shortages and skills needs. Migrant investment in housing, especially in origin communities, and entrepreneurship as well as ethnic/ diaspora tourism all help boost economic gains in cities of origin and destinations.

Platforms for exchange, consultation and cooperation must be developed

The reality is that many cities are insufficiently resourced and motivated to become truly inclusive. They remain socially and economically fragmented and exclusionary, and far from being able to become engines of global growth. Effective cities of the future need to be open and diverse, socially integrated, linked to other cities and global markets, and resilient to climatic, environmental and economic shocks. Not all cities are able to live up to these transformative expectations. This raises the question of how to balance knowledge, capacities and commitments towards good policymaking and practice for inclusive urban governance across countries and what roles international communities and organizations should play, while bearing in mind that the good practices of more advanced countries might not be globally applicable.

WORLD MIGRATION
REPORT 2015
Migrants and Cities:
New Partnerships
to Manage Mobility

191

The major global agendas for sustainable urban development, such as Habitat III[5] which is advising the UN on the global post-2015 sustainable development agenda, do not substantially address the role of migrants in sustainable urban settlements of the future. The absence of migrants from such major international programmes, which are aimed at drawing up a new urban agenda, reflects a serious gap in the international work on urban development. Taking the lead with the UN and IOM, the Mayor of Barcelona set up the first global Mayoral Forum on Mobility, Migration and Development in 2014 to discuss the role of local authorities in helping to manage human mobility.

In 2015, IOM dedicates its *World Migration Report* and a high-level International Dialogue on Migration conference to the issue of migrants and cities. The conference aims to assemble the collective wisdom on migration, mobility and urban transition and, together with city leaders and other experts from around the world, to draw a clear policy path towards improved migration management at all governance levels, which will benefit both migrants and cities. Specifically, the conference is being held:

- To support the efforts of individual cities to foster good practices for migrant-inclusive urban governance, international communities and organizations need to develop a coherent global agenda for migration and urbanization. An important first step could be the consolidation of existing yet scattered resources, data, indexes, tools and studies. It is important to assemble this information in a global database and promote greater information-sharing and dialogue among cities, multilevel government stakeholders and other partners.

- To improve existing efforts for data on urbanization and development by including migrants. With the prominence of cities as the site for sustainable development, city mayors and urban policymakers across the development spectrum are encouraged to consider the positive contribution of migration. Migrant-inclusive urban governance can start with establishing a clear understanding of where migrants reside and how they are organized, and then benchmarks can be developed for basic service provision as well as for measuring the levels of migrants' integration. This, in turn, could help formulate an effective policy from numerous programmes and practices on the ground.

---

5   Habitat III is the Third United Nations Conference on Housing and Sustainable Urban Development, to take place in 2016, decided in General Assembly Resolution 66/ 207. For details see: www.uclg.org/en/issues/habitat-iii

REFERENCES

Çağlar, A.
2014   Urban Migration Trends, Challenges and Opportunities. Background
            Paper for the *World Migration Report 2015, Migrants and Cities: New
            Partnerships to Manage Mobility*. IOM, Geneva.

Collier, P. and A.J. Venables
2013   Housing and Urbanization in Africa: unleashing a formal market
            process, CSAE Working Paper Series 2013-01. Centre for the Study
            of African Economies, University of Oxford, Oxford. Available from
            www.csae.ox.ac.uk/workingpapers/pdfs/csae-wps-2013-01.pdf

Glossary

WORLD MIGRATION
REPORT 2015
Migrants and Cities:
New Urban Partnerships
to Manage Mobility

195

GLOSSARY

Terms
Agglomeration economy
Circular migration
City competitiveness
Country of destination
Country of origin
Country of transit
Cross-border migration
Development
Diaspora
Diversity
Economic migrant
Emigration
Forced migration
Foreign-born
Gateway city
Global city
Governance
High-income countries
Host country
Immigration
Informal settlement
In-migration
Internal migration
Internally displaced person (IDP)
Irregular migrant
Irregular migration
Labour migration
Livelihoods

Terms
Low- and middle-income countries
Megacity
Metropolitan area/region
Migrant stock
Migration corridor
North
Outmigration
Peri-urbanization
Receiving country
Refugee
Regular migration
Remittances
Return migration
Sanctuary city
Seasonal migrant worker/migration
Secondary city
Sending country
Slum
Squatter settlement
South
South–South migration
Transit city
Urban
Urban agglomeration
Urban growth
Urban sprawl
Urbanization
Vulnerability

AGGLOMERATION ECONOMY	The benefits that come when firms and people locate near one another in cities and in industrial clusters, resulting in economies of scale and network effects, such as suitable infrastructures, availability of labour and savings in transport costs.
CIRCULAR MIGRATION	The fluid and repeated movement of people between countries of origin and destination or between national rural and urban areas including internal cross-country migration. This includes temporary or long-term movements which may be beneficial to all involved, if occurring voluntarily and linked to labour needs.
CITY COMPETITIVENESS	A set of factors, such as policies, institutions, strategies and processes that determine the level of sustainable productivity of a city. Sustainability encompasses economic, environmental and social issues.
COUNTRY OF DESTINATION	The country that is a destination for migrants (regular or irregular). See also: Host Country and Receiving Country.
COUNTRY OF ORIGIN	Generally speaking, the country of origin refers to the country that was the point of departure for the individual's migratory journey.
COUNTRY OF TRANSIT	The country through which migratory flows (regular or irregular) move.
CROSS-BORDER MIGRATION	A process of movement of persons across international borders.
DEVELOPMENT	The United Nations Development Programme (UNDP) defines development as the process of "creating an environment in which people can develop their full potential and lead productive, creative lives in accordance with their needs and interests... expanding the choices people have to lead lives that they value". This definition marks a shift away from the strict emphasis on economic development measured by growth or income indicators and encompasses the human dimension of the process.
DIASPORA	There is no single accepted definition of the term diaspora. Diaspora is broadly defined as individuals and members of networks, associations and communities who have left their country of origin, and maintain links with their homelands. This concept covers more settled expatriate communities; migrant workers temporarily based abroad, expatriates with the citizenship of the host country, dual citizens, and second-/third-generation migrants.
DIVERSITY	Diversity is understood in a social, cultural and demographic sense, whereby a society or group is made up of individuals from different national, racial or ethnic backgrounds.

WORLD MIGRATION
REPORT 2015
Migrants and Cities:
New Urban Partnerships
to Manage Mobility

197

ECONOMIC MIGRANT

A person leaving his/her habitual place of residence to settle outside of his/her country of origin in order to improve his/her quality of life. It may equally be applied to persons leaving their country of origin for the purpose of employment. This term is often loosely used to distinguish migrants from refugees fleeing persecution and is also similarly used to refer to persons attempting to enter a country without legal permission and/or by using asylum procedures without bona fide cause.

EMIGRATION

The act of departing or exiting from one State with a view to settling in another.

FORCED MIGRATION

A migratory movement in which there is an element of coercion, including threats to life and livelihood, whether arising from natural or from man-made causes (for example, movements of refugees and internally displaced persons, as well as people displaced by natural/environmental disasters, chemical/nuclear disasters, famine or development projects).

FOREIGN-BORN

The term "foreign-born" refers to residents of a country who were born in another country. Foreign-born residents can, under certain circumstances, change their status and become citizens through naturalization. When combined, both place of birth and citizenship status can be used to divide the population into three categories—native-born citizens, foreign-born citizens, and non-citizens—and define who among the foreign-born has acquired the full rights and responsibilities bestowed on all citizens.

GATEWAY CITY

A city that is a critical entry point and a settlement site for immigrants and that draws from a wide range of sending countries. For many immigrants, a gateway city is not the end in itself but rather a turnstile, with migrants moving in and out.

GLOBAL CITY

A strategic site in the global economy because of the concentration of command functions and high-level producer service firms orientated to world markets; more generally a city with a high level of internationalization in the economy and a broader social structure. A global city is both a centre of production and innovation as well as a home to markets.

GOVERNANCE

All processes of governing, whether undertaken by a government, market or network, whether over a family, tribe, formal or informal organization or territory and whether through laws, norms, power or language.

In politics, as opposed to the notion of "government", the notion of governance acknowledges both the increasing presence of networks in modern society and the non-governmental influences on policymaking. Governance comprises connections and relationships between government and stakeholders, civil society groups, and other agencies of government and the state.

HIGH-INCOME COUNTRIES

In accordance with World Bank country classification, high-income countries are identified on the basis of gross national income (GNI) per capita. In this report, high-income countries refer to all economies that had a GNI per capita of USD12,276 or more in 2010. High-income countries have the highest GNIs per capita of any World Bank income group, the others being (in descending order) upper-middle-income, lower-middle-income, and low-income countries. For the purposes of the current report, high-income countries are referred to as "the North".

HOST COUNTRY

The country in which a migrant is living. See also: Country of Destination and Receiving Country.

IMMIGRATION

A process by which non-nationals move into a country for the purpose of settlement.

INFORMAL SETTLEMENT

Areas where groups of housing units have been constructed on land that the occupants have no legal claim to or occupy illegally. Unplanned settlements and areas where housing is not in compliance with current planning and building regulations (unauthorized housing).

IN-MIGRATION

Move or settle into a different part of one's country or home territory.

INTERNAL MIGRATION

A movement of people from one area of a country to another for the purpose or with the effect of establishing a new residence. This migration may be temporary or permanent. Internal migrants move but remain within their country of origin (as in the case of rural to urban migration). See also Internally Displaced Persons.

INTERNALLY DISPLACED PERSON (IDP)

Person or groups of persons who have been forced or obliged to flee or to leave their homes or places of habitual residence, particularly as a result, or in order to avoid the effects, of armed conflict, situations of generalized violence, violations of human rights, or natural/human-made disasters, and who have not crossed an internationally recognized State border (para. 2, Guiding Principles on Internal Displacement, UN Doc. E/CN.4/1998/53/Add.2).

IRREGULAR MIGRANT

A person who, owing to unauthorized entry, breach of a condition of entry, or the expiry of his or her visa, lacks legal status in a transit or host country. The definition covers, inter alia, those persons who have entered a transit or host country lawfully but have stayed for a longer period than authorized or subsequently taken up unauthorized employment.

IRREGULAR MIGRATION

Movement that takes place outside the regulatory norms of the origin, transit and destination countries.

LABOUR MIGRATION

Movement of persons from their home state to another state or within their own country of residence for the purpose of employment.

WORLD MIGRATION
REPORT 2015
Migrants and Cities:
New Urban Partnerships
to Manage Mobility

199

LIVELIHOODS	Livelihoods comprise the capabilities, assets (including both material and social resources) and activities required for a means of living. A livelihood is sustainable when it can cope with and recover from stress and shocks and maintain or enhance capabilities and assets, both now and in the future, while contributing net benefits to other livelihoods in the short and long-term.
LOW- AND MIDDLE-INCOME COUNTRIES	In accordance with World Bank country classification, low- and middle-income countries are identified on the basis of gross national income (GNI) per capita. In this report, low- and middle-income countries refer to all economies that had a GNI per capita of USD12,276 or less in 2010. Low- and middle-income countries refer to all economies that are not in the high-income group. For the purposes of the current report, low- and middle-income countries are referred to as "the South".
MEGACITY	An urban agglomeration with a population of 10 million of more.
METROPOLITAN AREA/REGION	A region consisting of a densely populated urban core and its less-populated surrounding territories, sharing industry, infrastructure and housing.
MIGRANT STOCK	The number of migrants residing in a given location at a particular point in time.
MIGRATION CORRIDOR	Generally viewed as the migratory pathway between two different countries, whereby individuals born in, or holding the nationality of, a certain country move to another country.
NORTH	High-income countries, as classified by the World Bank.
OUTMIGRATION	To leave a region, community, etc., to move or settle into a different part of one's country or home territory.
PERI-URBANIZATION	The process of urban growth that creates hybrid landscapes with both urban and rural characteristics, immediately surrounding a city or town, between the suburbs and the countryside.
RECEIVING COUNTRY	Country of destination (host country). In the case of return or repatriation, it is also the country of origin.

REFUGEE
A person who, "owing to a well-founded fear of persecution for reasons of race, religion, nationality, membership of a particular social group or political opinions, is outside the country of his nationality and is unable or, owing to such fear, is unwilling to avail himself of the protection of that country" (*Art. 1(A) (2), Convention relating to the Status of Refugees, 80 International Migration Law Art. 1A (2), 1951, as modified by the 1967 Protocol*).

In addition to the refugee definition in the *1951 Refugee Convention, Art. 1(2), 1969*, the Organization of African Unity (OAU) Convention defines a refugee as any person compelled to leave his or her country "owing to external aggression, occupation, foreign domination or events seriously disturbing public order in either part or the whole of his country or origin or nationality". Similarly, the 1984 Cartagena Declaration states that refugees also include persons who flee their country "because their lives, security or freedom have been threatened by generalized violence, foreign aggression, internal conflicts, massive violations of human rights or other circumstances [that] have seriously disturbed public order".

REGULAR MIGRATION
Migration that occurs through recognized, authorized channels. See also: Irregular Migration.

REMITTANCES
Monies earned or acquired by non-nationals that are transferred back to their country of origin. More specifically, the International Monetary Fund defines remittances as the sum of compensations of employees and personal transfers from border, seasonal and other short-term workers who are employed in an economy where they are not resident and of residents employed by non-resident entities.

RETURN MIGRATION
The movement of a person returning to his/her country of origin or habitual residence, usually after at least one year in another country. The return may or may not be voluntary.

SANCTUARY CITY
The cities that do not use city funding to implement federal immigration laws. These cities have decided by legal regulation (de juris), internal memo or force of habit (de facto) not to enquire about the immigration status of persons with whom they come into contact.

SEASONAL MIGRANT WORKER/MIGRATION
A migrant worker whose work, or migration for work that, by its character is dependent on seasonal conditions and is performed only during part of the year (*Art. 2(2) (b), International Convention on the Protection of the Rights of All Migrant Workers and Members of Their Families, 1990*).

WORLD MIGRATION
REPORT 2015
Migrants and Cities:
New Urban Partnerships
to Manage Mobility

201

SECONDARY CITY A secondary city is largely determined by population, size, function and economic status. The population of secondary cities ranges between 10 to 50 per cent of a country's largest city. They will likely constitute a subnational or sub-metropolitan second-tier level of government, acting as centres for public administration and delivery of education, knowledge, health, community, and security services; an industrial centre or development growth pole; a new national capital; or a large city making up a cluster of smaller cities in a large metropolitan region.

SENDING COUNTRY A country from which a number of residents depart to settle abroad, permanently or temporarily.

SLUM A heavily populated urban informal settlement characterized by poverty, substandard housing and squalor.

SQUATTER SETTLEMENT Areas where people have built their own houses on land that does not belong to them and for which they have no legal authorization, lease or building permit, and usually built without following building and planning regulations. See also: Informal Settlement.

SOUTH Refers to upper-middle-income, lower-middle-income and low-income countries, as classified by the World Bank.

SOUTH–SOUTH MIGRATION South–South migration refers to the movement of people across international boundaries within and between low- and middle-income countries.

TRANSIT CITY A city where migrants stop over on their way from origin countries to the ultimate destination country.

URBAN The definition of "urban" varies from country to country, and, with periodic reclassification, can also vary within a country over time, making direct comparisons difficult. An urban area can be defined by one or more of the following: administrative criteria or political boundaries (e.g. area within the jurisdiction of a municipality or town committee); a threshold population size (where the minimum for an urban settlement is typically in the region of 2,000 people, although this varies globally between 200 and 50,000), population density; economic function (e.g. where a significant majority of the population is not primarily engaged in agriculture or where there is surplus employment), or the presence of urban characteristics (e.g. paved streets, electric lighting, sewerage). In 2010, 3.5 billion people lived in areas classified as urban.

URBAN AGGLOMERATION The population of a built-up or densely populated area containing the city proper, suburbs and continuously-settled commuter areas or adjoining territory inhabited at urban levels of residential density. Large urban agglomerations often include several administratively distinct but functionally linked cities. For example, the urban agglomeration of Tokyo includes the cities of Chiba, Kawasaki, Yokohama and others.

URBAN GROWTH   The (relative or absolute) increase in the number of people who live in towns and cities. The pace of urban population growth depends on the natural increase of the urban population and the population gained by urban areas through both net rural-urban migration and the reclassification of rural settlements as cities and towns.

URBAN SPRAWL   The uncontrolled and disproportionate expansion of an urban area into the surrounding countryside, forming low-density and poorly-planned patterns of development. Common to both high-income and low-income countries, urban sprawl is characterized by a scattered population living in separate residential areas, with long blocks and poor access, often over dependent on motorized transport and missing well-defined hubs of commercial activity.

URBANIZATION   Urbanization is defined mostly in demographic terms as the increasing proportion of a population that is living in urban areas. This increase can be attributed in general to three factors: natural population growth, net rural-to-urban migration, and also the progressive extensions of urban boundaries and creation of new urban centres. Urbanization frequently refers to a broad rural-to-urban transition involving changes in population, land use, economic activity and culture.

VULNERABILITY   The diminished capacities of an individual or group to anticipate, cope with, resist and recover from the impact of a natural or man-made hazard.